DATE DUE			
JUL 10 2001			

ACTION GUIDE FOR SUPERVISORS

ACTION GUIDE FOR SUPERVISORS

Claude S. George, Jr.

University of North Carolina at Chapel Hill

 Reston Publishing Company, Inc., Reston, Virginia
A Prentice-Hall Company

For Ella

Cartoons by Bruce Bollinger

Library of Congress Cataloging in Publication Data

George, Claude S.
    Action guide for supervisors

    Includes bibliographical references and index.
    1.   Supervision of employees.   I.   Title.

HF5549.G427   1979   658.3'02   78-23627
ISBN 0-8359-0122-X

10   9   8   7   6   5   4   3   2   1

Printed in the United States of America

CONTENTS

PREFACE

This guide deals with how to supervise people. It takes you step by step through the rough spots of supervision, giving helpful hints and demonstrating positive actions you can take. Because it was written to help you be a better supervisor, the book provides answers to a great many of your day-to-day questions. Not a book of theory, it presents instead those supervisory practices that have stood the test of time and application.

In today's complex business environment, practicing supervisors in every field recognize the need to gain new insights into directing the efforts of others. This book was written to help supervisors achieve this objective by giving them a clear and effective approach to understanding and dealing with the problems they face. Practically structured, it discusses ways to improve supervisory skills in such areas as motivating employees, building morale, handling discipline, making decisions, and communicating ideas.

Whether your are a newly appointed supervisor or a potential one, this guide will help you get acquainted with the overall scope of your job, introduce you to some of the many problems you will encounter, and offer you practical and timely help on how to face and solve these

problems. Written in a direct and easy-to-read manner, this book assumes no prior training or knowledge of the subject.

A great deal of the material in this guide came from my years as a
practicing supervisor in industry, from my experience in consulting
and teaching in business, and from my participation in scores of supervisory development programs. I also used research and publications
done by practitioners and scholars in the field as resources.

That is, therefore, a practical book — one that deals with real-world
problems and their solutions. I believe you will find it helpful.

CLAUDE S. GEORGE, JR.

PART ONE
YOU AND YOUR JOB

1
WHAT A
SUPERVISOR DOES

This chapter explains—

- What you will do as a supervisor
- The skills and qualities you will need
- What your functions and responsibilities will be

The key to success for any business organization is good supervision.

If you stop to think for a moment, you will see why this is true. For a firm to be successful, its employees must produce a quality product (or service) at a high level of efficiency and at a low cost. In fact, unless the employees fill out reports, attend to patients, assemble parts, type letters, test products, load trucks, wait on customers, dig ditches, take inventories, or do whatever needs to be done—and do it efficiently and effectively—then all the *top* management skills that the business possesses will not make it successful. Thus, it is the *first-line* supervisor who is responsible for seeing that work is accomplished. And unless he does his job well, the entire managerial pyramid will be weakened. It may even crumble and fail.

Good supervision, therefore, is just about the single most important factor in the success of our American economy. It is responsible for more than doubling our national output during the past twenty years. Because of good supervision we have produced a staggering array of new products, new homes, new automobiles, new clothing, new tools, new TVs, and so on. How have good supervisors done all this? They have done it by wisely directing the efforts of others, by wisely using the manpower available to them, and by wisely putting the right combination of men and materials together to get the work done. *The key to success for any firm is good supervision.*

IS A FORELADY A SUPERVISOR?

many names

Yes. Supervisors are known by different names in different companies. A supervisor might be called either a foreman or forelady, a leadman, a section chief, a front-line supervisor, a floor chief, a section head, or a department head. Whatever he or she is called, a supervisor must be able to understand people, be able to motivate them, be an energetic leader, be a good planner and allocator of work, be wise and just in making decisions, be knowledgeable about technical aspects of the work, and finally, be able to serve as an effective liaison between top management and the workers. All this sounds like a description of a superman—and it is! Most of us do not have all these attributes and capacities; therefore, we need to study what the supervisor does and how he does it so that we can grow in that direction—so that we can develop our capacities to the point where they meet the needs of a good supervisor.

HOW COMPLEX IS A SUPERVISOR'S JOB?

Supervisors' jobs vary widely in their complexities. For example, one foreman may be responsible for supervising a move gang whose duty is to load and unload trucks at the loading dock. He may do little more than tell the crew what to load into a truck and where to put material being taken out.

4

"Supervisors get things done
through the efforts of other people."

Basically, he sees what needs to be done and tells his men what to do. Notice we said, "tells his men what to do." This is what supervision is all about. *Supervisors get things done through the efforts of other people.* Supervisors, then, accomplish the objectives of the organization by directing the efforts of others.

    Some supervisory jobs, of course, are much more complex than the loading and unloading job described above. A complex supervisory position may require a full knowledge of computer operation and application, a full knowledge of health services, a vast comprehension of consumer needs and wants, and the issuance of directives to skilled men with advanced educations. But, although this job is more complex than the loading job, the supervisor's part is still the same: *getting things done through the efforts of others.*

*working through
others*

HOW MANY SUPERVISORY LEVELS ARE THERE?

Basically, there are three levels of supervision. Most of the time you hear people speak of them as (1) top-level supervisors (or managers), (2) middle-level supervisors, and (3) first-line supervisors.

    Top-level supervisors are the big bosses in charge of the whole operation. The president of a corporation is a top-level supervisor. A person in charge of a textile mill is a top-level supervisor, as is the owner-manager of a small firm. In each instance, the person holding down the top job is the top-level supervisor.

    Middle-level supervisors are higher up than first-line supervisors but are below the top-level supervisor. A department manager in a retail store who has several supervisors working for him would be a middle-level supervisor. A person in charge of purchasing or production for a business would be a middle-level supervisor. His title might be Director of Purchasing or *three levels* Production Manager.

First-line supervisors are the key men in the managerial family who carry out the policies and directives of middle and top management through face-to-face contact with the workers. Middle management's directives are carried out by first-line supervisors through the efforts of the nonsupervisory employees. Figure 1-1 indicates the typical supervisory groups by level and rank above the nonsupervisory workers.

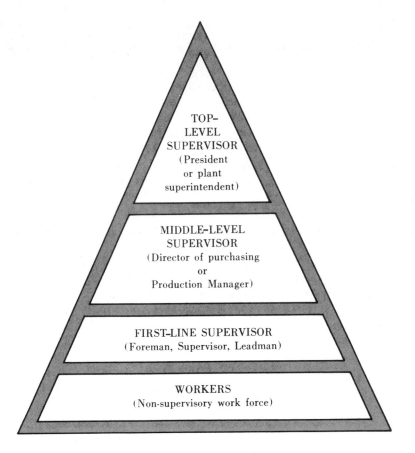

FIGURE 1-1.
The pyramid of different supervisory levels in a firm.

WHAT DOES A SUPERVISOR DO?

If you were to follow a supervisor about all day and list everything he does *as a supervisor*, the list would probably look something like the following:

- Talks to employees.
- Gives directions to employees.
- Dictates letters.
- Sets production or sales goals.
- Hires new employees.
- Reads mail, reports, etc.
- Attends meetings.
- Makes decision about new projects.
- Decides who will be promoted.

Note that this is a list of activities performed by a *supervisor*. He may, of course, perform nonsupervisory activities such as running a machine, looking up a letter in a file, or stapling sheets of a report together. Every supervisor performs some nonsupervisory work. His job may be 10% nonsupervisory and 90% supervisory, or it may be 20% nonsupervisory and 80% supervisory, etc. What is of interest to us is the supervisory activities that are listed. You will note that these activities, along with others you can think of, are one of two types:

1. Physical, or
2. Mental.

The *physical* activities usually involve some form of communication. The supervisor is *telling* someone something face-to-face or by *talking* to them over the telephone, *writing* to them, or *communicating* by gestures. When he is not talking and sending communications to others, he is receiving communications by listening or reading.

The *mental* activities, on the other hand, cannot be seen by us, but we know by what the supervisor says that he has been thinking and has made a decision—a mental activity. We can say, therefore, that all the acts performed by a supervisor are either physical (involving some form of communication) or mental (involving mental activity and decision making). The ultimate objective of these acts, of course, is to get work done through the efforts of others.

DOES A SUPERVISOR NEED SKILLS?

Yes. To be a good supervisor, you will need to be competent in several areas. You will need to possess these three skills:

1. Technical skills.
2. Human skills.
3. Conceptual skills.

Take a look at each of these.

You will need *technical* skills so that you can understand the technical aspects of the work done in your department. A supervisor in a machine shop, for example, needs to understand the operation of lathes, drill presses, punch presses, etc., in order to be able to supervise the men running them. An accounting supervisor needs to understand the operation of accounting machines, bookkeeping machines, and the techniques of double-entry book-keeping. A foreman in an electric firm, on the other hand, needs to know how to make a good solder connection, how to lace cable, and so on. A nurse supervisor needs to know how to give shots, change bandages, etc. In fact,

it's difficult to supervise people who are doing jobs or working with equipment you do not understand yourself. How, for example, could a man in a service garage be a good foreman if he does not understand what a dwell meter is and how it is used to set the points on a gasoline engine? To be a good supervisor, therefore, you need to have the *technical* skills necessary to understand the processes and equipment used. In many instances, these technical skills are acquired through on-the-job training or through vocational programs.

Supervisors also need *human* skills. Human skills are those skills that primarily concern working with *people*, whereas technical skills primarily concern working with *things*. Human skills involve being aware of your own feelings, beliefs, and attitudes about others. By being aware of himself, a supervisor with good human skills can *understand* and *accept* the beliefs and attitudes of others and can recognize that these may differ from his own. By understanding and accepting the beliefs and viewpoints that differ from his own, a supervisor will be more skillful in understanding what others mean by their statements and actions. By recognizing these differences, a supervisor can do a better job of communicating ideas to others. A supervisor, for example, may not be in favor of having a union in the company. Most of his employees, however, may be in favor of having a union represent them. By knowing and understanding his employees' feelings about unions and why they want to be represented by a union, the supervisor can create an atmosphere of under-standing in which employees can freely discuss unionism—an atmosphere in which they feel free to express their ideas without fear of ridicule. With human skills, a supervisor can be sensitive to the motivations and needs of others and can judge the probable effects various courses of action may have on his employees. He can then take steps that will tend to promote harmony and good effort within the group.

Human skills should be so much a part of a supervisor that he applies them continuously. Even when a foreman is not directly supervising his employees, everything he says or does will have some effect on them because what he does will reflect his true self to his men. Human skills, therefore, should not be thought of as techniques you can apply or use at will. On the contrary, a good supervisor should have developed human skills that are so much a part of him that they cannot be separated from him.

Most of us know people who have poor human skills. They are the ones who always seem to open their mouths and put both feet in. They rub others the wrong way. The supervisor who tells an employee, "I don't want to know why you are late; whatever your excuse, if this happens again, you'll be fired!" doesn't have good human skills.

Finally, a supervisor needs *conceptual* skills. Conceptual skills are those that enable a person to visualize something in its entirety. A person with good conceptual skills can "see" and understand all parts of a business and how each part contributes to the whole organization. He understands the role that accounting plays; how purchasing, sales, and finance relate to accounting; how personnel is a part of the total concern; how personnel functions in relation to each of the other divisions or parts of a firm; and so on. A supervisor with conceptual skills can visualize the part that the organization plays in the social, economic, and political forces in the community, state, or region. A supervisor needs these conceptual skills so that he can make wise decisions. With good conceptual skills, he can make wiser decisions because he will have the capacity to consider the impact that a certain decision will have on all parts and functions of a firm. He will understand, for example, how a wage increase would affect the whole business. He can see that a 10% wage increase might raise employee morale; but it would also increase the selling price of the product, which in turn could hurt consumer acceptance, and hence perhaps damage the long-run chances of success of the firm in the community.

With good *conceptual and human* skills, a supervisor will be able to visualize the effect that would result from giving a relatively new employee a choice job on a new machine. He could see, for example, that it might cause discontent among other employees, promote a possible labor slowdown or stoppage, lower product quality, and so on. You can easily think of other possible consequences.

A good supervisor, then, needs these three skills: *technical* skills so that he can understand and perform the technical activities required, *human* skills so that he can both motivate others and understand individual (and group) feelings and actions, and *conceptual* skills so that he can clearly understand and coordinate all the activities of the firm through wise decision making.

Technical skills are probably in greatest need in the lower levels of a firm. Human skills, on the other hand, are in real need throughout every level of the firm. Conceptual skills are more critical at the higher levels of the firm.

WHAT FUNCTIONS DOES A SUPERVISOR PERFORM?

Supervision deals with getting things done through others. A supervisor tells other employees what to do. As was previously indicated a supervisor can also perform some job—such as running a machine. While running a machine, of course, he is not supervising but is performing some work.

To achieve his job of getting things done through the efforts of others, every supervisor engages in a variety of functions:

1. He must plan his work and establish objectives. This is called the *planning* function.
2. He must organize people and materials in order to coordinate activities and actions. This is the *organizing* function.
3. He must secure qualified personnel to do the work—the *staffing* function.
4. He must direct the efforts of his employees—the *directing* function.
5. He must control the activities of his employees—the *controlling* function.

supervisory functions

Let's look at each of these functions and see why a supervisor needs to perform them.

Planning. A plan is a course of action to accomplish something—like a plan for a family vacation. Planning is the process involved in developing and formulating the course of action needed to accomplish your objective. Planning is not a function reserved just for top and middle management alone. On the contrary, first-line supervisors are actively engaged every day in planning—although their planning may not be as complex, or extended as far into the future, as top-level planning. A good supervisor plans what needs to be done, who will do it, when it will be done, how it will be done, and so on. Without this planning by the supervisor, his department's activities may well become disorganized, confused, and ineffective. In fact, thoughtful and careful planning by a supervisor can do much to change him from a mediocre supervisor to an outstanding one ready for promotion to a bigger job.

Organizing. Organizing consists of:

1. Determining what activities need to be accomplished to get the job done.
2. Grouping and assigning these activities to employees.
3. Giving the employees the necessary authority to carry out the activities in a coordinated manner.

All supervisors perform the function of organizing. Those at the top level are interested in the broader aspects of the firm, whereas the first-line supervisor is primarily interested in organizing his own department so that work can be accomplished in the best way possible.

Staffing. The staffing function covers all activities needed to recruit, hire, and retain individuals in the firm. In some companies this is done by a personnel department; in some it is a joint responsibility shared by the supervisor and the personnel department; in other companies it is the full responsibility of the supervisor. Staffing means putting people with skills and growth potential in spots where their skills are needed and they can grow.

Directing.   Directing deals with influencing, guiding, or supervising subordinates in their jobs. It consists not only of telling them what to do, but most important, of explaining *why* the job needs to be done. It involves a large amount of communication and, in most supervisory positions, consumes the greater part of a supervisor's workday.

Controlling.   The essence of control from a supervisory standpoint is, simply, that a supervisor must control people. If people are controlled properly, then actions and events will conform to plans. In essence, control is the check-up part of managing.

WHAT ARE A SUPERVISOR'S RESPONSIBILITIES?

In the past, many people felt that a supervisor had only one responsibility—making money for the business. Today, however, smart managers are developing a new sense of supervisory responsibility. Some people call it *business statesmanship*. Others call it *enlightened leadership*. Whatever its name, it refers to the fact that supervisors are beginning to realize that they have responsibilities not just to the owners but to many other groups both inside and outside the firm. Today good supervisors recognize a sense of responsibility to the community as well as to the people inside the plant. They recognize their responsibility to their owners, their employees, their customers, the general public, and the government. Let's look at each of these briefly.[1]

multiple responsibilities

Responsibility to Owners.   An owner (or stockholder) invests in a firm to make money. Perhaps more than anything else, the owner wants a good return from his investment, along with some security. He will, of course, agree that his company should treat its employees fairly and that it should be honest with the public and its customers; but primarily he wants dividends, and dividends can only come from profits.

A supervisor's responsibility to the owner of the business, then, is to operate his department so as to give him (the owner) the highest *long-run* return on investment. Working for the highest long-run profit will never conflict with obligations that a supervisor has to other individuals and groups. For example, an extensive program to construct new buildings and

---

[1]The following section is adapted with permission from Claude S. George, Jr., *Management in Industry* (Englewood Cliffs, N.J.: Prentice-Hall, Inc., 1959), pp. 564–69.

purchase new machinery may materially reduce profits for several years, but in the long run, profits would be greater than if the new programs were not undertaken. In fact, without the new building program, the business might lose its competitive advantage and fail.

Responsibility to Employees. An enlightened supervisor also recognizes that he has a very definite responsibility to his employees. Even as stockholders have invested their money, so have employees invested their time, their energies, and their efforts with a firm. Having thus cast their lot, employees are entitled to having a farsighted supervisor who recognizes their contributions as well as his specific responsibilities to them.

A supervisor is responsible for giving each employee a courteous reception when he starts on the job, and for placing him in a position for which he is both qualified and interested. Inasmuch as employees spend about 50% of their waking time at work, supervisors are also responsible for providing physical facilities that meet accepted standards of cleanliness, light, heat, ventilation, and safety. In addition, supervisors are responsible for providing leadership that will inspire employee cooperation and will allow the employees to work in a relaxed manner, confident that their best interests will be served.

Supervisors are also responsible to their employees for planning the work of the department so that a *steady* job will be provided. This may call for intricate planning of seasonal work, but the benefit to the employee and the community is obvious.

Supervisors have an obligation to stand up for their employees, to support and defend them when they rightly stick their necks out, and to tell them how they are getting along on the job.

Finally, supervisors are responsible for increasing the day-by-day satisfaction and well-being of their employees in relation to their work, their fellow employees, and the company. This responsibility includes the obligation to provide the opportunity for advancement and promotion within the limits established by the size and nature of the organization. It incorporates a moral responsibility to train employees so that they can attain the highest level of responsibility of which they are capable. And it includes the responsibility to recognize and respect the individual dignity of men—to treat each worker as an entity and not as an impersonal part of a group of humans.

Although the above list is not all-inclusive, it will give you some idea of the many responsibilities that enlightened supervisors should feel toward their employees.

Responsibility to Customers. A supervisor's basic responsibility to the customer is to help the company make a quality product that the customer wants, produce it when the customer wants it, and fabricate it at a price the customer is willing and able to pay—and all at a fair profit. In addition, the supervisor is responsible to the customer for building integrity into the company's products—for striving to improve the company's products so that they represent better buys for the customers and uphold the company's reputation for quality products.

Responsibility to the Public and Government.   Business exists because the public and the government *allow* it to exist. Corporations come into being and are allowed to operate because the citizens and the government of a particular state *agreed* through their laws that they (the corporations) could do so. Business owns property and locates buildings in accordance with the rights *granted* by local governments. Inasmuch as a business exists and operates through the consent of the public and government, it has a very definite responsibility to each of them.

To help meet these responsibilities, a supervisor should first of all obey the operating laws set forth by the local, state, and federal governments. This supervisory responsibility includes obeying not only the letter of the law but the spirit of the law as well. Where a law is vague and loopholes exist, the supervisor is responsible for operating within the total meaning of the law, considering the best interests of his employees and the community.

Many of the supervisory responsibilities discussed here were not recognized twenty years ago. Today, however, enlightened managers are developing an awareness and a philosophy of their multiple obligations and responsibilities. Managers are recognizing as never before that a firm will not prosper for any considerable time if its sole objective is to make as much money as quickly as possible. [*End of extract.*]

WHAT SPECIAL QUALITIES DOES A SUCCESSFUL SUPERVISOR NEED?

The characteristics or qualities that will make a successful supervisor are difficult to pinpoint precisely. Some qualities are more important than others, and some are difficult to describe. However, we do know that a successful supervisor must be able to inspire his employees, to motivate them, and to direct their work. As previously indicated, he needs to have technical, human, and conceptual competence. In addition to these qualities, he will also need to have an open mind. He must learn to search outside the everyday rut for a better method, a new policy, an improved way of doing things. He must, in other words, always be open to suggestions for a better way of performing any task.

A good supervisor needs to be able to discover what the problem is in times of trouble. Many people don't have this ability; they simply cannot see what is wrong when trouble erupts. They see and treat the symptoms of the problem rather than the causes of the problem. They may give aspirin for a headache (the symptom), when the real problem or cause of the headache is eyestrain. The cure, therefore, is to purchase glasses—not aspirin. Thus, a good supervisor needs to have the ability to get to the heart of the problem, to discover its real cause, and to take action to *cure* the trouble.

desirable qualities

To do a good job, supervisors also need most of the following qualities. See how many you have, and make plans to develop those in which you are weak.

1. *A good supervisor should have ambition—the desire to manage and grow.* He should always be willing to learn, to develop new skills, to broaden his job. He should not be afraid to take a chance but instead should possess confidence that he will succeed.

2. *A supervisor should be a self-starter.* He should think and move on his own initiative and not wait to be told by others to do something. To do this he needs self-confidence and courage to move ahead.

3. *A supervisor should be able to think.* This is perhaps the hardest task most people face. Most of us find it easy *to do, to act, to perform.* We have difficulty, however, in thinking clearly about a problem—our minds wander, we are distracted by noises or other problems, or we prefer to *do things* rather than *think* about how to solve problems.

4. *A supervisor should be able to express himself clearly.* The best idea in the world is worthless unless it is communicated well. As you know, supervisors spend most of their time communicating; therefore, they need to do it well. We aren't talking about great speaking or great writing. What we are talking about instead is the basic ability that a supervisor needs to get ideas across clearly to his employees so that they can understand what he wants them to do.

5. *A supervisor should be a salesman.* Any idea that you think up and communicate to others needs to be "sold." Selling an idea—convincing others of its worth—is one of a supervisor's prime tasks. Selling a plan of action is a vital part of a supervisor's job of communicating to his employees.

6. *A supervisor should possess moral integrity.* Truthfulness, honesty, and integrity should be so much a part of a supervisor that his subordinates will have total confidence in him and his actions.

7. *A supervisor should be able to organize.* This is another very important attribute, because a supervisor is constantly called on to organize his own work as well as the work of his men in order to maximize output.

8. *A supervisor should have the ability to work with and through other people.* He has to be able to get along with others and to get them to do what needs to be done for the organization.

9. *A supervisor should be willing to tackle hard problems and make tough decisions.* Anyone can make an easy decision, but a good supervisor must be willing to tackle the hard problems and make tough or unpopular decisions.

10. *A supervisor should be dynamic and have the ability to inspire others.* This is that special something, which you can't put your finger on, that makes you want to follow the directions of and work with some leader.

11. *A supervisor should have the ability to size up others and to recognize individual strengths and weaknesses.* This is a critical ability needed by supervisors in order to get the right man in the right job, as well as to reject the unqualified applicant.

12. *A supervisor should like people.* He should like to be with people and work with people. In fact, it is hard to visualize a supervisor who doesn't like his men, who doesn't have a sense of loyalty and feeling for his employees.

13. *A supervisor should be a balanced person.* This means that he should be levelheaded, understanding, firm, able to laugh, and fair.

14. *A supervisor should have the ability to delegate authority to others.* He should get satisfaction from seeing things done through the independent efforts of his employees.

WHAT OTHER SPECIAL QUALITIES DO YOU NEED?

In addition to the characteristics and qualities discussed previously, you will need to possess, if you want to be a good supervisor, a *willingness to subordinate your own desires and wishes* to those of *your* supervisors and bosses. You'll have to realize that you cannot have your own way over every matter but must instead submit to your bosses' wishes.

Also, despite all that can be done by you and others, disputes, grievances, and problems will sometimes arise among your employees. In each instance, you will need to call on every ounce of *levelheadedness and wisdom* that you possess to mediate these situations and render fair and impartial answers to the petitions.

You will need, of course, to have a thorough *understanding of what your job is* and what you are supposed to do. Knowing the technical aspects of your job will give you confidence and assurance in dealing with problems and in talking with employees.

special characteristics

You will need to *win the friendship, loyalty, and support* of your employees as well as of your other associates. In addition, you will need to possess and show a spirit of willing cooperation with other supervisors in your division as well as in other areas of the firm. No man is an island. You live and work with others, and to succeed as a supervisor you will need all the help you can get from your associates.

You will need *a good mind and a good education.* A good mind is reflected in an open and willing-to-learn attitude; that is, you don't mind tackling problems. A good education is reflected not in the number of years spent in school, but in the quality and amount of information you absorbed. Experience in many instances can compensate for formal education. For example, you will need to get along well with your associates and employees—a quality that is learned from experience rather than from schooling.

As a good supervisor you should always try to *see the whole picture* (using your conceptual skill) in order to understand what top and middle management want done and why. To be a successful supervisor you will need to understand the whole picture and communicate this in an understandable way to your fellow employees.

Patience is a virtue that you will need to be successful—patience to listen to and understand employees; patience to spend whatever time is needed to understand and improve work situations and worker relations; patience to take the time necessary to plan the total work flow and organize it in such a way that employees will feel comfortable in doing their jobs.

To be a successful supervisor you will need to be *flexible* in order to adjust to new procedures, new and changing conditions, and new ways of solving problems. Resisting change is one of the surest ways to slow down progress. Successful supervisors are the ones with open and receptive minds who do not resist change. They welcome new ideas, new ways of performing old jobs, and new concepts about how things can be improved.

To be a successful supervisor you must be *self-confident*. Therefore, you will need to have faith and confidence in your abilities and in your capacity to plan, organize, and direct the efforts of others.

Finally, and perhaps most important, you will need to possess *initiative* and the *desire to succeed*. If your desire to be a successful supervisor is strong enough, you may well overcome any shortcomings that you see in yourself. Determination, willingness, and the strong desire to be a successful supervisor will put you well on the way to achieving your goal.

HOW CAN YOU DEVELOP THESE QUALITIES?

The answer to developing the needed supervisory qualities lies in hard work, motivation on your part, and in formal and informal education. Managerial or supervisory courses will help in many instances. Experience can also teach you if you will allow yourself to profit from it. Another way to learn that has been used by a lot of successful men is to watch good supervisors at work. Observe what they do, see how they handle difficult employees, and watch how they solve tough problems. Learn from their good as well as from their poor habits. Accept and model your actions after their good habits, but reject their poor behavior patterns.

work, experience, and education   One of the most successful supervisors that I ever worked for had no formal education in the area of human relations and supervision. He didn't know what anthropology or sociology was. He finished high school and immediately started working and learning from the school of hard knocks. He worked hard and possessed many of the characteristics talked about above. A few years after starting work he was promoted to a supervisory position. As a supervisor he was well liked by his men; they could always count on his going to bat for them and getting a fair decision. He got along well with other managers and earned their respect and admiration. His employees could always be sure that he would recognize and reward hard work and talent, and they could always count on his being available to hear out a problem or mediate a tough decision. He was no patsy or easy pushover, but he did welcome the discussion of ideas that were at variance with his own. He was, in fact, one of the smartest, hardest-working managers I have ever known. And he developed into this position through extra effort and desire. If this is your objective, there is no reason why you, too, cannot succeed if you work hard enough at it.

ARE THERE OPPORTUNITIES IN SUPERVISION?

The opportunities in supervision are innumerable. Virtually every business enterprise, every governmental office, and every institution present possibilities for the application of supervisory skills. Every business is a potential source of employment for a supervisor. Young men and women who qualify as potential supervisors are being sought by business today as never before because their worth and contributions to a going concern are recognized.

As indicated throughout this chapter, you cannot be a supervisor by simply deciding to be one. Instead, the road to supervision involves a lot of study, hard work, and on-the-job training. Making yourself a successful supervisor, therefore, is a long but rewarding process. The field offers abundant opportunities for self-expression and financial reward if you are willing to work at it.

A Case Study
BILL WILDER'S OPPORTUNITY

For three years, Bill Wilder had worked as a clerk in the men's department of a large department store. He liked his job, the people he worked with, and his boss—Bob Teal. The men's department was one of the largest and best-run departments in the store. The fourteen clerks in the department consistently sold more merchandise than any others in the entire operation, and customer complaints and returns were at a minimum. In Bill Wilder's eyes, it was an "ideal department with a staff of dedicated, hard-working employees."

Because of the success of the men's department, Bob Teal had earned a reputation in the store as being the best supervisor in the business and was generally regarded as being groomed for higher-level positions.

Last week, Teal was called into the manager's office to talk about the poor showing that the home furnishings department had made during the past six years. Despite the fact that the store carried nationally advertised brands of quality merchandise, sales in home furnishings seemed to lag. Harry Vaughan, the department supervisor, planned to retire in two months, and the store manager offered the job to Bob Teal. For Teal, it would mean managing a larger department made up of four separate sections, employing twenty-seven clerks. In addition to the challenge it would offer him to improve sales, Bob Teal recognized the new position as a step up the managerial ladder with a generous increase in salary. He was eager to make the move, but his first job was to recommend someone to succeed him as manager in the men's department.

Bill Wilder seemed a likely candidate, so he asked Wilder to meet him in his office at 10:30 A.M. to discuss the opening. As he waited for Wilder to come, Bob Teal wondered what he should tell Wilder; how he should describe his supervisory role; and what "sales" approach he should take.

1. If you were Bob Teal, what would you tell Wilder? How would you describe the job of supervising the men's department?
2. Would you try to "sell" Wilder on the job or simply let him make his decision without a sales pitch. Why?
3. What managerial abilities would you stress as being most important when you describe the job to Bill Wilder?

A Case Study
SUPERVISOR HARRIS

"It looks like everything is going wrong," Bob Harris thought. "I come to work and what do I find? Nothing right!

"Four employees didn't show up today, leaving me short-handed. I have problems enough with this old equipment without having the added problems of workers who goof off, don't show up, or come in late. And they ought to know better. Yesterday I got them all together and read them the riot act. Chewed them out properly. A supervisor's got to show them who's boss. Let them know from the beginning that they can't get by with anything.

"Every time they have a problem—no matter how small—they call me. And I have to get in the middle of it all and do the job for them. It looks like I'm always repairing a machine, or adjusting a feeder, or taking an employee's place in the assembly line when he's absent. I'm always on the run. Always trying to catch up on a job. Always behind in production. If I didn't understand our production process as well as I do, I don't know how the company would get along. I know these machines and products inside out. I could run any one of them in my sleep. But my workers couldn't care less about the whole darn works!

"And these idiots don't seem to appreciate all I do for them. Every time I start to tell them something for their own good, they bristle and 'get their dander up.' If they want me to treat them like babies, they've got another thought coming! If a man can't take it and dish it out, he shouldn't be working for me."

About this time, Bob was interrupted in his thoughts by one of his men saying, "Hey Bobbie, we've run out of lag bolts."

"Well, what do you expect?" Bob shouted at him. "If you don't order material you won't have any!" The employee shrugged his shoulders and said, "Ordering ain't my job."

Bob immediately picked up the phone and called a local supplier to see if he could let him have three gross of the bolts.

Bob just didn't understand why things like this were always happening. He had told every one of his employees that they should watch out for things like this. He made it clear whenever a new man came on the job that his job was to "keep the machines going—to keep production rolling." He felt that his employees ought to have enough "get up and go" to look after things like this and not have production always being held up because they were out of materials, or a machine needed to be repaired, or for some other darn reason.

18

Lately, Bob's boss, Mr. Nelson, had been on Bob's back because he was behind in his orders. Customers were calling for parts, and Bob's department was holding up the works. In fact, Mr. Nelson was always telling Bob about how his work affected other parts of the company. "Hell," Bob thought, "all I'm interested in is the work in my own department. If I can keep it going, the rest of the plant can take care of itself. I can only do so much. Haven't got time to look after everybody else's job. A man shouldn't have someone on his back all the time, and I'm fed up with Mr. Nelson always telling me something. This is the second time this year he has jumped on me."

1. What kind of supervisor do you think Bob Harris is?
2. What are his good points? His weaknesses? Cite evidence in the case study to support your conclusions.
3. If you were Mr. Nelson, what would you do about Bob Harris?

2
LEADING AND SUPERVISING OTHERS

This chapter explains—

- The qualities you need to be a good leader
- How leadership is important in supervision
- The four types of leaders

A good leader is the person who knows where he is going and can persuade others to join him. He's out front *leading*, rather than staying behind *pushing*. He is the most valued man in any organization today. Most of us recognize a good leader but can't discover precisely what makes one.

Leadership is an elusive quality that inspires others to perform. It is a quality that enables a supervisor to influence others to accept his directions freely and willingly. Good leaders seem to have a special knack of getting others to follow them and to do what they want done.

Although you might be a good leader, you may not necessarily be a good supervisor. One man, for example, can be a good leader of a rowdy mob. He might have the capacity to excite the mob and get them to break windows and follow his directions. This same leader, however, might be a poor supervisor under calmer conditions. He may well lack the qualities we talked about in the previous chapter—qualities of supervision dealing with technical skills, human skills, and conceptual skills. He may not be able to plan, organize, and perform the other functions that supervisors are expected to perform. A good leader, therefore, does not have to be a good supervisor. On the other hand, if you want to be a good supervisor, you will need to possess many of the necessary qualities of a good leader. Let's take a look at some of these qualities of leadership and see what they are.

"Most of us recognize a good leader, but can't discover precisely what makes one."

Many people are concerned about what it takes to make them good leaders. Believe it or not, it is almost impossible to find the correct answer. Although you and I can recognize a good leader, we cannot say with certainty that if you possess certain traits or characteristics, you will be a good leader.

By observing outstanding leaders, however, we can list a few qualities that most of them possess. We can say, therefore, that if you want to be a good leader, you will probably need to possess the following characteristics:

1. *You will need a desire to excel.* A leader is never content with being second. He always wants to be out front. He is a self-starting individual who is willing to work long hours to achieve success.

    needed characteristics

2. *You will need a sense of responsibility.* A leader is never afraid to seek and accept obligations to others. He always willingly discharges any responsibility he assumes.

3. *You will need a capacity for work.* Good leaders are always willing to accept the demands of leadership success—long hours and hard work.

4. *You will need a feel for good human relations.* Leaders are always involved with their fellow workers, studying them, analyzing their needs and demands, and trying to understand their problems. This interest and ability to discover what their fellow workers need is in all probability the single most important characteristic of a good leader.

5. *You will need to exhibit a contagious enthusiasm.* No one wants to follow a dull, uninspired leader. Enthusiasm is something like mob appeal—once we are caught up in it, we move along with it. And once workers are caught up in the web of enthusiasm for their jobs and their work, they take on a new sense of enthusiasm and commitment to the jobs they are asked to do.

6. *You will need to have a high sense of integrity.* Any leader who succeeds has to be honest with himself and with his followers. You may fool some of the people for a while, but sooner or later a lack of honesty will force you out of a position of leadership. Few men who are insecure and undependable succeed as leaders.

Obviously, these are not the only qualities you will need. Many of the prerequisites of a supervisor previously discussed also hold good here. Such qualities as intelligence, character, and loyalty are important too.

WHAT TRAITS INDICATE A POOR LEADER?

Poor leaders send out signals that indicate that they are doing a poor job. You can probably recognize many of these traits in leaders you have known.

Make every effort to observe the following nine rules if you want to be an effective leader.

1. *Don't pass the blame.* If something goes wrong and it is your responsibility, don't blame someone else. Be willing to accept blame as well as praise.
2. *Don't be self-centered.* Leaders who think mostly of themselves lose the support and help of their employees. Show interest in the group, not in yourself. Encourage others to participate.
3. *Don't ask an employee to do something that you wouldn't do.* And, likewise, don't do something that you wouldn't let your employees do.
4. *Don't be aloof, cool, unfriendly. Don't talk down to your employees.* These tactics only serve to isolate you and lower employee morale. Instead, be easy to see and talk to.
5. *Don't be a "Big I."* Don't lord it over your employees.
6. *Don't drag your feet.* When something needs doing—do it!
7. *Don't say "yes" and not mean it.* Always be truthful, honest, and fair.
8. *Don't agonize over decisions.* Look at the facts, use your best judgment, then commit yourself.
9. *Don't jump to conclusions.* Too quick a decision can frequently cause more harm than good. Don't be a procrastinator nor a gun jumper. Get the facts, use your best judgment, then make your decision.

WHAT IS THE CONNECTION BETWEEN LEADERSHIP AND SUPERVISION?

Although most people recognize that leadership is a part of supervision, they sometimes fail to see that supervision isn't the same thing as leadership. As we have indicated before, supervisors must make plans, establish a satisfactory organization, hire people to staff the organization, tell them what to do, and set up controls. A leader doesn't necessarily do these same things. All we expect of a leader is that he get other people to follow him. A supervisor, however, is asked to perform all of the functions associated with supervision in addition to being a leader. We can see, therefore, that although a strong leader may be a weak supervisor, a strong supervisor must be a good leader too.

The leader of a group is not always the foreman appointed by management. In other words, the leader of a group doesn't necessarily have to be the supervisor of the group. Leadership roles are often assumed by members of a work group. For example, a nonappointed leader of a work group would be the member who could get the group to, say, reduce or hold their output to a level that would be below what the supervisor wants. This indicates that leadership is something that is an active process and not necessarily something that grows out of a position of authority, such as a supervisory position.

Before leadership can exist, you have to have—

1. Leaders and followers who agree on a common cause or goal.
2. Leaders and followers who agree on what needs to be done to reach that goal.

To illustrate this theory, consider the above example of the work group that followed one of its own members in restricting output. Here you had a leader and followers who agreed on their goal, as well as agreed on what they needed to do to reach their objective. Thus, although the leader needs only to get his associates to follow him, the supervisor must perform all the functions associated with supervision.

WHAT IS AN INFORMAL LEADER?

Every work group has a leader. This leader may be officially *appointed* by the management of the firm and be thus accepted by the group, or he may be an *informal* leader unofficially selected by the group itself.

An *informal leader* chosen by a group may well be chosen because he is taller and can be seen, or because he has a loud booming voice and can be heard, or because he has work seniority and is thus most respected, or because he says funny things and can relieve group tension. Whatever the reason, an informal leader's reign is a precarious thing. He might be the leader today and be replaced tomorrow. This is particularly true where the composition of the work group changes rather frequently or where the work location or product worked on changes.

Leadership in a group depends on what the group's objective is. If the group centers its attention on getting work done, like producing 400 units per hour, then the leader will probably be the person who can generate the most enthusiasm. On the other hand, if the work group needs to have tension relieved because of the stress and critical nature of the job, the leader may well be one who can reduce tension through his humor. A work group may, however, have both of these objectives (400 units per hour and relief of tension), in which case it may choose two leaders—if it can't find one person possessing both attributes.

*source of
leadership
authority*

WHAT IS THE DIFFERENCE BETWEEN JOB-CENTERED AND EMPLOYEE-CENTERED SUPERVISION?

Some supervisors are *job-centered* in their approach to leadership. They spend most of their time initiating and directing their employees' actions toward solving production or job-related problems. The job-centered supervisor is more interested in the things of production than in his employees.

He arranges working conditions so that the human element—the worker—interferes to a minimum degree. He keeps his employees at their jobs and insists that the work be accomplished in accordance with directions. He forces his employees to think "things," to think "job," to think "achieving production."

Other supervisors are *employee-centered*. They spend a great deal of their time in helping and in satisfying members of the work group. This type of supervisor is more interested in people than in things. He wants to avoid frustration on the part of his employees. He wants his employees' personal needs satisfied. He wants to develop a comfortable, friendly atmosphere or environment in which his employees work. He wants to boost their morale, reduce their tensions, and help them realize their personal needs for social sanction and work satisfaction.

approach to job

A good leader manages to combine both qualities in his leadership style. He knows that if he emphasizes the job only, he will be considered a driver and a hard taskmaster and thus risk the possibility of loss of group cooperation and support. On the other hand, if he emphasizes only the employee or social aspect, then he will be regarded as a popularity seeker; he may be used by his men for their personal advantages, and productive output will suffer.

To be a good leader, therefore, you should strive to combine both qualities. You should try to provide a balanced approach, giving emphasis to maintaining morale, and at the same time getting an adequate work performance. In other words, you should be thoughtful and help promote employee satisfactions, but at the same time you should recognize the role that productive output plays.

WHAT ARE THE FOUR TYPES OF LEADERS?

Some leaders are very bossy, some are very strict, others try to get their men involved in making decisions, and still others just leave their employees alone. These four types of leaders are:

1. Dictatorial.
2. Authoritarian.
3. Democratic.
4. Laissez-faire.

You will easily recognize each type when you see him.

supervisory styles

The *dictatorial* leader is exactly what the name implies. He is a negative leader and holds threats of punishment, discharge, and fear over the heads of his employees to get them to do his will. Although he gets results in some work situations, most managers doubt that the quality and quantity of his results can long remain at a high level. This type of leader almost invariably promotes unrest and dissatisfaction, and sooner or later his employees "revolt" by implementing a work slowdown or by simply transferring to other jobs. Dictatorial leadership seldom lasts over long periods of time.

The *authoritarian* leader exercises strong control over his men. You have probably seen this type: he always resists help from others, and he plays his cards close to his chest—withholding information from his men, making them dependent on him for decisions. He is the strong "captain of his ship" and controls all coordination and interface between workers in achieving the group's goal. Because of this leader's strong control and the group's dependence on him, the group is virtually lost in his absence.

The *democratic* leader, on the other hand, solicits aid and advice from his men—trying to get them involved in work problems and their solutions. This is the type of leader whose group can function effectively even during his prolonged absences. The reason, of course, is because the men are used to working with problems and their solutions and are aware of the group's situation and progress. In the leader's absence, therefore, they can take over and move ahead.

The last type of leader, the *laissez-faire* leader, is really not much of a leader at all. He is a leader in name only, and his position of leadership is one decreed by upper management. He sometimes is the boss's son, or he may have married the "old man's" daughter to get the position. He is more or less a figurehead with little or no power and is virtually never listened to or respected by the men. In situations like this where the appointed leader is really a leader in name only, the true position of leadership is usually assumed by some other individual (perhaps the leader's assistant) or by some senior man in the work group whom the men like and respect.

Which Type Is Best?   We can't say that one particular type of leadership is best. What is best in one situation may be worst in another. It depends on you, the work, and the men you are working with. In general, the democratic form is probably the all-around best. However, in situations where close control must be maintained, your group might well prefer an authoritarian type of leader. For example, if you are supervising a rescue effort, then an authoritarian type might be best. But if you are supervising a group of highly skilled self-starters (such as research scientists), then the laissez-faire or let-them-alone type of leadership may be best. In most work situations you will have to judge which type would be best suited or which combination would be best for your particular operation.

DO LEADERSHIP PATTERNS AFFECT TEAMWORK?

Both experience and studies have shown that the one factor that affects a group's behavior and motivation is the behavior pattern of the leader.

If you are the *dependent* type of leader, you are afraid to make decisions—to take chances. You are primarily concerned with saving your own hide; therefore, you follow rules and regulations to a "T." You communicate with your men only when absolutely necessary. As a result of all this, your employees have no spirit and lack incentive, and in general an atmosphere of apathy and doing nothing prevails.

If you are *dictatorial,* then your actions promote anger and antagonism. You exercise close control and generally limit your communications with your employees to giving them orders or directions. You may get work done by being dictatorial, but your employees are unhappy, antagonistic, and rebellious.

If you want to concentrate on your own personal advancement, then you may try to be the *diplomatic* leader. If you are this type, you know how to handle people and get along reasonably well with both your employees and your superiors. You have frequent contacts with your employees, but largely on a superficial basis. You tend to manipulate people, and your employees are not team-oriented. Instead, they are interested in their own selfish ends.

If you want to promote an air of cooperation and teamwork, you should try to be the *coach* or *team* leader. Using this style of leadership, you aim at building a team, at coaching the individual members. The group as a whole, instead of the individual, is dominant in your thinking. You have free and easy communications with your employees, and a sincere two-way exchange

effect of leader's behavior pattern

of ideas takes place. Your entire team seeks to achieve productive goals *as a team,* and thereby the whole team wins advancement as well as security in the organization. Using the coaching style of leadership, you emphasize the "we" versus the "I" or "you" approach. You discuss problems and solutions rather than give orders. You decide on action by mutual agreement instead of by rules and direct orders. You promote an atmosphere where two-way communications can easily take place between you and your employees. And, finally, you promote teamwork and loyalty instead of apathy.

The team leader is probably the ideal type of leader. He is concerned both with his employees and with production. He is successful at motivating people to achieve goals. His employees are committed to doing the job that needs to be done. They see the relationship between their personal job satisfaction and work achievement. The true coach or team leader thus successfully shows his men the need for the existence of a mutual relationship of trust and respect between them and promotes respect among them for their individual jobs and accomplishments.

WHAT TYPE OF LEADER DO EMPLOYEES LOOK FOR?

No two leaders are exactly alike, and no one type can be singled out as the ideal leader that employees are looking for. One person might look for one aspect of leadership, whereas another employee might emphasize another aspect. Despite these differences, surveys show that there are specific qualities that most employees look for in a leader. A majority of employees, for example, want a leader who gives recognition and credit for doing a job. They like to be patted on the back. They also want to work for a leader who is friendly and keeps them informed about what is going on in their department—not one who rarely communicates, who plays his cards close to his chest.

Employees also indicate that they like to work for a leader who lets them know where they stand, how they are doing, and what their chances for promotion or advancement are. They also want a leader who gives them a sense of importance—who makes them feel that they are a needed member of the team. They like to work for a leader who is ordered in his work—who plans his work, then works his plan—who has well-defined jobs and everything in its place.

*leaders who
promote teamwork*

Workers like leaders who promote teamwork in their department by emphasizing the positive rather than negative aspects of their performances, and who provide the opportunity to get their ideas heard and tried out.

Finally, employees like to work for leaders who are fair, impartial, and just in their dealings, thereby promoting a feeling of trust and security.

ARE LEADERS BORN OR MADE?

No one is a "born" leader. You may have certain capacities that enable you to develop into a leader, but you have to work at it. What are the capacities that you need if you want to lead other men? No one can say for sure. However, if you look at good leaders, you will probably find that the common traits in the majority of them are as follows:

1. *Intelligence.* Leaders are usually a bit smarter or a bit more intelligent than their followers. This does not mean that a successful leader must have an excess of intelligence over his average follower. But it does mean that he is a bright and alert person with above average intelligence.

   leadership traits

2. *Understanding.* A leader needs to have an understanding of and feeling for other people. Because a leader works with people and gets things done through the efforts of others, he must be accurately attuned to the feelings of others, to their goals, and to their problems. A good coaching leader should be sensitive to the values of the entire group in addition to those of the individuals.

3. *Social activity.* A good leader needs to be active socially. He needs to participate actively in group functions. He needs to initiate actions for others and for the group as a whole.

4. *Communication.* A good leader needs to be able to make his employees understand him and his ideas. He needs to be able to communicate

messages accurately and clearly. If he can't communicate his "million-dollar" idea, it is worthless.

5. *Criticism.* A good leader can't let other people "get under his skin" with their criticisms. If he does, he's headed for failure. A good leader can and does, however, take and welcome deserved criticism while shrugging off tactless, heavy-handed attacks from his adversaries.

As you can see, you can work on and nurture most of these traits. You probably have the native intelligence required to be a good leader. Using this native ability and intelligence, you can improve your capacity to understand others, your social activity, your communications skills, and your ability to accept criticism. With good native intelligence, most people agree that a person can develop into a position of leadership.

You must remember, however, that a leader is one who operates in a particular work situation relative to the intelligence, attitudes, and abilities of his workers. This means that although you could be a leader in one work group, you might not be able to be a leader in another work group. A man who has the capacity to be the governor of a state and to lead legislators might be a miserable leader in a work group in a manufacturing plant. The capacity to lead is always relative to those being led. You can be a leader in *many* situations but not in *all* situations.

WHAT ARE POINTS TO REMEMBER ABOUT BEING A LEADER?

Remember that leadership is the capacity to get others to follow you willingly and to do what you want them to do. As a leader, you will be called upon to make decisions that will be unpopular with some of your employees. You can't, therefore, be a "good Joe" to everyone. What you want to strive for is your employees' respect and their satisfaction with your leadership. Leading is, to a degree, a lonely job, but at the same time a rewarding one. You will have a sense of accomplishment for your company and for your workers. You will possess status and prestige among your friends in the community as well as among the employees at work. And, of course, you will have a higher income with the higher (and more difficult) job.

A leader always depends on his employees for support. In fact, without their support and cooperation, he cannot lead. Thus, the authority or control you have over your employees is what they give you. Resist pulling your rank, therefore, except in cases of real demand. If you are just, fair, and impartial, you will earn the support and respect of your employees, and you won't have to pull your rank by telling them that you are the boss and they must do what you say.

leadership check points

Handle different employees in different ways. Be firm and authoritative with the insecure and dependent type of employee as well as with the pushy and hostile employee. Be cooperative and willing to discuss problems with your cooperative, aggressive, and willing worker. Be democratic and give a free rein to employees who are self-starters, who know their jobs, and who work best with the least supervision. In any critical or emergency situation, however, always use the authoritarian approach. If the boat is sinking, you don't want to call a conference to discuss who should dip water!

Don't try to take credit for what the group has done. Most great leaders are modest and are quick to give credit to others for their accomplishments. A good leader doesn't have to tell how good he is—the loyalty of his men and their work will speak it "loud and clear" for him. Employees respond positively to the leader who doesn't try to hog the credit.

Be genuine. Don't try to give the "know-it-all" air. If you don't know the answer to a problem posed by an employee, say so. Then ask the employee for his opinion. If he doesn't have an answer, tell him you will get an answer to the problem and will let him know. Getting help and suggestions from others makes for better human relations.

Be consistent. Your employees will want to be able to predict what your answer will be today as well as tomorrow. Always show enthusiasm for a job well done and disapproval for slovenly work. Don't sometimes avoid the job of disapproving because it is unpleasant.

Try to understand your employees. Try to put yourself in their shoes; if you do, you will be able to predict their needs and responses better. You will know your men better and can give them better advice and instructions.

Finally, always be fair and just. Treat all of your employees in the same way. Don't show favoritism. Not only will having a "teacher's pet" cause dissension among your employees, it may well wreck a good team that you have worked hard to build.

A Case Study
TI IE CASE OF I HE OILY RAG

Ben Adams had worked eight years for a textile firm specializing in double knits when he was promoted to supervisor of the packing and shipping department. Although he had been well liked by the men prior to his promotion, an incident that occurred raised a question in his mind.

His story goes like this. The men in the packing and shipping department, according to him, had fallen down on their jobs and were "goofing off" at least 30% of the time before he was made their supervisor. Aware of this, he instituted a strict work program, telling every employee work group exactly what to do, when he expected the job to be completed, and what their next job assignment would be. This information was communicated by a departmental "work order" that he designed. Men who were caught away from their assigned work areas without excuses were subject to layoff or dismissal. Reporting late to work from rest breaks or lunch periods also brought reprimands from him.

The men, sensing that he was trying to make a good showing, tried to cooperate with his "new broom" approach until the day he caught one group cleaning up in the washroom a good 10 or 15 minutes before lunch time. He immediately sent them back to their work stations with a promise of a penalty deduction from their pay. According to the men, this was the last straw; they knew that their old buddy had deserted them.

The next day, as Ben walked through his department checking up on his men, a dirty, oily rag in some mysterious way sailed through the air and hit him squarely in the face. In a fit of rage, he vowed to fire the individuals responsible for the act. Although the men declared their innocence and indicated that perhaps the rag had been thrown from one of the moving arms on a packing machine, it was obvious that they were amused by the incident.

1. What was wrong with Ben Adams's supervision?
2. How should he have behaved in his new assignment as supervisor of the packing and shipping department?
3. What action, if any, should he take about the incident of the oily rag?
4. If you were Ben's boss, what advice would you give him?

A Case Study
BUNNIES BURGERS

As president of Bunnies Burgers, Ken Johnson was always on the lookout for a potential manager for one of the chain's outlets.

Founded in 1972, the chain had grown from a sales of $230,000 during its first year to an annual sales of $673,000,000. It was known as the leader in its field, and no small part of its success was due to the shrewd and capable management of Mr. Johnson. In his words, "Our most valuable asset is our employee. And our most valued employee is a qualified leader who can manage one of our food centers." He believed what he said and spent the greatest part of his time in looking for, interviewing, and recruiting potential managers.

His latest applicant was a young man named Robert Nicosea. Robert's experience was not too exciting: work in a supermarket as a checker, and summer work during his school as a construction laborer and as a clerk in an accounting firm. Not too impressive a record, to be sure, but what struck Mr. Johnson was Robert's burning desire to get ahead—to succeed—to make something of himself.

Robert's job in the supermarket was head checker, and as such he was responsible for hiring, training, and manning the eleven registers. The job also entailed checking out each register daily to be sure that the tapes and the money checked. The store manager wrote a glowing account of Robert's job performance but did indicate that he was a little impatient to move ahead—to get promotions and salary increases.

When interviewed by Mr. Johnson, Robert exhibited an almost contagious enthusiasm for honest work, belief in his fellow man, and a desire to move ahead on the job. According to his personal data sheet, Robert Nicosea was the leader and informal spokesman for his local bass fishing club, and in addition was president of his town's Young Man's Fellowship Group. When asked about his prior work and his current involvement in other groups, Robert pushed it aside as only routine—nothing to brag about.

When Mr. Johnson asked Robert about why he wanted to be the manager of one of their outlets— why he thought he would be a good leader—Mr. Nicosea thought for a moment and replied, "First of all, I know I can do the job. I've had experience in food handling in a supermarket, and I know figures and book work. Also, I think I know how to handle employees. I believe that people who work for you like to see their boss have a strong hand and exercise sound and strong control. They like a superior who is not afraid to make decisions and will make them quickly. They like a boss who runs a taut ship. And I think that all of these things apply to me.

"I don't mind sticking my neck out. I'm not afraid to make a decision. And I surely don't mind telling an employee to do something—to give instructions. Furthermore, if an employee doesn't follow through

32

with what I give him to do, I don't mind reprimanding him, even firing him if he doesn't prove that he can do the job.

"I believe that I'm a born leader. I've always wanted to tell others what to do. Even when I was a little kid, I always wanted to lead the rest of the kids on my block—to tell them what we would do—to be the captain of the outfit.

"For these reasons, Mr. Johnson, I know that I could be one of your best managers within a year. I'm sure that I can run one of your outlets and increase business and profits. I'm a hard worker. I don't mind long hours, hard work, and tough goals. Give me the chance, and I will prove to you that I can get results."

Thanking Mr. Nicosea for coming to see him, Mr. Johnson indicated that he was interviewing several other candidates and would let him know his decision within a couple of days. The two shook hands and Nicosea departed.

Mr. Johnson was clearly impressed with Mr. Nicosea. But he wondered whether or not Robert Nicosea would fit in as the manager of a fast foods outlet. Did he have the leadership abilities he was looking for, or would he be too dictatorial in running an outlet catering to the eating public?

He was mulling over these ideas when his secretary announced the arrival of another appointment.

1. Would you hire Robert Nicosea? Why?
2. What leadership qualities do you see in Mr. Nicosea? Are they the type of qualities that would be effective in a fast food outlet?
3. Do you see any qualities that could be detrimental to Mr. Nicosea's success in Bunnies Burgers?

3
HOW TO COMMUNICATE CLEARLY WITH YOUR EMPLOYEES

This chapter explains—

- Why good communications are important to you
- How you can communicate more effectively
- Why communications break down
- Your role in good communications

The skill and expertise with which a supervisor communicates are in direct proportion to his skill and expertise as a manager. The better a manager communicates, the better a manager supervises.

In managing his department, a supervisor needs to communicate with his employees to explain the work that must be done, discuss who is to do it, show how it should be done, and so on. He must give orders or directions to his employees, describing what they should do and what is expected of them.

Not only do good communications tie together a group of employees making them work as a team, but good communications also tie together various component parts of an organization. Without communications, for example, the sales organization would not know what to sell, production would not know what to produce, and finance would not know the amount of money needed. In all of our organizations, communications serve to transmit information from one person to another, so we will know what to do. Communications also help us form opinions about the company as a good (or bad) employer. Through communications we are motivated to perform certain jobs with skill and vigor, and communications help to orient us in our social and economic environment. All of these types of communications are a part of and are important to the job of supervising others.

WHAT IS A COMMUNICATION?

importance and definition

A *communication* is simply the transfer of information and understanding from one person to another. It is successful only when a mutual understanding takes place—when both the sender and the receiver of the communication understand it. It is not necessary that the two parties *agree* with an idea in order for them to have a successful communication. It is, however, necessary that they *understand* the idea in order to have a successful communication.

When a communication involves the supervisor and his employees, it is often called an *employee communication*. This is a big part of a supervisor's job. In fact, it is so important that most first-line supervisors spend between 50 and 60% of their time communicating with their employees.

Communications, of course, can take place in many ways. You can communicate directly by talking or writing, or *indirectly* by gestures (thumbs down meaning "no good"), by actions (a pat on the back, drumming your fingers, or tapping your foot), by facial expressions, by tone of voice, and so on. In fact, more than half of our communications are indirectly expressed through facial expressions and body movements.

ARE YOU COMMUNICATING WHEN YOU TALK?

Not necessarily. Although speech is the most frequent form of communication, we still make a lot of mistakes when we communicate by talking.

Words are symbols that we use to transmit ideas to another person. In oral communications, you have to *conceive* of an idea first. Then you have to *choose and say the words* that you think will communicate your idea to another person. And, finally, before a communication has taken place, the other person must *understand* your meaning of the words.

Suppose, for example, that your car breaks down and you want to get a ride to work with a fellow employee. You might say, "Joe, can you pick me up in the morning?" To which Joe might reply, "Sure," thinking that you are asking him if he is physically strong enough to lift you off the floor (pick you up) during the morning hours. In this instance, communication has not taken place because the other person did not understand the meaning of your words. Or suppose you say, "Joe, how about stopping by my house after work for a drink?" You might mean a cup of coffee or a soft drink, but Joe might say, "no" because he thought you meant an alcoholic drink. Communications have to be *understood* before they are communications.

speaking vs.
understanding

DO WORDS MEAN DIFFERENT THINGS TO DIFFERENT PEOPLE?

Most of us "hear" with our hearts as well as with our ears. This is because we may give words an added meaning that is not intended. You usually don't say *mill* workers and *clerical* workers, for example, because these words might have a negative emotional connotation to some people. Rather, you might say *hourly* and *staff* employees. Or instead of saying that *union membership is compulsory* to work in a plant, you might say that you have a *union shop*.

Because we have this tendency to "hear" with our hearts, you have to be careful in communicating to others to be sure that they understand what you mean. To do this, you should try to learn ahead of time how others feel about certain situations and what their "hang-ups" and biases are so that you can express yourself with words and ideas that say to them the true meaning of what you have in mind.

word overtones

WHAT IS FEEDBACK?

When you communicate through writing, you can never be sure whether or not the person receiving your letter or note understands exactly what you are saying. You can't see his expression (a smile, a puzzled look) when he reads it. In other words, you don't have any feedback. You can't check to see if he understands the message. When you talk to another person face to face, however, you can observe his expressions. You can ask if he understands. You can repeat yourself so that he can grasp the true meaning of your words.

need for feedback

Because of feedback, two-way (face-to-face) communication is a better way to get ideas across to others than one-way communication—where the other person doesn't have the opportunity to ask questions. As a result, most communication by supervisors is oral, two-way communication.

Two-way communication is valuable because it gives the other person an opportunity to question and speak freely. In fact, you may find in two-way communication that the other person is critical of your ideas and says so quite frankly and openly. This would not be true in a one-way communication. To be a good supervisor, therefore, you should promote open, face-to-face communications between yourself and your employees, encouraging them to ask questions freely and to express their ideas openly.

WHAT ARE THE RULES FOR LISTENING?

understand the meaning

A good supervisor not only needs to listen to the words an employee is saying, he also needs to work with an employee so that he can understand the meaning the employee is placing on his words. Listening is hard work. It is easy for us to "close our ears" or "listen with only one ear" when we have other things on our minds. Sometimes when others talk to us, we are not interested in what they are saying and don't pay close attention. When we listen in this frame of mind, we are not going to get the message regardless of its importance. We need to listen attentively and sympathetically. The rules for listening, therefore, include the following:

1. *Be interested in the message.* Give the sender your full attention. When you are listening to others speaking to you—*listen.*
2. *Resist distractions.* Be completely attentive to what is being said.
3. *Don't let personal biases turn you off.* Sometimes you may not like the way a person approaches you, or you may not like the sound of a person's voice. These biases can cause you not to hear the correct message. As a supervisor you will need to get the true and correct message about what is being communicated. You should not, therefore, let your biases and preferences cause you to fail to pay proper attention to what the other person is saying.
4. *Try to understand the words and the implied message.* Just getting the facts is not enough. Try to listen with your heart as well as with your ears and thereby get the real implications. For example, an employee might talk to you about wanting to quit or getting a transfer because of the type of work she is doing. Yet when you analyze the work in the department she wants to transfer to, you can see it is the same type she is now doing. The real message, therefore, might be that she can't get along with her work partners, or that she thinks you are unfair in assigning jobs. Try to understand the whole message—the implied meaning as well as the actual words.
5. *Work hard to understand difficult ideas or material.* Don't shut your mind to what is hard to grasp.

6. *Don't hesitate to ask questions.* Be sure you understand what the other person is saying. Don't let outside distractions (from a noisy machine, a ringing telephone, or another person waving to you) cause you to miss the meaning. When such distractions do interrupt, don't be afraid to ask questions. The person doing the talking felt it was important enough to talk to you and should, therefore, welcome this sign of interest and attention on your part.

WHAT ARE THE CHANNELS OF COMMUNICATION?

Virtually every organization has two ways in which information is transferred to employees. One is the *formal* channel set up by management, and the other is the *informal* channel often called the *scuttlebutt* or *grapevine*.

Formal Channels. Formal Channels usually follow the company's organizational lines of authority from the top man to the bottom of the totem pole. Communications and directives may go down this line of communication as well as up. In theory, there should be a two-way flow. In practice, however, this is often not true. Although orders and directions tend to flow from the top down without interruption or distraction, the flow of information from the bottom up is often sidetracked or stopped. A supervisor, for example, may feel that a certain piece of information should not be passed on up to his boss because (1) he doesn't want to bother him with trivia or (2) he may feel it would not reflect well on his ability as a supervisor. Upward communications are usually questions, complaints, or grievances, and many supervisors consciously or otherwise tend to stop the flow of such communications.

channels to use

In addition to communications up and down the line of authority, we also find formal communications that are horizontal; that is, they are between employees or supervisors on the same level. These horizontal communications are necessary in order to coordinate the work of various individuals within a section or coordinate the work of various sections within a department.

Informal Channels. Regardless of the formal channels established, an *informal* channel of communication variously known as the grapevine, or rumor mill, or scuttlebutt, always exists. It is born of both curiosity and insecurity. It grows out of people working and talking together about their jobs. It is natural for it to exist because all of us want to "be on the inside" or know what the latest information is. The grapevine thus provides a channel for employees to express their apprehensions or wishes in the form of rumors or speculations.

News that comes from the rumor mill, the grapevine, or the scuttlebutt is typically more gossip than truth, is unreliable, unconfirmed, and unauthenticated. Despite this lack of reliability, it draws people like a magnet, and rumors fly. We find it everywhere: in social circles, in small towns, in churches, in schools, and in businesses. The information generated by the rumor mill is not only unreliable, it also constantly changes in character in order to suit the purposes of the individual passing it on. For these and similar reasons, the "gospel" passed along by the grapevine as the "unmitigated truth" is typically incorrect.

As a consequence of the above, the grapevine should never be used to give information to employees. Tell them yourself. Don't rely on others. In fact, the grapevine is found to be most active in companies where supervisors do not communicate openly and freely. If you don't tell your employees about job changes that will affect them, if you don't combat rumors, the grapevine will begin to manufacture speculations, and rumors will fly in all directions. Most employees would rather get the story straight from you. As a supervisor, therefore, you can do much to stem the flow of rumors by answering all questions as promptly and truthfully as you can. If employees know that they can get the right information from you, this will do much to scotch the rumors.

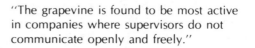

"The grapevine is found to be most active in companies where supervisors do not communicate openly and freely."

Communications break down because barriers often exist that hamper or distort the flow of communications between people. These breakdowns in communications frequently can (1) cost time and money to the company, (2) cause employees to lose work, (3) create misunderstandings, (4) cause a breakdown in team effort, and (5) seriously damage morale. Because of these serious consequences of poor communications, you should attempt to recognize and overcome barriers that might cause you to be an ineffective communicator.

The choice of words, which we have already mentioned, can cause a breakdown in communication. Status can also be a barrier to clear communication. An employee listening to his supervisor talk about production output may evaluate what he hears in relation to his own position and background—not his supervisor's. He may also assume that the supervisor doesn't understand him and his needs because the supervisor has never had to work like he does nor been in his financial position. As a consequence, he may not hear (or at least he may pay little attention to) what the supervisor is saying. Status also keeps us from speaking freely to those "up the ladder" from us. When we are in the presence of the big boss, for example, we may not express our thoughts, ideas, or complaints to him because he is so far removed from us on the company's status scale.

barriers to communications

When communications take place over some distance, misunderstanding often occurs. Telephone conversations, for example, are not as effective as face-to-face communications because you cannot see expressions, gestures, and other body signals that help the speaker communicate the true meaning of a message to you. And since you cannot see these additional means of communicating, you are not in a position to ask questions and check on meanings that you might otherwise do if you were talking face to face.

Sometimes a supervisor may prejudice a person. He may, for example, already have his mind made up about this employee's ability, and he might let this prejudgment show. The supervisor, for example, might say to the employee, "You probably won't understand this, but I'll try to explain it to you." The employee, knowing that the supervisor has no confidence in his capacity to understand, as shown by the supervisor's statement, might therefore make little effort to understand.

Or a supervisor may block communication by saying to his employee, "Where did you get such a wild idea?" Even a good idea and communication would probably die with such an introduction.

Another barrier to effective communication can be caused by either the "know-it-all" attitude on the one hand or the "I'm-so-inferior" attitude on the other hand. A person might consider himself such a know-it-all, so superior, that he feels that others don't know what they are talking about—and as a result, he doesn't bother to listen. At the other extreme, an employee who feels so inferior that he thinks he cannot understand what the boss is trying to tell him sets up a barrier to good communications and understanding by failing to listen.

Sometimes age indirectly acts as a barrier to communications. The older supervisor, for example, may have a crew-cut hairstyle, and the young employee may have long hair. They both understand the words that are being spoken, but because they are alienated by the generation gap as expressed in their hairstyles, neither one accepts the other person for what he is, and good communications are hampered.

We all have known the individual who sees himself as a certain type of person with a certain social status or position. Any communication that might tend to threaten this position of prestige would cause a breakdown in communications. Calling a supervisor by his first name, for example, might cause such a breakdown.

Physical disabilities and inadequacies should also be considered when we talk to others. A person who is hard of hearing, for example, may have difficulty hearing what we are talking about. He may even feel we are talking in a low tone to frustrate him. Such feelings can obviously create resentment as well as erect barriers to good relations and communications.

HOW DO YOU OVERCOME COMMUNICATIONS BARRIERS?

Overcoming the barriers to communications mentioned in the previous section is more a matter of common sense than of any special skill. On occasion, we all use the techniques needed to overcome these barriers. The trouble is we don't use them enough. What we need to do, therefore, is become aware of the barrier problems and then utilize more frequently the techniques that we already know.

Face-to-face talks are always better than other forms of communication. For one thing, talking directly to a person enables us to ask simple questions during our conversations in order to clear up any misconceptions. Watching facial expressions, such as a frown or a raised eyebrow, can also give a clue to lack of comprehension. Expressions of bewilderment or misunderstanding are good feedback clues. If a friend looks quizzical when you are explaining the floor plan of a house, this feedback is your clue to explain it again or perhaps make a drawing of it.

how to be understood

Simple, clear, clean-cut language does much to break down barriers to understanding. When we talk with others, we aren't out to win a speaking contest. Long, complicated sentences and words are a sure road to confusion. Avoid them at all costs. Use language that the other person can readily understand. For example, don't use "exactitude of verbiage" when what you mean is "precise words."

Repetition is another way to overcome communications barriers. For instance, repeat a message several times using different words. Try to say the same thing using simple expressions that the other person may readily understand. The frequency and degree of repetition will depend, of course, on the other person's experience, his background, and the nature of the message.

Try to place yourself in the other fellow's shoes. In other words, try to understand his feelings, his opinions, and his attitudes. We call this *empathizing.* If we try to understand how another person feels, then we can communicate to him in ways that he should understand.

Always be genuine and concerned about the welfare of the other person and about the possible effect that the communication will have on him. Whether you are "chewing out" an employee for taking too many coffee breaks or simply reminding him that lunch is from noon to 1:00 P.M., the way you express yourself and your obvious concern for the total long-run welfare of the employee will have a positive effect on the way he receives, understands, and takes your conversation.

Finally, when possible, choose a physical location that will help and not hinder good communications. Talking over problems in a quiet office free from noise and distractions is quite different from trying to talk over problems on a machine shop floor. There are, of course, emergencies, and we cannot always choose the best spot to talk, but we should be aware of what makes a bad place to communicate with others.

WHAT IS A SUPERVISOR'S ROLE IN GOOD COMMUNICATIONS?

The communications climate in your organization depends to a large extent on you. If you as a supervisor establish sound and clear communications with your associates and employees, an air of healthy open exchange will exist.

Although every person is involved in communications and has a responsibility to communicate effectively, the supervisor is the one on whose shoulders will rest much of the responsibility for the success or failure of a firm's communication program. The supervisor, like everyone else, communicates with others. In addition to this, however, the supervisor is charged with maintaining a good climate for communications among his employees. He is responsible for seeing that his employees understand each other, their jobs, and their objectives. He is also the key person responsible for communicating between his department and other departments in the company. He is, in effect, the linking chain between departments, and as such he must realize that the total communications climate in a company is no stronger than the weakest supervisor.

the supervisor's
part

In a large company, clear communications might well be stopped or hindered by a supervisor who is weak in communications skills, thereby preventing a clear concept of the boss's wishes from reaching the rest of the organization. In like fashion, a first-line supervisor is responsible for good communications and understanding within his unit. Despite the importance of communications, however, and despite the fact that supervisors recognize

"How well a supervisor communicates
is in direct proportion to his
skill as a manager."

the problem of good communications, most supervisors would readily tell
you that poor communications cause more problems and troubles than any
other single item.

Communications that are effectively and properly made can have a
healthy and positive effect on the climate and production of an organization.
And the supervisor is the key person in this chain. An employee typically
cannot understand a statement any better than the supervisor explained it.
Poor communications make for poor understanding, and poor understanding
makes for poor cooperation. An employee, for example, can't be expected to
generate enthusiasm and support for a new wage payment plan if his supervisor didn't explain why the employee would be better off financially under
the new plan.

The supervisor needs to be a better communicator than the average
employee because his scope of influence is greater. He may well have fifteen
or twenty employees depending on him for clear instructions, and his influence on the firm's success is, therefore, very great indeed. Through his
communications, he can have a significant influence on production, morale,
quality, and profit—because his communications affect a large number of
employees.

Supervisors, therefore, should always be informed. If a supervisor does
not know and understand, he cannot communicate effectively to others. And
if he is asked a question that he cannot answer, he should not be afraid to say,
"I don't know the answer to your question, but I will find out and let you
know." In addition to being informed, supervisors should be genuinely concerned about how they communicate with others. To say they are concerned
about good communications is one thing; to show that they are concerned by

practicing good communications is another. An employee readily sees this difference; he should not be left wondering what the supervisor said.

A supervisor should gain his employees' confidence by being consistent in his communications—he should not say one thing today and another thing tomorrow. This confidence that an employee has in his supervisor will make for easier communications between them. What the employee hears depends to a large degree on his confidence in the supervisor. If he has confidence in the supervisor, he will accept the communication at face value. If he doesn't have confidence, he will begin to read and search between the lines for hidden meanings. Did the supervisor mean this or that? Why did he say it the way he did? Was he trying to tell me something? These and similar questions are the type that arise to hinder and impair clear and easy communication when the supervisor does not have his employees' confidence.

HOW CAN A SUPERVISOR AID UPWARD COMMUNICATIONS?

One area that the supervisor needs to be particularly concerned about is upward communications. As we have said, communications and orders come down the line easily, but information from the worker that needs to go up the line may be sidetracked unless helped.

Many supervisors don't seem to realize how difficult it is for their employees to talk to them. The supervisor, of course, feels free to walk over to the employee and talk to him. But the prestige and status of the two are different. The employee may be a blue-collar worker and because of his dress may hate to go to the boss's desk or to the front office in his work clothes.

The boss, because of his years of experience, is frequently able to express himself more easily than his employee, and as a result, the employee may hesitate to initiate a conversation. Then, too, the employee doesn't know his supervisor and his job as well as the supervisor knows the employee and his job. Because of this, the employee cannot speak with the same understanding and assurance.

Another barrier to upward communications is the fact that the supervisor controls the employee's job and pay. The employee, therefore, may be hesitant to say something that may in some way affect his job. In other words, the employee is dependent to a large degree on his supervisor, and this may cause him to hesitate to "speak up" to his boss. For these and similar reasons, the upward flow of communications is hampered and in many cases is stopped altogether.

making communications easier

Managers should be aware of the existence of this difficulty and should make every effort to make it easier for the worker to "speak his mind." Rules and regulations, for example, can be used to tell an employee what he should or must call to his supervisor's attention. For example, rules such as the following can be used to encourage an employee to talk to his boss:

1. An employee should inform his superior of any change in his work that would require coordination or notification of other departments.
2. An employee should keep his supervisor informed of any controversies that might cause trouble between units in a plant.

You can readily think up other rules to aid upward communications.

In addition to rules, management should establish alternate channels of upward communication—channels other than through the employee's immediate supervisor. Many companies, for example, have industrial chaplains, counselors, suggestion systems, opinion surveys, and open group meetings where the employee may feel free to express himself. These are excellent alternate channels of communication.

What we have discussed here are *techniques* that supervisors can use to enable employees to express themselves freely. But better than all these techniques is the strong desire on the part of supervisors to have their employees express themselves openly and freely. This genuine desire by the supervisor to have free communications can be promoted only through his creation of a climate of free expression, a climate where he openly encourages his employees to communicate, and a climate where he takes and shows a genuine interest in their ideas, suggestions, and complaints. As is true in so many other instances, the supervisor is also the key man here in the promotion and encouragement of the important and necessary upward flow of communications.

WHAT ARE SOME ADDITIONAL POINTS TO REMEMBER?

A supervisor can't know too much about employee communications. He supervises his employees by communicating to them, and the skill with which he communicates will be reflected in the skill with which he manages. To be a good supervisor, therefore, you need to muster all of the skill you can to influence your employees—your work team—to do what is needed to accomplish the goals you have communicated to them. There is no one best way to communicate to everyone. Depending on the person, the situation, and the information to be covered, you communicate in different ways to different people. Your communication may be a smile or a pat on the back to one employee; it may be a brief talk to another telling her what a good job she is doing; or it may be a formal letter to another.

communicate clearly

You can, however, overcommunicate. Like the man who wears suspenders, a belt, and a safety pin to hold his pants up, you can overdo it. Communicate enough to let your employees know everything necessary but not so much that they will "tune out" old blabbermouth when you start talking. Talk to them about things they want to know about and are interested in—their jobs, their pay, the things that affect them at work. But avoid controversial nonwork subjects such as politics and religion.

Be sure your employees understand what you are saying. Check on their comprehension by asking questions about what you have said. Choose exact words to say what you mean. Instead of asking an employee to "work harder," you might ask him if he can increase his production from 600 to 650 units per day.

Be a good listener. This is a big part of good communications. Don't interrupt an employee when he is telling you something. Let him have his say—let him get it off his chest. Don't try to outguess him and help him along with his comments. Listen carefully to what he says. Try to understand his reason for talking to you. Give his comments thought; then give him your reply.

WHAT ARE THE EFFECTS OF GOOD COMMUNICATIONS?

The effects of good communications within a department or a plant cannot be easily measured; however, they are reflected in several ways. For one thing, an employee's attitude toward the company and his job will be improved, as will be his morale, his cooperation, and his job satisfaction. With this healthier work climate, other more tangible effects may also result. For example, employee turnover, as well as absences and lateness, may be reduced. In retail establishments, a reduction in returned purchases and customer complaints may result. This is not to say that good communications will make all of these things come true. It is to say, however, that when a healthy attitude toward work and a free climate of communication exist in a company, it is natural that these other happy results should follow.

A Case Study
GRACIE'S COMPLAINT

Jane Carlos was generally regarded by the girls in the typing pool as being a fair and just supervisor. She distributed the work equitably on the basis of quantity as well as difficulty. However, one recent employee, Gracie Haywood, seemed to have difficulty right from the beginning.

From time to time the other girls had seen Gracie Haywood crying at her work. When they offered to help, she replied, "Oh, it is nothing. I'll be all right."

Gracie was an excellent and careful typist, and Jane was pleased to have her as a member of the pool. She didn't, however, show Gracie any favoritism. After three months, Gracie applied to the personnel office for a transfer to another department—any department where typing needed to be done. In the transfer interview in the personnel office, Gracie told her story.

From the beginning she was tense, afraid she would not make a good employee and afraid she would lose her job. When Jane Carlos hired Gracie, her instructions were brief and to the point: "Do your job; don't talk; don't slip away to the restroom for an extra break; don't come in late; don't wear perfume; don't wear pants suits; and don't flirt with the men." After six weeks on the job, Miss Carlos had sent Gracie a note to be in her office at 9:45 A.M. the next day to discuss her work.

Miss Carlos handled the appointment in her usual, routine, businesslike way. She cautioned Gracie about several errors and carbon smudges, then told her she was being moved to the wide carriage typewriter starting the next Monday. When asked if she had any questions or complaints, Gracie managed to say, "No, ma'am," and got back to her typewriter as quickly as she could.

Her work on the wide carriage typewriter worried Gracie. It involved lots of tabulation and tables, and as a consequence her output had dropped considerably. This worried her, and she was sure Miss Carlos was keeping a record of it and would soon descend on her with rebukes.

Because of bus problems, Gracie had been a few minutes late a couple of times. She had always gone straight to Miss Carlos and explained the reason for being late, to which Miss Carlos always replied, "Don't let it happen again." For these and other reasons, Gracie said she didn't feel that Miss Carlos liked her or approved of her as an employee, and, therefore, she wanted a transfer.

When the personnel interviewer called Jane Carlos to say that Gracie wanted a transfer, Jane couldn't understand why. She indicated that Gracie was one of the best, most promising typists she had hired in ten years.

1. What was the basic problem in the typing pool?
2. What mistakes did Jane Carlos make?
3. What should Jane Carlos do now?

A Case Study
THE CHRISTMAS PARTY

The annual Christmas party for the Baker Tire Company was being held this year on December 22. As was typical, it was an all-family affair, with spouses of all employees invited to attend and have fun. At the end of the party, Santa Claus always appeared with bags of goodies for the small children, presents for the spouses, and bonus checks for the employees. Mr. Goodman, the owner and manager, always "said a few words" on the occasion. After a polite round of applause, the wishing of "Merry Christmas," and a handshake with Mr. Goodman, the individuals usually left for home.

This year was no exception. Everything went as usual. Then Mr. Goodman arose and made the following remarks.

"Fellow employees and friends. Tonight marks the 25th Anniversary of the founding of the Baker Tire Company. It has had twenty-five years of existence. Some years were good; some were trying. But in all, they have been good years for most of us. Some few of us, of course, haven't always worked with the Company. And some of you will not be here next year.

"This year has been a difficult one financially. Inflation has constantly eaten into profits, and expenses have pushed steadily upward. All this has had a dampening effect on profits, and as a consequence we are not in as strong a position as we have been in the past. The only hope I can see for a continued strong growth and a financially sound business is for us to cut expenses. This means we will have to reduce labor costs—along with any other expenses that we can control.

"I know that many of you are restless. Some of your children are hard to manage at this hour and you want to be on your way, but I did want this opportunity to say a few words to you. This business is our entire lives. We all have to nurture it like we do our children, if we want to see it develop and grow.

"I know that most of you have heard from the grapevine that business has been increasing at a decreasing rate and that profits and bonuses will suffer this year. Part of this rumor is true.

"I am very concerned over those who will remain with me through the future years. I want to see your children develop into strong and loyal young people. I want to see them married and establishing homes of their own.

"New ideas call for new wage plans, and I hope that in the coming months we can generate new ones.

"Finally, let me wish you all a Merry Christmas. In summary, this has been a memorable year, and I am happy to give each of you employees a bonus remembrance." With that, Mr. Goodman called out names, and the various employees came forward to get their checks.

When they later opened their "gifts," every employee found that his bonus had been increased significantly over last year's bonus. When the party broke up, some families started drifting toward the door to shake hands. A good many of the men, however, started gathering in small groups and talking. "What did the old man mean? Will some of us be fired?" were the types of questions they were asking.

1. What do you think Mr. Goodman had in mind for his message? Why do you think this?
2. What errors or mistakes do you see in his speech? Why do you think he said it in the way that he did?
3. If you had to correct or make suggestions about changing his remarks, what would you suggest? Why?

4
PUTTING HUMAN RELATIONS TO WORK

This chapter explains—

- How human relations affect supervision
- How you should treat your employees
- How you can rate yourself on the human relations scale

As a supervisor, you will work with people, equipment, and materials. Although all three factors are necessary for you to do your job, your employees are by far the most important. The success of your department and your company is dependent on them. Loyal employees who have the ability to feel, to think, to plan, and to make things are by far your most valuable asset. At the same time, however, people are difficult to motivate, control, and inspire.

Many managers seem to think that all they need to do to be a good supervisor is to tell an employee what to do and provide him or her with the tools and materials necessary to get the job done. Nothing could be farther from the truth. Employees are human beings who have basic drives, needs, and wants that they seek to satisfy through their work as well as through their home life. As a supervisor, therefore, you will need to know how to handle people, how to influence them to do the things that you want done, and how to get along with them. One of your top priority jobs, therefore, is to try to continually improve the relationships that exist between you and your employees. Remember that a firm is made up of *people,* that what you get accomplished is through *people,* and that your personal success as a supervisor will depend on how good a job your *people* do for you.

WHAT IS MEANT BY HUMAN RELATIONS?

Some people say that practicing good human relations simply means applying the golden rule. Others say it is the application of psychology to people—sort of winning friends and influencing people. Some define human relations as an ethical approach to personnel problems. Others say it is what *motivating* takes place (the relationship) between workers. All of these factors are a part *employees* of good human relations.

To a manager, practicing good human relations means getting his employees to work together harmoniously, productively, and cooperatively to achieve economic as well as social satisfaction. It means *motivating his employees to want to do productive and personally satisfying jobs.* Note that we have said that the manager's job is to *motivate* his employees, not to *drive* or *push* them to do their jobs. This is a key part of human relations—to motivate people. You can see, therefore, that practicing good human relations is more than backslapping, more than "being a nice guy," and more than glad-handing.

WHAT MAKES EMPLOYEES DIFFERENT?

Good human relations result from knowing how to work with groups as well as with individuals. The employee who works for you is a member of your organization for only *part* of his time. He is also a member of his family, a member of his church and of his clubs, and a citizen of his community. Knowing this, you as a supervisor should recognize that you cannot change an employee simply by bringing him into a plant, having him punch a clock, and assigning him a place to work. The employee still has his own physical and mental makeup. He still has his own feelings about things. Even though he works for you, he still has his own personal problems and attitudes. And you must remember that these feelings and attitudes come with him to the job, and he will continue to be influenced by his associations in other organizations.

When you assign a person to a job in a retail store or a manufacturing plant, you should remember that you have limited the freedom of that individual. He may, for example, be required to stay in one location. If he is the type of person who likes freedom to move about, this may frustrate him. His actions may be paced by a machine, which may irritate him if he is by nature a person who likes to change his work pace. And, finally, he may be forced to associate and work with certain employees with whom he would not normally associate if left to his own choice. Such limitations as these may produce problems for some employees and, therefore, hamper their effectiveness in working with others.

Other employees, however, adapt themselves more readily to an industrial environment, and often these are the employees who are the easiest and most pleasant to work with. Supervisors should be aware of the individual differences that employees bring to the job, recognizing that these differences might make the employee frustrated and discontent. By taking these differences into account when employees are initially placed on jobs or are later transferred to other work, the alert supervisor may well ward off trouble and create for himself a healthier, happier work force.

*employee
differences*

In addition to these individual differences, some employees come to the job with a predetermined set of requirements that the job should fulfill. It might be that the job should appeal to their social status, or it might be that it should satisfy their need to belong—to be part of a group. These and other expectations make for differences in the way that employees look at their jobs, how they react to them, and how effective they are. Some women, for example, may look at jobs quite differently from men. For some women, a job may be a temporary thing before marriage— a source of some extra money and social contact. It may not be her life's work, and other people may not depend solely on her for support. A man, on the other hand, is frequently the chief breadwinner in the family and is concerned for his welfare *and* for that of his family.

Age likewise influences individuals. Older employees are often more security-conscious than younger ones, and as a result they are more interested in maintaining their present positions than in transferring to other positions with unknown opportunities.

These are a few of the individual differences you will find among your employees, and they serve to point out to a degree why different employees have different needs, different attitudes, different personalities, and different demands from their jobs. As a supervisor, you will want to recognize these needs so that you will be in a position to effectively deal with them and thereby create a harmonious and well-directed work force.[1]

WHAT DO YOU NEED TO REMEMBER WHEN WORKING WITH OTHERS?

As a supervisor, you will be working with and leading people. Because you will be supervising and leading your employees, you should remember several basic facts about them as individuals.

1. Remember that all of us are different. We are different in thousands of ways. Just as our fingerprints are all different, so are we different in other ways. From the day of our birth, we develop differently. We each have our own individual minds, our own thoughts, our own ideas about life, our own wants.

   Because we *are* individuals, therefore, the study of human relations starts with the individual. It starts with *you* as a person. You may be part of a work team, but remember that the team is made up of individuals like yourself, and the team exists and has power because of the individuals who make it up. The *team* cannot make decisions. The *individual members* of the team are the ones who make decisions.

   the individual on your team

2. Remember that when you are working with a person, you are working with the *whole man*. You might wish you could employ him as a *hired hand*, but you can't. Even if you want only his hand to work for you, you also get his mind and his thoughts. You get his desires and motivations. You get the reflections of his home life, which affects his work even though it is separated from his work place. As a supervisor, you should remember that every employee is different and that you must work with him as a whole man.

3. Remember that all normal behavior by an individual is *caused* behavior. It is caused by what the individual needs or wants. He does things because he feels that by doing so he will achieve some goal that he feels is worth working for. Your employees are not motivated by what *you* think they ought to do and have but by what *they* think they ought to do and have. To you, the things that another person wants and the reasons he wants them may appear foolish. To him, they are important, real needs. These needs cause the behavior with which you will be dealing.

4. Remember that people are not machines to be knocked about and thrown out when you are through with them. As human beings, we

[1]This section adapted with permission from Claude S. George, Jr., *Management for Business and Industry* (Englewood Cliffs, N.J.: Prentice-Hall, Inc., 1970), pp. 320–21.

need and ought to be treated with dignity and respect. No matter what a man's job is, no matter how "low" you may think it is, he deserves to be and should be shown the proper respect for his choice of jobs and his own abilities.

If you will always keep these four aspects of people clearly in mind, you will find that your understanding of other people and your ability to work with them effectively will be significantly improved. For example, when you recognize that people differ from each other, you will not try to categorize them or put them in certain molds such as, he is a "good mixer," or she is a "cold fish." You won't try to handle every person in the same way because you will recognize that you are working with or supervising the whole man—an individual who is unique. You will more clearly recognize the dignity of work and better understand the respect another human being deserves.

HOW DO YOU AFFECT YOUR EMPLOYEES' ATTITUDES?

Your job is to get things done through people, and your effectiveness as a supervisor will be measured by how productive your employees are. You are dependent on them for your success. Inasmuch as this is true, your employees are a very real asset to you and should, therefore, be treated with respect and consideration. Remember that your employees probably want to please you. They want to do what you want them to do. Remember also that their jobs are one of the most meaningful aspects of their lives and that they hope to find personal satisfactions and rewards from them. Whether or not they find these rewards depends on you as a supervisor and how well your style of management presents the job to them. Remember that the employee is the only one who can decide how hard he will work. And this decision is closely tied to the way you understand him, the way you treat him, and the way you help him. The effective supervisor, therefore, is the one who can create a work climate in which the employee will willingly strive to do his best.

your impact on employees

DO YOU UNDERSTAND YOURSELF?

It has been said that if you want to understand others, you should first understand yourself.

When you begin to know yourself, you have taken the first step toward understanding others. When you recognize, for example, that you have certain attitudes about how you should dress, how fast you should work, and how as a supervisor you should behave—you then realize that others, too,

"The effective supervisor creates a work climate in which employees willingly strive to do their best."

have ideas about dress, work pace, and supervision. You recognize that you are not the only one who has goals and ambitions that are being worked for in an aggressive manner. Your employees, too, have ambitions and goals that they are working for with equal vigor. Understanding yourself will enable you to understand others, and when you come to understand the other person, you will be in a position to treat him fairly and justly.

know yourself   This is certainly true of the relationship that exists between the supervisor and his employees. Whenever you become critical of what someone else has done or said, first ask yourself what *you* have done to help create the situation that needs correcting. More than likely you will find that some of the blame is yours. If not, shift your point of view and look at the situation from your employee's point of view; this will enable you to better understand him and his problem. As a result, you will treat the employee and the situation with understanding, compassion, and integrity because you know how you would like to be treated in similar circumstances.

Understanding yourself means looking at your strengths as well as your weaknesses. It is easy to see your strong points, but you will have to work harder to see your bad points. You should recognize that you have limitations and hang-ups just like the next person: that you have such things as a short fuse and a quick temper, or that you may be prejudiced against female employees, and so on. When you recognize these types of shortcomings, you will be in a position to try to control them and thereby be a better supervisor.

You will recall that we previously talked about understanding the other fellow by putting yourself in his shoes. When you do this, you are *empathizing*; that is, you are trying to see the problem from the other fellow's point of view. This does not mean, however, that once you see the problem from his point of view, you agree with him and decide in his favor. On the contrary, it means that once you understand and see the problem from his point of view, you are in a better position to deal with it effectively and fairly. You are in a position to appreciate his point of view and his feelings without getting yourself involved in his personal life. When a problem arises between two employees, for example, you can empathize with both. You can truthfully say that you understand each person's point of view, that you understand the problem, and that you understand why each feels the way he does. Once you have achieved the ability to truly empathize, you will be in a sound position to make a clear and fair decision. And having made your decision, you will be in a position to state in clear terms why you made the decision and, if necessary, why the decision could not be made the way they wanted it.

the other point of view

We have said that all normal behavior is caused by something—that there is a reason for behavior. As a supervisor, you should try to recognize and understand the cause for the behavior of your employees. The reason why an employee does something may not be logical; it may not be reasonable; it may even be ridiculous in your mind. But it is important to the employee and is the cause of his action. The challenge facing you as a supervisor, therefore, is to understand why a particular employee behaves the way he does, and not to turn off his actions as absurd or ridiculous. In fact, when you state that another person's actions are absurd, you may well be admitting your own inability to see the other fellow's point of view to see the reasons for his action. If you are unable to see the reasons for his action, then perhaps you are at fault as a supervisor.

A good supervisor must work at empathizing with his employees. You should make it so much a part of yourself that it comes as easily as shaking hands. It should be so much a part of you that you will be able to quickly settle a dispute, prevent a grievance from arising, or shed new light on a tough problem.

HOW WELL SHOULD YOU KNOW YOUR EMPLOYEES?

The better you know your employees, the better you will be able to understand them, their points of view, and their problems. As a supervisor, therefore, you should make every effort to see and understand the whole man. You should know about his family because it is a part of him and influences his work and behavior patterns. If you know the size of his family, the age of his children, what their names are, where they go to school, what their

the whole man

the
whole
man

accomplishments are, and so on, you will know and better understand your employee.

In like manner, you should know something about the employee himself. Where is he from? What work experience has he had? Does he have special skills or hobbies? What is his educational background? What are his goals and ambitions? Knowing these types of things about an employee enables you to talk with him about the possibility of better placement within the company, about his opportunity for advancement, or, if he aspires to be a supervisor, whether or not he has the educational and personal makeup that the company requires.

To be a good supervisor, it is almost impossible to know too much about an employee. Knowing the types of things mentioned above, you will be in a better position to understand the employee, to understand his problems, to see his point of view, and to empathize.

SHOULD YOU TRY TO CHANGE YOUR EMPLOYEES?

The fact that employees differ widely in their abilities and capacities is a fact of life that you must face. Some of your employees will have real mechanical ability, whereas others are almost lacking in mechanical aptitude. Some may be bright, others dumb. Some may be quick to catch on to a new job, whereas others are slow learners. People are different, and as a supervisor, you must learn to accept people as they are.

accept people for
what they are

Your employees bring to the job these differences they have developed over their years of living and countless experiences. It would be unrealistic, therefore, for you to try to remold or change them. You must accept people as they are and work with what they have. If you try to do otherwise, if you try to change them, you will be doomed to a life of needless frustration.

This is not to say that you should not attempt to help your employees help themselves. Many of their mannerisms or work habits, for example, might well be improved in time with your friendly help and suggestions. Accepting people as they are does not rule out trying to help them. You accept an employee as a person and as a sensitive human being—not as a commodity that you can remold. The supervisor who sees this difference, who accepts employees for what they are but is willing to try to understand and help them, is the supervisor who will succeed because of his success in handling the human problems of supervision.

WHAT IS DIFFERENT ABOUT WORKING WITH GROUPS?

In your work, you may find that much of your time is spent with a group of employees. This may be a *formal* group, such as an assembly team of which you are a member, or it may be an *informal* group, such as a blackjack club that plays cards during breaks and lunch periods. Formal groups are set up by management to enable employees to work together on a job. Informal groups are formed by employees who have some common interest. Inasmuch as you will be supervising people who work and play in groups and who achieve their personal needs through groups, you should have some knowledge of what groups are and how they work.

Groups differ greatly in the attraction they hold for members. Some groups are loosely formed and members drift in and out, such as the blackjack group. Other groups are highly cohesive; they are strong, stick together, and are highly effective. They command and get active support from their members. In highly cohesive groups, pressure will be put on extremists to conform to what the *group* thinks should be done. This is not true, however, in low-cohesion groups. In highly cohesive groups, some of the members will try hard to get the nonconformist to change. However, if the members fail and the nonconformist refuses to change, then the members will give up trying to influence him. Instead, they will "cut off" the *group attractions* dissenter and will no longer accept him as belonging to the group.

One peculiarity of groups that you should recognize is that the people who are most vocal and try the hardest to influence the other members of the group are usually the ones who are most willing to accept the opinions of others. This may seem contradictory to you at first, but it is a characteristic of the behavior of employees in groups. If one employee wants desperately to influence the others, if he wants to be the leader and spokesman, then he will be most willing to accept the views and suggestions of the other employees so that he can "lead" them. The stronger the ties of the group and the more cohesive it is, the more this rule holds true. If it didn't work this way, then the employee who was vocal and said things the group did not agree with would soon be cut off from the group if he did not accept their views.

These are characteristics of all groups whether they are formal or informal. Recognizing and understanding these group characteristics are important to you from a human relations point of view. As a supervisor you will be achieving many of your goals through groups; you should, therefore, carefully study and analyze your employees' actions in groups in order to make your work groups operate as harmoniously as possible.

WHAT DO EMPLOYEES WANT FROM THEIR JOBS?

All of us have certain basic needs that we want fulfilled. We all need food, clothing, and shelter, and we all have the same desire for self-respect, recognition, and self-esteem. Individual employees, however, place different weights or values on different needs. A starving man, for example, places a high value on food, whereas a man with plenty of food but little clothing might place a high value on clothing. If you know the different needs or wants that individual employees have, you will be in a better position to do an effective job of motivating and supervising them. You can, perhaps, help each employee to satisfy his needs and thus become a better employee.

Although different employees have different wants and place different values on these wants, studies have shown that the basic wants or desires of the average employee will include the following:

1. *Fair pay.* The average employee wants fair pay for his work and comparable pay for comparable work. An employee resents others getting more money for the same or comparable work. He also wants his pay to be in line with those in the community. A deviation from the normal is a sore spot and may well be a source of employee discontent and dissatisfaction.

2. *Recognition as an individual.* An employee wants to feel important in the eyes of his fellow workers. He wants to be recognized for doing a good job. Words of encouragement, a pat on the back, or a pay increase could help supply this need.

3. *Opportunity for advancement.* Most employees want the opportunity to move ahead on the job. New employees frequently look for this in seeking a job. Moving ahead is vital, and blind-alley jobs may explain why an employee is dissatisfied and may eventually quit. In addition to the opportunity to advance, most employees want *job security* to go with it—they want to feel secure enough in their jobs that they can plan ahead, buy a home, and settle in a community. This is particularly true of the employee who is the head of a household and is supporting several other people.

4. *Interesting work in a good place to work.* This factor will be high on many workers' lists. Safe, clean, pleasant working conditions are desired along with employee facilities such as parking lots, cafeterias, lockers, and shower rooms. A good place to work, however, is to little avail if the employee is not interested in his work. Various jobs, of course, hold different attractions for individual employees. What is one man's pie is another man's poison. You should exercise real care, therefore, in choosing and placing employees in jobs.

5. *Acceptance by the group.* The desire to belong is strong in most workers. As was stated before, employees seek social acceptance and approval by their fellow workers. If they do not get this, their morale may be low, their efficiency lacking, and their productivity suffering. Not only do employees need to belong to employee groups, they also need to feel that they belong to and are a *part of the company group*—that they are "in." Every worker wants to feel appreciated and needed by the company to the extent that he participates in discussions about possible shift changes or a new method of work. Getting this informa-

job needs

tion directly from supervisors rather than through the grapevine will do much to make an employee feel a part of the company group.

6. *Good and just leadership.* An employee needs to have confidence in his superior. He wants to work for a person who knows his job, who is sure of his decisions, and whose actions are impartial and fair.

The weights placed on these needs and desires by various workers will differ. As a supervisor, you will need to recognize these and other individual needs and the different weights that each employee places on them. Opportunity for advancement might be of first importance to one employee, whereas job security might be most important to another. It won't be easy for you to identify individual wants, so be on guard. What an employee says he wants and what he actually wants may be two different things. He might, for example, express dissatisfaction with his pay, but his real need is to be accepted by the shop employees. Recognizing these and other wants can help you understand why employees behave as they do, as individuals or as members of a group. To practice good human relations, you should be aware of these desires and insofar as possible create conditions favorable to satisfying most of the major desires of the individuals. Supervisors who strive to do this contribute considerably to making a group of employees get along well together and work in an efficient and harmonious manner.

WHAT CAN YOU EXPECT FROM GOOD HUMAN RELATIONS?

The concept of human relations means something takes place between one person and another, between a worker and his supervisor, or between fellow workers. By practicing good human relations, a supervisor will be able to help his workers satisfy some of their needs. A supervisor might, for example, introduce a new employee to the blackjack club members, saying, "Fellows, this is Joe Brown, a new employee on the punch press. He is a great worker and a humdinger at blackjack. How about showing him the ropes and dealing him in?" This might make Joe a member of the group and thus satisfy his need to belong.

Practicing good human relations, of course, doesn't mean that everybody will be all smiles and happiness. We all have our problems, but practicing good human relations enables us to work around the difficulties that problems present. What you should aim for in your work is to have: *human relations impact*

1. Peace among your employees.
2. Openness and understanding.
3. A friendly air between workers.
4. Employees expecting and receiving a fair and just hearing and decision.

Achieving these human relations objectives will pay off. The rewards may be difficult to measure, but you can rest assured that they are there. Practicing good human relations may mean that a difficult problem of employee coordination or a problem of poor work performance can be avoided—can be stopped *before* it starts—rather than be patched up at a later date. Practicing good human relations may mean uninterrupted work rather than a slowdown or stoppage. Thus, practicing good human relations will manifest its value in numerous ways that will provide you with the personal satisfaction of a job well done, as well as provide your employees with the opportunity to develop and practice their talents to the fullest.

HOW HIGH DO YOU RATE ON THE HUMAN RELATIONS SCALE?

Your job is to supervise the employees working for you in your department. In doing this, you will have an opportunity to test all of your human relations skills. Answer the following questions honestly to see how high you are on the human relations scale. Give yourself 4 points for each "yes" answer. A score of 80 or better places you high on the scale of practicing good human relations with your employees.

1. Do you know each employee well?
2. Do you talk to your employees about their homes, their hobbies, and their families?
3. Do you tell your employees how they are getting along?
4. Do you give them credit when credit is due?
5. Do you tell them in advance about changes that will affect them?
6. Are you open-minded? Do you ask for suggestions?
7. Do you respect all jobs and make them seem important?
8. Are you courteous in your treatment of your employees?
9. Are you honest, impartial, and fair in your dealings and judgment?
10. Do you treat your employees with dignity and make them feel that they are a part of the company group—that they belong?
11. Are you generally cheerful?
12. Do you try to be a good listener?
13. Do you always consider every complaint?
14. Are you equally strict (or lenient) with all employees?
15. Do you praise good work and criticize poor work?
16. Can you say "no" to an employee without making him feel antagonistic toward you?
17. Can you empathize—see the other fellow's point of view?
18. Can you give clear and easily understood orders?

19. Do you explain why changes have to be made?
20. Do you do everything you honestly can to get your workers promoted or transferred to better jobs?
21. Do your employees come to you freely with job or personal problems?
22. Do you try to explain each employee's job and its relation to the whole company in order to show the employee that his job is important?
23. Can you freely accept personal criticism from your employees about how you operate as a supervisor without getting upset?
24. Do your employees respond positively when you talk to them about doing a better job?
25. Do you know yourself as well as you know your employees?

A Case Study
THE CASE OF THE PERFECTIONIST SUPERVISOR

Bart Richmond is supervisor of the Plating Department for the Southern Liberty Company. In his mind, his department is the best-operating and best-disciplined department in the whole company. And he views himself as being a tough but fair supervisor with his only real problem being that he can't get reliable help. "They always come in like a new broom," he states, "but within a couple of months their work begins to slip, and within six months they move on to other jobs."

Bart is a perfectionist and expects everyone to work the same way. He is a stickler for following rules to the letter, never making exceptions, regardless of the reason. For example, one company rule states that an employee will not be paid for a holiday if he is absent on the day prior to or following the holiday. Henry Sizemore, who will retire next year, failed to show up for work on the day following July 4. He had stayed with his wife who had an emergency appendectomy on that day, July 5. Despite his age, his years with the company, and his superior attendance record, Bart treated him exactly as he did the new motorcycle rider who was also absent at a race on July 5. "You've got to be firm and fair—treat them all alike," was the way he put it.

Likewise, he views everyone as an individual who is entitled to his privacy. He never talks to his employees about their outside work or hobbies unless he feels these activities are interfering with their work in the Plating Department. "What the employee does outside of work is his own business," Bart says. His only concern is what the employee does on his job in the Plating Department. However, when an employee's output drops, Bart is quick to talk with the employee and "jack him up." He feels an employee is paid to perform at a satisfactory level, and if he doesn't, Bart is the first to point this out. As long as the employee's work is OK, he never bothers him.

Bart doesn't believe in coddling people. In his view, his employees are paid to do their work, and he expects them to do it. When he got a new man from the personnel department, Bart put him to work where he was needed, without discussing the position with him, assuming that the employee wanted to work or he wouldn't have applied for the job.

Despite the fact that he is just, never stands in an employee's way in promotions, and treats all his employees with the same degree of firmness and fairness, Bart's production record has gradually slipped during the past eight months. In his mind, the reduction in output is directly related to the "poor help" that the personnel people send him. "The guys I get are picky and choosy about what they want to do and will leave at the drop of a hat," Bart explained. Other departments, however, haven't experienced these same problems.

1. What do you think is the problem in Bart Richmond's department?
2. What human relations mistakes do you think Bart is making?
3. If you were called in to give Bart help, what would you tell him?

A Case Study
LAZERBEAN'S

As supervisor of inventories for Lazerbean's, a large chain operation, John Rogers had six separate storerooms under his control. Two of the six storerooms were located in the Auto-Servi-Center where automotive products were sold and repairs were made, with the remaining four storerooms located in the main building, which housed various departments in a six-story building.

The storerooms were specialized in their inventories and were located near the particular areas using their supplies. As a consequence the six storerooms were fairly widely scattered throughout the Lazerbean complex of buildings and floors.

In organizing these storerooms, Rogers had appointed one employee to be head storekeeper in charge of the operation of the particular storeroom as well as of the other employees working in it. Although the men in charge were not called supervisors, they were recognized as having potential for promotion to supervisory positions and were paid wages higher than the other employees.

One Saturday during the noon lunch hour, Lazerbean's District Manager, Mr. J. J. Swamore, came by Rogers's office and asked to be shown through the various storerooms. Rogers had developed a reputation in the Lazerbean chain as one of their outstanding supervisors and organizers. Because of this, Mr. Swamore was interested in seeing how Rogers organized and controlled his operations. It was obvious from Mr. Swamore's comments that he was much impressed with the operations of the storerooms, the layout of the rooms, the personnel assignments, and the manner in which material was controlled.

Everything went well until they entered the upstairs storeroom in the Auto-Servi-Center building. Here they found the room open with no one apparently in attendance. As they walked through the back of the room, they found the head storekeeper sound asleep on a pile of cleaning rags. Rogers was embarrassed for himself, ashamed of his storekeeper asleep on the job, and indignant that the District Manager had come upon the scene. As Rogers started for the storekeeper, Mr. Swamore suggested that they continue with the inspection, indicating that he (Rogers) could deal with the sleeping employee later.

As soon as the inspection was completed, Rogers returned to the storeroom and found the employee still asleep on the rag pile. He awakened him, and without waiting for any explanation, fired him on the spot.

In his exit interview in the personnel office, the employee indicated that he liked his job, was sorry he had fallen asleep, and would like another chance. He stated he had been up the previous night with virtually no sleep because of a sick wife and baby.

1. Should Rogers have fired the storekeeper under the conditions? Why?
2. If you were Rogers, what action would you have taken? Why?
3. What effect would your actions have on other employees? What effect would Rogers's actions have on other employees?

5
HOW TO IMPROVE MORALE

This chapter explains—

- How your supervision affects morale
- How to measure morale
- How you can help build morale

Your morale is your state of mind—how you feel about things. If your morale is "good" or "high," you feel good about things. You are optimistic. You work with enthusiasm and energy. And you feel that you are making progress. Low morale is just the opposite. You feel "down" or "low." You have a negative attitude toward your work.

Many things can affect your morale: your health, your work environment, your family experiences, your supervisor, the company you work for, and so on. Your reaction to these and many other factors causes you to feel a certain way about things. Morale, therefore, is not the result of a single attitude or feeling, but a combination of several or many factors. And your morale or your attitude about your work, will affect your job performance and your willingness to work.

WHY DOES MORALE VARY?

Some of us are very intense in everything we do. We don't do anything halfway. If we decide to do something, we enter into it with 100% enthusiasm. If we aren't given this opportunity, we don't like it, and our morale suffers. Other people, however, may have a sort of take-it-or-leave-it attitude. They are indifferent as to whether or not they do something. They are seldom highly excited or very low. Theirs is a steady monotonous existence. There are also people who are moody—bright and happy one day, down and depressed the next. Their morale varies with their moods.

approach to worker

We all have different ideas about things. We have developed attitudes from our experiences at home, at school, and with friends. Some people, for example, may have been taught that "idle hands are the devil's workshop" and that they should always approach work with vigor and a positive frame of mind. Employees with this background are not happy and do not have good morale unless they are working at a meaningful job. Other people, as a result of their home environment, may find work distasteful and put a high premium on leisure time. Their morale is highest when their jobs provide leisure time for other activities.

As you can see, these and other similar factors are the reasons you feel as you do about things. These are the types of things that affect your attitude about your job and your morale.

DOES SUPERVISION AFFECT MORALE?

Yes. The way you manage and supervise employees has a direct bearing on their morale. As you know from experience, morale is always present in some degree. Sometimes it is good, at other times low. But it is never

"The way you manage employees has a direct bearing on their morale."

absent. It always exists at some point between extremely good and very poor. What you do as a supervisor affects the point where your employees' morale will be on this scale.

As a supervisor, you can't use your authority to order your employees to have high morale. You can't buy it. The only thing you can do is help create a climate in which high morale can develop. Good morale grows out of good human relations, good employee motivation, respect for the individual, recognition of individual differences, good supervision, good communications, understanding, counseling, and other good supervisory practices.

authority and morale

Because of the importance of good morale, every supervisor should be concerned with the level of morale among his subordinates. The supervisor more than any other person affects the morale of his employees through his day-to-day contacts. It is a long-run proposition—not something that can be cultivated by a brief pep talk. Good morale comes about as a result of long-run actions taken by you to create a work environment in which your employees will willingly participate.

Morale may vary from day to day. It may spread in a contagious manner, but it can erode quickly if something is wrong. As a supervisor, therefore, you will need to exert your energies to maintain a satisfactory level of morale among your employees. Good morale among your workers will mean a happier, healthier work force, one that tackles jobs with a better work attitude. With good morale, better production and better product quality typically result.

Your employees are all individually affected by the morale you help to develop. Good morale for an individual employee makes his work a pleasure, not a chore. Good morale makes working with others a source of satisfaction rather than a source of ill feelings. Employees with good morale are usually pleased with their jobs, have confidence in their abilities to get their work done, and participate willingly in getting the work out. These factors are all important to the employee because they make his day of work a pleasure rather than a miserable experience. They are likewise important to the supervisor because quality products and good productivity can be expected from an employee who has a healthy attitude toward his job. One of the major tasks of a supervisor, therefore, is to build or create a climate in his department where high morale can develop and grow.

WHAT INFLUENCES MORALE?

Almost anything you can think of can have some bearing on morale. Some things are in the control of management; others are not. As a supervisor, for example, you can do little to change the family relationships that each employee experiences at home, his associations with friends, his hobbies, his ability to repair a faulty water heater. Yet these things affect an employee's attitude. An argument with his wife can easily cause him to face the day in a negative way. His lack of success and frustration in repairing a water heater may likewise cause an employee to approach his work with less than a positive attitude.

Although you cannot do anything as a supervisor to control these factors, you should be alert to their existence and do whatever you can to reduce their impact on your employee. One of the best things you can do to help ease the impact of outside events on an employee's morale is to help him "get it off his chest." Encourage the employee to talk to you about what is bothering him. Just telling our problems to others seems to help, and in the process you may be able to help the employee put his problem in proper perspective, or even point out an alternative solution. You might, for example, give him a good tip on how to repair the water heater. With a possible solution in mind, the employee will probably stop his worrying and concentrate on his work with renewed vigor and a more positive frame of mind.

Employee morale is also influenced by factors that are within management's control. These include such things as job security, adequate compensation, good working conditions, interesting work, and recognition for a job well done. All of these factors affect morale, and neglecting any one of them may cause the extra effort you put on the others to go for naught. For example, if you neglect to give recognition to your secretary for her good work, for her help and loyalty, and for a job well done, her morale may suffer even though she is well paid and works under good working conditions. So take time out and say to her, "Sally, you are really a great secretary. Don't know how I could manage all of these things without your help. Even though I don't always tell you, I want you to know that I do appreciate all your efforts and everything you do to make things run smoothly here." *things that affect morale*

Employee morale is particularly affected by what the supervisor does and the way he acts. His general approach to supervision, his direction, and his leadership all have a direct effect on his employees' morale. For example, a supervisor who expresses appreciation to his employees for their good work will exert a positive effect on their morale. If he talks with them and shows them how important their work is to achieving the overall company objective, they will have a healthier mental attitude toward their jobs. The *way* in which a supervisor does these things, the way he acts, likewise affects their morale. If he compliments an employee's work with a lighthearted, off-the-cuff remark, it will not have the impact that a serious compliment would. Consider, for example, how you would feel if your supervisor said to you, "Oh, by the way, that repair job you did the other day was OK." Contrast how you would have felt if instead he had said, "Joe, I want you to know that management appreciates the skill and speed you used in repairing the press. Because you did such a good job, we'll be able to ship the government order on time. All of us are grateful to you."

If a supervisor loses his temper, shows he is worried, or indicates that he is unsure of himself, these factors too will affect his employees' morale. If an employee sees that his supervisor is mad and worried, the employee will feel that things are not going well in the department and will be depressed and his morale will suffer. A supervisor, therefore, should remember at all times to lead in a positive way. He should acknowledge his difficulties and should seek his employees' help to correct an error that has been made rather than try to hide his problems and show that he is worried. He should remember that "worry begets worry" and that confident leadership creates a work climate where morale can be high.

HOW DOES MORALE AFFECT PRODUCTIVITY?

Some people think that high morale and high productivity go hand in hand. This is not always true. Generally, however, there is some positive correlation between the two; that is, if morale goes up, productivity usually goes up. But if morale goes down, productivity usually goes down too. *morale and work*

Your morale reflects your attitudes about many things, some of which do not influence productivity. For this reason we can't say that an increase in morale will always increase productivity. It is fair to say, however, that high morale puts an employee in a frame of mind to be productive, and if good supervision and good working conditions are also present, then productivity will usually go up.

An employee's morale is high only when his happiness, his satisfaction, and his personal adjustments make him want to contribute his efforts to reaching the company's goal. Reaching the company's goal, of course, enables him to reach his own goals of food, clothing, a home, and so on. A good supervisor, therefore, should always try to show the employee that he will personally benefit, that he will reach his own goals, if he will help the company to reach its goals of producing goods. It is possible, of course, to have good productivity and low morale, but it is highly questionable whether this condition would last for any length of time. Low morale, reflecting negative attitudes, would sooner or later affect output.

CAN YOU MEASURE MORALE?

It's difficult to measure morale because morale is an attitude or frame of mind. It is how you feel about something. However, as we have said, maintaining high morale is important to supervisors because high morale results in a better, happier, more satisfied work force, one that produces better products at a higher output. Managers do, therefore, try to measure morale through morale surveys, or opinion surveys, or attitude surveys. All of these terms mean the same thing. In a morale survey, questions like the following are asked.

opinion surveys

1. Do you like to work for this company?
   - ☐ Dislike.
   - ☐ It is OK.
   - ☐ Like the company.
   - ☐ Very happy working here.
2. Does your supervisor keep you informed about what's going on?
   - ☐ Never.
   - ☐ Rarely.
   - ☐ About half the time.
   - ☐ Yes, always.
3. Does your supervisor listen to your complaints or gripes and handle them quickly and fairly?
   - ☐ No. Very unsatisfactory.
   - ☐ He tries but doesn't do enough.
   - ☐ He handles them well.
   - ☐ I never have any complaints.

By analyzing the answers to these and similar questions, management can tell how its employees feel about their jobs, what parts of the jobs they feel strongly about, how they feel about their supervisors, their attitude toward the company, which departments are weak, where training needs are apparent, where poor communications exist, and so on. It is important for management to take immediate action to correct these problems once they find out what they are and where they exist. By correcting them, supervisors can help create a better work climate where employee morale can be shifted to a more positive position.

WHAT ARE THE ADVANTAGES OF A MORALE SURVEY?

In addition to showing management how employees feel, morale surveys also give the employee the opportunity to say what is on his mind. They enable him to communicate freely up the line. This can be important because it tells management what the employee is thinking, and it makes the employee feel better because he is provided the opportunity to get some things off his chest. Morale surveys are also important because they indicate to an employee that the company is interested in him and his opinions—that the company cares.

Morale surveys have another advantage: they focus management's attention on morale and its importance to the company, making supervisors "morale-conscious."

A morale-conscious supervisor is in an excellent position in a company *importance of* to sense and control the attitude among the rank and file employees. He can *surveys* talk with an employee and learn why he feels the way he does. He can help an employee see another point of view. He can teach an employee new ways of looking at things, both by example and by talking with him. For example, Sam, a newcomer, might think the company is unfair to him because he has been assigned to the oldest press on the floor. It is an old and slow machine, and as a result, his output is low. He gripes about this and thinks it is unfair. A good supervisor recognizes Sam's gripes and helps him see the situation from the company's point of view. Sam is the youngest man in the department, still a "learner." His supervisor explains that all new employees are put on the slower press until they get the hang of the job, usually about three months. After this they are transferred to newer and faster equipment where they can meet their production quota. With this explanation, Sam's attitude changes. He can see that the company is giving him an opportunity to learn and to make his mistakes on a slower machine, and he knows that as soon as he develops skill on the job, he will be assigned a newer machine.

ARE THERE SIGNS OF LOW MORALE?

We don't always need a morale survey to tell us how well things are going in a company. We can also tell how morale is by signs, such as the following, which point to low morale.

1. High labor turnover.
2. No respect for supervisors.

3. Low productivity.
4. Excessive waste.
5. Large number of grievances.
6. Large number of accidents.
7. General lack of cooperation.
8. Poor quality of production.
9. Low regard for the company.
10. Excessive lateness.
11. Excessive sick leaves.
12. Leaving work early.
13. Long lunch periods.
14. Excessive one-day absences.

Of all the workers in a company, assembly line workers, by and large, have the lowest morale. Because of the monotony of their jobs, they generally find little satisfaction in their work. Frequently they feel they are overworked, not appreciated, and have little or no opportunity for advancement. These same things can be said about other workers; however, assembly line employees seem to be most subject to low morale. Since the supervisor is in most frequent contact with these employees, he is in the best position to help improve their attitudes. He should, therefore, keep these signs of low morale in mind and should take immediate steps to change the conditions and help change the attitude causing the low state of morale.

WHAT CAN A SUPERVISOR DO TO HELP BUILD MORALE?

As you can see, it is of utmost importance to a company that its employees' morale is high and that their attitudes and job satisfactions are not low. You might be asking what you as a supervisor can do to help satisfy a worker's needs. For one thing, you can develop an understanding and appreciation of the employee as a person, seeing his individual qualities and capacities. You should treat him courteously at all times, and let him know that he is a needed and valuable member of the work team. Give him credit where credit is due. Criticize an employee when it is justified, but do so in private, not in front of his fellow workers.

building morale

Talk over an employee's job with him, getting his ideas and suggestions for changing and improving it. Be sure that his pay is just and fair, and in line with pay for comparable jobs in the community. Look after general working conditions, making sure of comfort, safety, and cleanliness. Periodically talk with each employee about his job performance, his progress, and the opportunities that might lie ahead for him. Point out his need (if any) for additional skills, training, or education in order for him to take advantage of future opportunities.

By doing these and similar things, you will have the opportunity to raise the level of morale among your employees and at the same time you will be able to observe and study them for indications of dissatisfactions. As a supervisor, you are in a position to constantly study and observe the attitudes and behavior of your employees. You can listen to what they are saying as well as to what they are implying. You can sense changes in their attitudes toward the company and their willingness or unwillingness to cooperate.

Because of your close day-to-day contact with your employees, you should know them well and should be able to sense and observe minor changes in their morale. The closer you are to your employees, the easier it will be for you to recognize changes in morale before they grow to the point of disrupting the work of your department. It is in this area of day-to-day supervision that you can do the most to raise and maintain the level of morale in your department.

A Case Study
ALLISON AUTO PARTS

In 1927, Henry Allison opened his first auto parts store in connection with his garage and service station. He sold high-quality products at fair prices and in the years that followed developed a reputation as a reliable source for replacement parts.

With continued growth in the auto parts business, he sold his garage and service station and in 1934 opened a mail-order auto parts store. By 1954, his staff had grown to 60 salesmen, 15 warehousemen, and 5 office employees.

Mr. Allison was an iron-fisted man who ran a "tight" shop. His word was law, and everyone knew it. His hiring practices were simple. If an applicant for a job wore a hat, he concluded that the man would make a good salesman. If he did not wear a hat, Mr. Allison, depending on his mood, might consider him as a possible warehouseman. He always asked a prospective employee, "Do you repair your own car?" If the prospect answered "no," he was turned down for the job. When an applicant was hired, Mr. Allison personally took him into the store or warehouse, depending on his assignment, and told him precisely what he wanted him to do. Then he turned the employee over to the supervisor. Any worker who contradicted or strongly disagreed with Mr. Allison was fired without question.

Allison Auto Parts had no formal system of pay or merit increases. Instead, every employee was paid what Mr. Allison thought he was worth, and his pay was increased whenever Mr. Allison thought it should be increased. Mr. Allison was a firm believer in hard work and didn't "baby" his employees with fringe benefits, paid vacations, or sick leave.

In 1967, Mr. Allison's son Dick came to work in the business as vice-president and general manager. In school, Dick had taken some courses in personnel and human behavior and felt that the company's personnel practices were not ideal. His first act was to devise an application blank for all employees. One was filled out for each new applicant, and to complete the files, he also had one made out for each old employee. In addition, he made arrangements with a local physician to give every new employee a physical examination to determine his physical fitness for the work. Dick also wanted to install an employee as well as a supervisory training program, but he was not able to convince his father of such a need.

Labor turnover during the past ten years had increased from 6 to 26%, and absences had increased in proportion. Although most employees who left the company said they did so because the work was too hard, they also stated dissatisfaction with their jobs, and some complained about pay. When Dick checked the average wage, however, he found that it was above the community average for similar work.

In trying to figure out the cause of the trouble, Dick decided that what was needed was a system of job specifications. He also indicated that he thought morale could be improved by an employee suggestions system. Mr. Allison vetoed the idea of job specifications but agreed tentatively to an employee suggestions system. Accordingly, Mr. Allison placed on the company bulletin board an announcement indicating that a suggestions system was in effect and that employees should make their suggestions to their supervisors. If an employee's suggestion was adopted, he would be awarded a cash bonus to be determined by the value of the suggestion to the company.

After a month and a half had passed with no suggestions, Dick found that several had been made, but the supervisor in question had decided they were of no value and, therefore, had not passed them on to Mr. Allison. Dick then got his father's permission to install a new suggestion system, and during the next month over 41 suggestions were received covering such topics as changes in manufacturing methods, changes in plant layout, job classifications, employee leaves, vacations with pay, a system of promotions and transfers, and materials handling. Mr. Allison patiently read each suggestion aloud to his son and explained why it could not be adopted. When employees heard nothing from their suggestions, they stopped submitting them. Labor turnover continued to increase, up to 32%.

Dick Allison knew that employee relations and morale were getting out of hand, but he could not decide what steps he should take next.

1. What do you think the trouble is with Allison Auto Parts?
2. What would you do to correct the situation?

A Case Study
GENE HUBBARD

Gene Hubbard had been in business for four and a half years. Opening up his office supply store with virtually no capital, he had worked night and day to make it a success. It had grown, was well accepted in the community, and Gene felt that with his nine employees he could now afford to work less and enjoy life more.

But things didn't seem to work out for him that way. There always appeared to be problems that he personally had to solve. A customer who didn't get what he ordered, an employee with a personal complaint or grievance, employees not showing up for work at the designated hour, and thus the list went on.

Gene was a self-made man and really didn't know what to do. He wanted to give his employees authority to make decisions, to run his store, but he didn't trust them. He felt that they couldn't be relied on to do what they were hired to do. In fact, in his mind they weren't worth the pay that they received each week. It seems that every one of them had complained about his or her job, indicating they were all overworked and not appreciated. He always laughed at the employees when they started talking along this line, telling them that what they needed to do was to roll up their sleeves and get to work. This usually shut them up and they returned to their jobs.

In fact, this was one of the things that always annoyed Gene—that his employees were always complaining, telling him that they needed a better washroom, or that they wanted an area where they could sit down for a coffee break or eat their lunch. He laughed at such ideas, telling them that this was a place to work, not a home where you could lounge around. In Gene's mind, his employees just didn't seem to appreciate all that he was doing for them. They always wanted more.

It seemed to him that they had forgotten what their status was before he gave them a job. Most of them had been unemployed, looking for work, and with a family to support. They had forgotten that he had found them at the unemployment bureau and had offered to give them an opportunity to make something of themselves.

Gene wanted to have a prosperous business. He wanted his employees to like him. And he wanted to be known as a successful businessman. But he didn't know how to go about telling his men what he wanted from them. He had never been "good with words," and he figured his actions would tell them a whole lot more than any fancy words. He always stayed an hour or so after the store closed, for example, and he hoped some of them would too. But instead of staying late, he found two of them slipping out ten minutes early last Tuesday. However, he figured he had stopped that type of action by docking their pay and letting everyone else know about what they had been trying to get away with. He had said on many occasions that he didn't plan to treat any of his employees with kid gloves.

1. Do you think that morale was high or low in Gene's store? Why?
2. What would you say were the main qualities that Gene Hubbard possessed as a supervisor?
3. If you were hired as a consultant to help Gene Hubbard, what advice would you give him?

6
HOW TO SOLVE PROBLEMS AND MAKE DECISIONS

This chapter explains—

- How to identify and solve problems
- What errors you should watch for in making decisions
- A practical approach to making decisions

The job of supervising and managing employees is the job of making decisions—decisions about hiring new employees, about promotions, about training, about equipment, about productivity, about communications, about morale, and so on. In fact, when all is said and done, supervisors are paid for doing primarily one thing—making sound decisions. As a supervisor, this is your job. To do a good job, therefore, you must make good decisions because making good decisions is the essence of good supervision and the key to success as a supervisor.

WHAT TYPES OF DECISION MAKERS DO YOU FIND?

People make decisions in different ways. Some supervisors pride themselves on making quick decisions. You know this type. This supervisor gives little thought and consideration to people's feelings, to analyzing the facts, or to the impact the decision will have on others. His main concern is to do it fast and move on to the next problem, which frequently is caused by some other quick decision he has made.

At the other extreme is the supervisor who takes weeks to decide on an answer that should have taken a few hours at most. He never gets excited, always puts off taking action, and tells you things will work out OK in a few days.

making decisions
Between these two extremes there is the middle-of-the-road supervisor who hesitates to make decisions that will upset anyone. He wants to be everyone's friend and can't bring himself to make a decision that would be against someone's wishes. He is the pussy-footing middle-of-the-road type who never makes a solid decision. Instead, his answers are all watered-down compromises that seldom upset others and seldom really solve the problem.

Sometimes we find the research-type supervisor who refuses to make a decision until he has looked into every facet of the problem. He wants all the facts before he will move. Frequently, "all the facts" aren't available, so decisions aren't made—or it takes so long to get "all the facts" that the opportunity to take action has passed.

Of course, you will recognize other types of decision makers. There is the worrying type who agonizes over every decision, no matter how small (should we buy *one* or *two* boxes of paper clips?), and worries everyone else by asking their opinion when it really doesn't matter. Or the shy and timid type who never has the guts to face a problem head on. He sort of gives it passing glances and tries to fool himself and others that he is "working on it."

What we are interested in here is not these types of poor decision makers, but supervisors who have an open and willing-to-learn approach to making sound managerial decisions. Some problems, of course, can be decided on by past experience. For example, past experience will tell you how much paint to order for stock and what colors consumers want most. Other problems that have to be solved are not so easy. They are the one-of-a-kind type that cause most of the difficulties that supervisors experience. Let's take a look and see how you should tackle this type of problem.

HOW DO YOU MAKE A DECISION?

If you were to ask various supervisors how they make decisions, they would probably say: "I don't know. I just do what has to be done." Or: "I have a gut reaction. There are no rules. I just do it." Or: "It is something that I do naturally. I don't know what steps I take." Despite what they say, however, they all agree that making good decisions means they are good supervisors. And even though they are not aware of it, virtually every good supervisor follows a fairly well-developed series of steps in his decision-making process. These steps to making a decision are:

1. Be alert to possible problems.
2. Clearly define the problems.
3. Systematically analyze the problem.
4. Solve the problem.

Let's examine each of these steps in detail.

Be Alert for Problems.　To be a good supervisor, you need to be sensitive to the possibility of problems developing. You should be aware that trouble is brewing long before it bursts into the open and becomes critical. You need to be alert to areas that will cause potential problems and to keep a sharp lookout. A good supervisor always tries to nip a problem in the bud, solve it in its early and easy stages—rather than wait for a crisis to develop. For example, a disagreement between two employees should be settled to their satisfaction before the whole department takes sides and work is stopped.

sensitivity to developing problems

You might be wondering how you develop this skill. It's not hard to do. If you'll review most problems, you will find that some evidence or symptom that something was wrong appeared long before the problem itself surfaced. What you need to do, therefore, is systematically observe these small symptoms and see if they could possibly lead to larger problems. Once you get yourself used to thinking along these lines, you will become alert to any small symptoms that occur and can then do something about them. For example, if Tom's machine is producing a little more scrap than normal, what does this mean? That the machine is wearing out? If this is the trouble and the machine breaks down, it will cause a week's delay in production. Or does the excess scrap signal that you have a batch of poor-quality raw material that will run up costs and make poor-quality products? Or does it tell you that Tom is having some sort of personal or moral problems that have affected the quality of his work? Whatever it is, this small signal should alert you to look

"A good supervisor needs to be alert
to the possibility of problems developing."

into the matter and to make some corrective decisions before the problem gets out of hand.

In the same way, other symptoms of problems should not go unnoticed. For example, if you have a slight increase in labor turnover, look into it. Likewise, you should check such things as an increase in absenteeism, in lateness, accidents, down time of machines, or in sickness.

Communications between you and your employees can also provide clues to future problems. If there are no communications where there used to be a free exchange, what is wrong? If an employee starts giving a brief "Good morning" instead of the old warm "Good morning, Harry! How are things going with you today?" this may signal some problems in the making. None of these incidents may be anything unusual, but it is possible that each could be a signal that something is brewing. Check them out! Look into them. Train yourself to be alert to these and other signs that may point to larger problems.

Define the Problem.   Believe it or not, clearly defining the problem is frequently the biggest part of solving the problem. Once we know what the problem is, we can usually find an answer for it. If an automobile engine sputters and stops, for example, we might guess that the problem is we are out of gas. So we put gas in the tank, but the engine still won't run. We next say our problem is that we need new points. So we put in a set of points. The *problems vs* car still doesn't run. Finally, we put in a new gas filter, and the engine starts! *symptoms* We "solved" two problems that didn't exist, but we did not initially define and solve the real problem that was causing the trouble! Instead, we stumbled on it by trial and error. If we had checked the gas tank for gas, the spark plugs for spark, and the carburetor to see if we had gas going through it, we would have found the real problem—"no gas was going into the carburetor."

And we would have found it *before* we had wasted a great deal of time solving nonexisting problems.

As a supervisor, you may be faced with all sorts of symptoms. You may recognize from reports dealing with waste, employee absences, machine breakdowns, and goods returned by customers that something is wrong. You may feel frustrated, disturbed, even dismayed at all the things you see that could be the root of the problem. But remember you are like a doctor carefully analyzing all these symptoms before making a diagnosis; your job is to diagnose and state specifically what the problem is. Once you are sure of the problem, then you can look for a solution. But before you start taking action, you need to know what the problem is.

You must be careful, however, not to treat symptoms instead of causes. For example, if your head hurts, you may treat the symptom (a headache) with an aspirin, but as soon as the aspirin wears off, you may find your head still hurts. Later you find out that the real problem is eyestrain. You need glasses, therefore, to solve the problem and eliminate the headache symptom.

Practice in sifting through facts and defining the real problem will improve your problem-solving ability. The more you practice, the better you will be. And the better you are at determining the real problem, the more confidence you will have in yourself as a decision maker.

Analyze the Problem—Get All the Facts. After you have defined the problem, your next job is to systematically analyze it. To do this, you will need to get all the facts that are available to you. Until you define the problem, however, you will not know what information you will need. This is why it is so important for you to define the problem *before* you start collecting the facts. Once you have a clear definition of the problem, you can then decide what is important and what additional information you will need.

Some supervisors are always complaining that they can't make a decision because they don't have enough facts. This is frequently just an excuse for putting off a decision. You will never have *all* the facts. What you must do, therefore, is make decisions with the facts you have, plus those you can get without too much delay and expense. Without the facts, you are "shooting from the hip." You are making snap decisions, and the consequences may be disastrous.

Getting the facts that bear on a problem is so basic to good decision making that it is almost impossible to overemphasize the importance of this step. Even when it means delaying the decision somewhat, it is frequently worth it to get the facts.

understand the problem

To reach a sound decision, a supervisor frequently needs information or facts pertaining to a host of things in his company. He may need to know what company policy is. What rules and regulations exist. How similar cases have been handled in the past. Have any precedents been set? Do union contracts have any bearing on the problem? Are any excessive costs involved? What effect will a possible decision have on work procedures? On employee morale? And so on. These are the types of things that a supervisor will need to investigate. He needs to have a searching and questioning frame of mind in order that important data that would have a significant bearing on the problem will not be overlooked.

Having identified the problem and gathered the facts, the supervisor then needs to make sure that the problem was correctly identified. He needs to review the situation to see if the real problem has changed from what he originally thought it was.

At this point, with the problem defined, the facts gathered, and the causes of the problem understood, the supervisor is ready to try to solve the problem.

Solve the Problem.   As the old saying goes, "There is more than one way to skin a cat." Likewise, there is more than one solution to most problems. To find the best answer to a problem, therefore, a supervisor needs to develop several possible solutions so he can select the best one. This is a difficult step in decision making because we need to keep an open mind to all logical solutions to the problem. Most of us have certain tendencies, or preferences, or preconceived ideas about how something should be done. If we aren't careful, we will solve a problem using these preferences or preconceived ideas without ever looking at other possibilities.

To solve a problem, most supervisors find it helps to take two steps:

solving the problem

1. Look at all logical solutions. Consider all the ways in which the problem can be solved.
2. Select the best solution from all the possible solutions that you recognize.

Let's look at these two steps in a little more detail.

Look at All Logical Solutions.   At this point in making decisions, you need to make a firm rule that no decision will be made until all possible logical solutions have been considered. Remember that the decision you make will be no better than the solutions you consider. To do your best job, therefore, you should have as many solutions as possible to choose from, so that you will be sure to select the best. If, for example, you have to choose the color to paint a house and you only consider red, blue, and purple, you will probably not make a wise decision. If, on the other hand, you considered all shades of yellow, green, blue, red, purple, black, and white, then you would probably make a wise decision because these alternative colors (solutions) from which you can select one color (the decision) give you a greater selection to choose from. You have looked at all logical choices of color. You have considered all logical solutions to the problem of what color to paint your house.

Don't fall into the trap of seeing only one or two solutions to a problem. True, it is easier to choose when you have only two alternatives; just as it is easier to make a choice of ice cream if you only consider cherry and vanilla. If you consider all 37 varieties, however, your decision will be more difficult to make. But the outcome will probably be better. The same is true of more complex decisions. Remember, the rule here is always consider all possible solutions before you make a decision.

Select the Best Solution.   Once you have looked at all possible solutions, your next job is to choose the best one. To do this, you will need to sit down and carefully consider each solution. Every alternative solution has some good points and some bad points. What you need to do, therefore, is to size up each solution. Recognize the good features that would help solve your problem as well as the negative aspects that the solution offers. To do this, try to visualize how using each solution would affect your department, your employees, and so on. Try to foresee the desirable as well as the undesirable consequences of putting each solution into effect. For example, try to foresee what effect the solution would have on production. Would it help production or slow it down? What effect would the solution have on your employees? Would it help morale or hurt it? What effect would the solution have on product quality? What expenses would be involved? Do you have the necessary tools? Would the solution be in line with stated company policy? These are the types of things you should consider for each proposed solution.

After having thought through each of your solutions in this manner, you will be in a position to see which one would work best for you and would cause the least amount of friction. The one that appears to have the most good points and the smallest number of bad points would be the one you would choose. This would be your best solution.

You must remember, however, that every decision involves some risk. There is no such thing as a "sure-fire" decision—one without any risk. No matter how carefully you have thought through the decision, things can come up and go wrong that you didn't foresee. So be prepared to work with the solution to make it work.

In choosing a solution, some supervisors rely on previous experience. This is not a bad idea, but you should remember that history does not always repeat itself. What worked before may not work this time. Although past experience is helpful to a manager, it would be dangerous for him to follow it blindly without considering every possible solution. Conditions, people's feelings, and economic situations vary, and what worked last time may be a poor solution now.

HOW DO YOU MAKE ROUTINE DECISIONS?

Some problems occur frequently enough so that you can set up a routine way to solve them. For example, if an employee has been absent on a day prior to or following a paid holiday, should he be paid for the holiday? You might decide that if he were absent on both the workday prior to and the workday following a paid holiday, he should not be paid for the holiday. If he were absent only on the day prior to the holiday, you might decide he should be paid for the holiday. Having set up this procedure, you would follow the same routine in deciding future similar cases.

common problems

Before you decide on a particular routine decision, however, you should go through the same procedures we discussed previously in order to determine which solution would be the best one. In other words, you should consider all possible routine solutions before selecting the best. In the holiday pay case above, for example, you should consider these possibilities:

1. No pay for any time not worked.
2. Pay for the holiday under any conditions.
3. Pay for the holiday only if the employee worked the day prior to and the day following the holiday.
4. Pay for the holiday if the employee worked either the day prior to or the day following the holiday.

Each of these four possible solutions should be evaluated, recognizing the impact each would have on employee morale, expenses, output, union negotiations, and so on. The choice would be the solution that had the largest number of good points and the smallest number of bad points.

CAN BRAINSTORMING HELP MAKE DECISIONS?

Yes. Brainstorming is the "ten-heads-are-better-than-one" approach to solving a difficult problem. It's a simple idea but frequently turns up some pretty good answers to perplexing problems.

The first thing to do is get your group (any manageable number) together in a quiet place. Tell the group what the problem is that needs solving. Then ask them to throw reason to the wind in coming up with answers. Ask them to think wildly—without reserve—not considering such things as lack of funds, lack of space, etc. As suggestions and answers come forth, don't stop to examine them as to their feasibility. Instead, let every proposed solution—no matter how wild it may sound—serve to trigger another person's thinking. Keep this type of activity going for a set length of time, and then go back and examine every individual suggestion. Perhaps one or more suggestions can be combined and modified to come up with a pretty good solution to a perplexing problem.

think broadly

Just for a start, try brainstorming with a problem like: "What use can we make of 100,000 venetian blind slats?"

WHY DO WE PUT OFF MAKING DECISIONS?

In many cases we put off making a decision for good reasons. Often, however, we put off making a decision because down deep inside we want to avoid making it. We don't want to face the consequences of the decision. You might, for example, be faced with making a decision about spending a large sum of money that will put you deeply in debt. You don't relish the thought of this and are, therefore, subconsciously looking for ways to put off making the decision. You look for all sorts of "legitimate" excuses. You may not be aware of what you are doing, but you are trying to avoid making the decision. Whenever you find yourself in this position of having to make a decision that you want to postpone, you should stop and ask yourself if you are trying to duck making the decision. To help you answer this question, see if you are postponing the decision for any of the following reasons:

reasons to
postpone
decisions

1. You decide that there aren't enough facts to make the decision. Therefore, you decide to postpone making it until you can get *all* the information.

2. You decide that it is not important enough to bother with—then you assign it to a subordinate to make.

3. You assign the problem to a committee to decide. This will probably delay the decision indefinitely.

4. You undertake research on the topic to find out how such a problem was previously decided. This could cause the decision to be put off for months.

5. You postpone making the decision because of "illness" or a "more pressing problem."

6. You decide that you don't have the authority to make the decision—that it should be made by someone else.

7. You decide to wait until next week when you will have more time to devote to giving the matter your undivided attention. Next week, of course, seldom comes.

If you find yourself not making decisions for these and similar reasons, *be sure you understand yourself* and know what you are doing. Recognize that in all probability you are ducking the decision making responsibility. Of course, if you actually want to delay making a decision, then any one of the above excuses could serve you well.

The rule, however, is to understand yourself and postpone making decisions only for good sound reasons.

HOW DO YOU PUT THE DECISION INTO EFFECT?

We don't make decisions just for the fun of it. A decision is made to solve a problem, and one of the most satisfying experiences that a supervisor can have is to see his carefully thought-out solution to a problem put smoothly into effect. This doesn't happen by itself, however. Instead, it involves a well thought-out plan of putting the solution into operation. A *wise* decision that is *poorly* implemented is worse than a *mediocre* decision that is *well* implemented. As a supervisor, therefore, you need to carefully plan *how* your decision can best be implemented.

Most of the time a decision will result in some type of change that will affect one or more employees. It is human nature to resist changes. A change moves us from a routine we know to one we don't know. Therefore we resent the change. A supervisor who recognizes this human resistance and carefully plans the implementation of his plan will be a successful supervisor.

Putting any decision into effect involves several steps:

1. *Plan* how you will put the decision into operation. You need to consider such questions as What needs to be done? Who will do it? How will it be done? and When will it be done? Many a good decision has failed simply because it was introduced at the wrong time. Decisions sometimes fail because the work is introduced out of sequence. By planning ahead, a supervisor can foresee possible trouble spots and can take action to avoid them.

2. *Communicate* the decision. Most decisions involve people, and the wise supervisor is the one who gets the employees who will be affected by the decision into the act. This may mean consultation during the decision-making process if the decision is one where an employee can help. It also means prompt communications to all affected employees. Any supervisor who has learned from one of his employees about a management decision to add a second shift will readily understand the need for prompt communications through the proper channels. This same sort of logic applies to the implementation of your decisions. Communicate them promptly to your employees, and try to get their support. Answer their questions carefully and truthfully. You will depend on them to get the decision carried out and if your employees do not support your idea, they can make you as well as your ideas look pretty silly.

3. *Follow up* the process. No matter how well you have thought out a plan and how carefully you have discussed it with the employees involved, it is always possible for it to go wrong. Things may come up that you don't anticipate. Maybe everyone is not doing his part to get the decision implemented. Maybe some group of employees has developed resistance to the change. Maybe raw materials are not coming in on time. These are the types of things that could make the decision not go into effect smoothly. You will need, therefore, to follow closely every step in the implementation of your decision. Following up is your insurance that things are going according to plan, that your decision will be implemented. This is not to say that you have to be involved in every detailed step, but you should not give your employees a plan or decision and then forget it. You will need, instead, to make routine checks just to be sure that everything is going according to your plan. This is the point where small deviations can be caught that could save time and money later.

4. *Evaluate* your results. Did your decision achieve the desired results? If not, why did it fail? Where did it fail? All of us can learn by our mistakes, but we cannot learn unless we study our mistakes and see where we went wrong. Examining your failures, therefore, can point out errors to avoid so as to achieve future success. If your plan was successfully introduced, you should look at what you did that made it succeed—and then use these ideas again. By evaluating successful plans, you may also see some weak spots that you could improve next time, thus making your plan even more successful.

As was said at the beginning of this chapter, supervisors are paid to make good decisions. The only way to consistently improve your decision-making ability is to follow the procedures outlined above.

WHAT ARE SOME PRACTICAL TIPS ON MAKING DECISIONS?

Now that we have discussed the process involved in making and implementing decisions, let's look at some day-to-day practices that you might well remember.

1. *Decide whether the decision is a big decision or a small one.* If it is a big problem, give it the full treatment that we have discussed. Weigh all aspects carefully. Big problems deserve all the time, attention, and skill that you can give them. Little problems, on the other hand, don't deserve the trappings of a summit conference. If it is a small problem, don't spend hours agonizing over what to do. For example, don't spend hours trying to decide whether to give a coffee break at 10:15 or 10:30, or whether you should paint the employee lounge a beige or egg-shell color. Major concern over little problems isn't worth your time, and if you are not careful, the small problems may take your attention away from more important matters.

   aids to making decisions

2. *Don't make a snap decision.* Take time to get the facts and then analyze them carefully.

3. *Rely on established company policy and practices where possible.* If company policy is to suspend an employee found drinking on the job, this is the answer if you face such a problem.

4. *Seek the help of others when you are in doubt.* Ask other people what they think, especially people who are well informed and whose judgment you trust. Seek the help of experts if the decision involves technicalities you are not familiar with. For example, don't try to solve a safety problem involving electricity. Instead, call the plant electrician or an electrical engineer to give you help.

5. *Avoid crisis decisions.* Most of the time, decisions don't have to be made under crisis conditions—even though you might think they do. Stop and consider the situation. Ask yourself when the decision has to be made. Then utilize the time available to make the best decision. If you do have a crisis, however, remember that you are the boss, and your employees are looking to you for a decision. Don't panic. Instead, take a moment to go through the major decision-making steps we have previously discussed; then give your answer to your employees.

6. *If a decision has to be made, make it.* Don't put off making a needed decision. This will only cause your work to pile up all the higher.

7. *Don't brood over a decision once action has been taken.* Evaluation? Yes! Brooding? No! The thing is done. You can't be 100% right every time. Poor decisions are made every day, from the President of the United States on down. We are all human. This is not to excuse a poor decision. This is not to say we should not analyze a decision once we have put it into effect. What we are saying is don't worry yourself into ulcers trying to decide whether or not you made the right decision. As a note of consolation, we seldom make any really wrong decisions. Instead, most of the time, it is a matter of how good (or how poor) the decision was. It is a question of the degree of correctness of our decision. So, once you've made a decision, put it into effect and don't worry over it.

A Case Study
DECISIONS! DECISIONS!

Gene Hamlin, the supervisor of the small parts assembly line, had just returned to his desk from his weekly production conference to find himself faced with the following:

1. Mattie Smith, one of the best assemblers he had ever known had been offered a job by a competitor at an increase in pay. She wanted to talk with Mr. Hamlin about opportunities in the company.

2. A note indicated that Mr. Ashmore, the plant manager, wanted to talk to him about a new departmental layout.

3. The digital tester on the subassembly line was giving "funny" readings. The employee wanted to know what she should do.

4. The welding group of four men said they were quitting work at 4:00 P.M. unless the company took some action to make the welding equipment faster and safer. They had already had two lost-time accidents this week.

5. A note from his wife requested that he call her immediately.

6. His secretary, according to her note, was sick in the women's lounge. She didn't know whether to go home or try to stick it out and wanted his advice.

7. The personnel director had three candidates for a job opening in his department waiting to talk to him.

When he reviewed all the things facing him, Mr. Hamlin heaved a sigh and put his head in his hands.

1. What priority should Mr. Hamlin give each decision?
2. Which problem should he tackle first, second, and so on? Why?

A Case Study
ALLEN MANUFACTURING COMPANY

The Allen Manufacturing Company, located in South Planes, manufactures and distributes small electric tools such as hand-held electric drills, light drill presses, hedge clippers, sanding machines, buffers, etc.

The company is well established and has operated at 80% of its capacity since 1974. Sales last year amounted to $1,000,000, but gross profits were only $100,000. When Mr. Allen, the president and owner, began checking into the cause of this rather low gross profit, he found that the manufacturing and distributing costs had increased. He found, for example, that labor costs last year had risen to $500,000 and that the costs of raw materials had increased to $300,000.

At the next staff meeting, Mr. Allen presented this problem of dwindling profits to his staff and asked for their recommendations. The Chief of Manufacturing suggested that the trouble was that the products were priced too low, and suggested, therefore, that an across-the-board price increase of 25% would place the company back in a sounder profit position. The Sales Manager, however, objected to the rosy picture painted by the Chief of Manufacturing, and indicated that a 25% price increase would surely reduce sales. The Chief of Manufacturing regretfully agreed with the Sales Manager, and the two of them estimated that the proposed price increase would reduce the utilization of plant capacity by 10%.

The Chief Engineer, on the other hand, indicated that he did not think it would be wise to attempt any price increase at this time. Instead, he proposed to make some improvements in the old operating equipment, purchase some new labor-saving machinery, and incorporate processing changes. In fact, he estimated that with an increase in fixed costs of $100,000, he could reduce labor and material costs by 25%.

Mr. Allen pondered the two proposals: one to increase prices and suffer a reduction in volume; the other to purchase new equipment, thereby increasing fixed costs but reducing out-of-pocket expenses.

1. How would you go about making a decision in this case?
2. What action would you suggest that Mr. Allen take? Why?

7

HOW TO PLAN AND LEAD A MEETING

This chapter explains—

- A supervisor's role in meetings
- Why you need to hold meetings
- The fine points of speaking at meetings

Supervisors often complain about having to go to meetings, stating that meetings take up too much time—maybe so much that there's no time left for work.

Some meetings are a waste of time, yet it seems we have more and more meetings every day. Despite all the noise made against meetings, however, there's no readily available substitute for them. Without meetings it would be very difficult for an organization of any size to operate efficiently.

WHY DO WE HOLD MEETINGS?

We hold meetings because we haven't found a better way to get information across to employees and to get problems solved. There are, of course, many ways other than meetings to get information to employees, and there are ways to get employees' ideas about how to solve problems. We could, for instance, use bulletin boards, letters, and surveys instead of meetings. But employees like meetings best. They like to hear the story straight from the boss. And they like a chance to ask questions and express their own ideas.

need for meetings

In addition, an informal meeting is a great way to get employees to participate in departmental matters. They are more enthusiastic about carrying out directives and plans that they have helped develop than plans handed down from above. When you get a group of people together to talk about a problem that is of interest to all of them, there seldom is a dull moment.

Under a friendly atmosphere of exchange of experiences and opinions, better solutions to departmental problems will develop than could have been made by one man alone. A group of people bring a wide background of experiences and education to bear on a topic, and it is only logical, therefore, that you can reach a better decision. This is the brainstorming effect we discussed in Chapter 6.

Meetings can also bring about coordination between employees and departments. When members discuss and understand the other fellow's point of view, they usually are more tolerant of the problems that other employees present.

In addition to the above, meetings are also held for the following reasons:

1. To give subordinates the opportunity to express themselves and be in on making decisions.
2. To enable you to communicate your departmental "party line" to your employees and to explain why.
3. To provide a forum where friendly debate can take place to explain key problems or selected topics.
4. To teach others, by example, how meetings should be conducted.

5. To allow employees to indicate their emotional reactions to proposals or suggestions, allowing them the opportunity to hear all sides and arrive at a compromise.

6. To promote teamwork by making the participants all equals in the development of a final decision.

WHAT TYPES OF MEETINGS ARE THERE?

Four types of meetings are typically held in business situations. These are:

1. The Informational Meeting. This is held to get information across to the participants. It may take the form of an address or lecture, or it may be visual, using motion pictures, filmstrips, slides, and so on. Although there is some discussion and questions may be asked, the major emphasis is on imparting information to the participants.

2. Opinion-Seeking Meetings. These meetings are used when the supervisor wants the ideas and opinions of others to help him make a decision. He asks questions, solicits employees' opinions, and wants to know how an employee would handle the situation.

*varieties of
objectives*

3. The Problem-Solving Meeting. A problem-solving meeting is called to get the facts before the group so that they can be considered and discussed and so that a solution to a problem can be agreed upon. This type of meeting typically produces free and lively discussions. In problem-solving meetings, the group has been given the authority to make a decision, and even if their solution is not the best one, it is one they have agreed upon and will be implemented by them.

4. The New Ideas Meeting. The purpose of a new ideas meeting is to *generate* new ideas, to elicit full participation in the development of new concepts. The purpose is not to take action but to develop new concepts and ideas that may later prove useful.

WHERE SHOULD MEETINGS BE HELD?

Of all the factors that can make or break a meeting, nothing is more important than where you hold it. In fact, where you hold it is so important that the location can positively or negatively affect the participants and can make the meeting a success or a flop. Therefore choose the meeting place carefully. Be sure it is comfortable and relatively quiet. Some companies provide conference rooms. A brief, informal meeting might even be held right in your own department. However, where difficult problems have to be tackled, meetings are most effective when they are held in a quiet, well-lighted, temperature-controlled room, arranged so that all members can see and talk with each other. Chairs set in rows like theater seats are poor because people are speaking behind others and are not facing them. A blackboard or other writing surface is frequently needed to list group ideas and to summarize what has been said. Finally, the area should be isolated so that the meeting will be free of phone and personal interruptions.

WHAT IS A LEADER'S ROLE IN THE VARIOUS TYPES OF MEETINGS?

Depending on the type of meeting, the leader's role will vary. An informational meeting needs a leader who is a good speaker, who can explain ideas, and who can get the group to agree to go along with what the leader is telling or "selling."

The opinion-seeking meeting requires a leader who can get people to express their ideas. He has to have the ability to suggest questions that will stimulate the group and convince them of his sincerity in wanting their ideas. He needs the ability to make every member feel that he has made a significant contribution to the discussion at hand.

The problem-solving meeting requires a leader with the greatest abilities because his task is the most complex of all. His job is to get ideas accepted. He also must elicit discussion, get all the members to give their ideas, and keep the meeting moving on the target. He has to have the ability to tactfully shut up those who want to hog the show and to get the quiet ones into the act. When discussion goes astray, he has to move it back on target without offending the speakers. His job is *not* to tell people what *he* thinks, but to get them to say what *they* think. The purpose of the meeting, after all, is not to learn what the leader thinks, but to get the group to express its ideas and solve the problem—make a decision. The good leader, therefore, deemphasizes his own ego and, instead, constantly strives to secure maximum group participation. He has to artfully curb the talkative and stimulate the timid to speak. He writes what people say on the blackboard so they can see the point. He talks only enough to equalize participation and reflect the sentiments of the group.

Most of the time, the group is at its best when discussion is high and members are participating back and forth with each other rather than with the leader. The leader's role here is to listen, make notes on the board, and summarize occasionally what has been said.

The leader of a problem-solving group needs to get the members to agree on a solution. If at all possible, the leader should try for a unanimous agreement. Otherwise, some of the members will be forced to carry out some action that they did not support or even openly opposed. Unanimous agreement, however, should not be sought when it would destroy the group or excessively prolong a meeting. It is frustrating for members who have already made up their minds to listen to extra hours of discussion trying to convince one or two members to go along with the decision of the group. In such cases, there is no reason why a minority report could not be made along with the findings of the majority.

As you might well imagine, the leader of a new-ideas meeting should attempt to promote an atmosphere that encourages a free and easy discussion of the topic at hand. He should never criticize or evaluate an idea. Instead, his role is to elicit ideas, encourage participation, and promote a full discussion of any concepts that the group may evolve.

WHAT ARE THE MAJOR STRENGTHS OF MEETINGS?

Probably the biggest byproduct of a meeting is that the participants feel more strongly motivated to carry out the decisions of the group. In fact, in a lot of companies, this is one of the reasons, if not the main reason, for holding meetings—that is, to get the participants to agree to carry out the decisions of the group. A person who participates in making a decision is much more interested in seeing it work and will work harder to see that it does succeed.

A second bonus from meetings is that nonparticipants are also more apt to go along with decisions made by the group than by an individual. Even superiors are more likely to abide by group decisions because they feel that controversies have been ironed out in the meeting and that the group should stand behind its recommendations.

*motivation
through
participation*

Meetings are also important to industry because employees are working together instead of simply talking together. Members begin to know each other by individual capacities and by jobs or positions. When this occurs, members begin consciously to want to work together as a team. Thus, the desire to cooperate is stronger, and the individual's team efforts are considerably increased.

Meetings bring the talents of many different individuals to bear upon a problem. From their diverse backgrounds and experiences, these individuals should be in a position to bring out all pertinent facts and arrive at a sound decision.

Because of the thorough discussion that most problems get, participants tend to have a better understanding of what everyone thinks, and they recognize all aspects of a problem. Understanding the complexity of the problem, they may see that there is no simple solution.

Finally, meetings are especially good at getting employees innovating, thinking up new ideas, or brainstorming. As you know, brainstorming gets the members to express new ideas about a problem or product in a meeting. Their ideas in turn start other members thinking and communicating their ideas. Out of all the ideas discussed may emerge an innovation in the form of a new product or new concept that no one individual can claim as his own. It is a product of the entire group—each person contributing his idea to make up the whole.

WHAT ARE THE WEAKNESSES OF MEETINGS?

Meetings take up a lot of time, and many of them are unproductive. Meetings are complicated, and although the supervisor may wish for the simplicity of individual decision making, meetings are here to stay, and we may as well learn to live with them. It's no longer a matter of whether to have meetings, it's a matter of how best to use them.

Meetings take money as well as time. It's not uncommon for a meeting of fifteen people to last three hours. This means that 45 man-hours of effort at a large cost in dollars went into the making of an agreement or decision. When we see the outcome, we sometimes wonder if the money was well spent.

costs, time, and compromise

Meetings tend to make people seek the lowest common denominator of agreement, to compromise rather than take a stand that they would have taken individually. When we meet, we have a strong feeling or urge to reach an agreement. As a result, people compromise their feelings to reach this end. Of course, this leveling effect is not altogether bad. It serves to curb radical ideas and keeps the group from going off half-cocked.

Individual responsibility is not felt in meetings. Participants feel that the responsibility is shared among all the members present, and as is frequently the case, "everybody's business is nobody's business." No one feels responsible as a result, and this somewhat limits the usefulness of meetings.

Even with these weaknesses, meetings are still an important part of our business and social lives. They serve an important and unique function that cannot be served by any other device.

HOW SHOULD YOU HOLD A MEETING?

have objective and plan

The key to a good meeting is to plan in advance what you will do. First, *be sure you know why you are holding a meeting.* What is your objective? That is, what do you want to accomplish? After satisfactorily answering this question, next ask yourself if some other technique could be used that would be less expensive. If the meeting is still your answer, then you should prepare a *list of participants.* Be sure to include specialists from different areas in order to get proper representation as well as a balanced group for proper deliberation. The composition or *mix of the group* is important. If possible, select participants who are about equal in rank. A group that includes the plant manager, the controller, the division manager, and supervisors, as well as workers, would inhibit the participation of most of the workers as well as of the lower-level supervisors.

Next, *prepare a discussion outline* listing the objective of the meeting, probable topics to be discussed, questions that you should ask, and materials and handouts that you will need. Doing this will force you to think the whole thing through in advance and will allow you to anticipate the participants' reactions to points of discussion. It also provides you with an agenda for the meeting, thus making sure that an important point is not omitted.

List the materials you will need—materials like slides, demonstration models, or printed handouts. Be sure you have a blackboard or a chart pad handy. When you write things on the board for the group to see, you focus their attention on the topic. You can also use the board to list key points that are brought out in a discussion, as well as to summarize what the group has covered.

Choose a time and place. Select a time during working hours that is most convenient for everyone. Meetings held outside working hours are seldom effective because employees reason that if the meeting isn't important enough to hold on company time, the subject matter must not be too important.

Find a meeting place that is comfortable, quiet, and well-lighted and that provides ample work space. Arrange the seating to form a "U" so that

"Before you call a meeting, be sure you know why you are holding it— what the objective of the meeting is."

each participant will have maximum visibility and so as to give the discussion leader better control. Be sure to *notify all participants* well in advance of the meeting.

When the day of the meeting arrives, *open the meeting on time by clearly stating the objective* of the meeting. Indicate precisely what the group is expected to accomplish. If specific items need to be considered, list these on the blackboard for general guidance.

Start the discussion by introducing noncontroversial material that the group can tackle without fear of ignorance. Then move toward the objective by helping members express themselves and by calling for illustrations to clarify points. Get the group to suggest different ways that the objective can be met. Then discuss each way suggested, looking at its strong and weak points.

Up to this point, you've gotten the meeting going, and a lot of discussion has taken place about different ways the problem could be solved. For the informational, problem-solving, and opinion-seeking meetings, the stage is now set to *get the group to compromise and agree.* This will test your leadership ability because you must get those who disagreed to reconcile their views and to agree to a compromised position. You can tactfully point out faulty thinking, biased judgments, and narrow points of view. You can summarize positions, pointing out the advantages and disadvantages of each recommendation. With all this, you will need to keep up group interest and not let a good meeting "go to the dogs" as a result of poor control.

Don't drag out a meeting unnecessarily. When you sense that the group has reached an agreement, ask them, "Are we in agreement, then, that this is what we should do?" If you get agreement, restate the proposal and ask if you have made any errors or omitted anything.

Then *close the meeting on time.* If some members want to continue the discussion, tell them that they are welcome to do so after the meeting adjourns.

WHAT KINDS OF QUESTIONS SHOULD A LEADER ASK?

Depending on the response you want, various types of questions can be used. You might direct a question to an individual who doesn't mind opening a meeting. However, be careful how you use directed questions because you might embarrass a timid member. Instead, you can use overhead questions directed to the group in general, such as, "What do you think we can do to correct this problem?"

If you want one of two answers, use a question like, "Would you give this person a merit raise or reprimand him?" This gives the respondent only two choices. If you want to stimulate his thinking and get his ideas, then say, "What would you do in this case?" If you want to provoke discussion and controversy, you could say "To be successful, does a businessman have to be religious?" Then listen to the controversy that follows! Avoid catch questions

99

*How to Plan and
Lead a Meeting*

such as, "Have you stopped drinking on the job?" If the person answers with
either "yes" or "no," he is caught.

Don't let the group put you on the spot. When they ask you questions
like, "Mr. Boss, what is meant by a ratio-delay study?" throw the question
back to the group by saying, "That's a good question, Sam. Henry, can you
explain a ratio-delay study to Sam?"

Finally, use a "yes or no" type question to get a commitment; then
follow it with a "why, when, or where" question. For example, "Joe, do you
think attending meetings like this is worthwhile?" He'll either say "yes" or
"no." Then ask, "Why do you feel it is (or is not) worthwhile?" You've caused
him to tell you what he thinks; now you can get him to express his reasons for
his belief.

WHAT DO YOU DO ABOUT MEMBERS WHOSE ACTIONS DISRUPT MEETINGS?

As a leader, what do you do about members who are compulsive talkers, or
members who won't say anything, or participants who tend to argue over
every point, or digress, or carry on private conversations? All of these individuals present problems for the leader. Perhaps a discussion of each would
be of help.

The Compulsive Talker.   Some people just talk too much. They like to hear
themselves talk, and it seems they use every meeting to monopolize the
discussion. If you know this type in advance, seat him to your extreme right
or left; then you can "avoid" seeing him trying to get the floor. If he gets the
floor, let him have a reasonable amount of time; then interrupt by saying,
"You've got some good points there. Now let's hear what some other members think." If this doesn't work, set a time limit of, say, two minutes for any
one person to hold the floor.

The Member Who Won't Say Anything.   Some people are timid and get
all tongue-tied when they try to speak before a group. Don't embarrass this
kind of person by asking a difficult direct question. Instead, ask a question
you know he can answer. A question about his work, his family, or how he
handled a particular situation. Give him praise and a pat on the back
whenever possible to help him get over his hesitation to speak out.

Private Discussions.   When one member starts a conversation with his
neighbor that is disturbing to the group, what should you do? The best thing
is to ignore it if possible. There are always people who are inconsiderate
about other people's feelings, and you'll just have to tolerate them. If the
conversation reaches a point where something has to be done, try interrupt-
ing him by asking a direct question. Or you might stop talking and wait for

him to get quiet. If this doesn't work, you could say to the talker, "If you have anything to say, please speak up so that everyone can have the benefit of your comments." And, finally, if you want to put him on the spot, ask him to summarize the last few proposals and evaluate their feasibility. He probably hasn't gotten them clearly in mind and will have trouble. He'll get the point.

The Guy Who Argues over Every Point. The type of participant who argues over every point can cause an otherwise good meeting to fall apart. You'll need a lot of skill to handle him. If you can, try to find out why he is against everything. Once you detect this, maybe you can handle him. Don't get upset by his criticism. Treat his caustic comments and questions as though they were normal and routine. If possible, rephrase and restate them so that they appear to be conforming with the group. If you cannot tactfully control him, then refer his questions to the group. They'll probably be disgusted with him by this point and will not pull any punches in letting him know how obnoxious he is. This should quiet him. If not, see if you can avoid having him at your next meeting!

Digressions. Irrelevancies tend to crop up in meetings that try the skill and tact of even the best leaders. When this happens too often, the meeting is sidetracked, and progress is retarded. Your job as leader is to get the group tactfully back on the track. Several techniques can be used.

You can say, "This is an interesting observation. How does this fit into our problem?" This may cause the group to see their digression and get them back on the topic for discussion. Or, if you can, gradually tie in the remote discussion to the problem at hand and thus lead the group back on the track. If this doesn't work, try summarizing what has been said up to this point. This should serve to orient them and focus their attention on the main discussion. You might have to point out, "This discussion is interesting, but may I suggest that we postpone it until next month's meeting when that topic will be discussed." If none of this works, you might have to be rude and simply rule the discussion out of order.

DO YOU NEED AN AGENDA?

A well-prepared agenda distributed to members before the meeting will do more than anything else to keep a meeting from wandering off the track. In fact, more meetings fail because of this one reason than any other: that is, an agenda was not distributed in advance telling the members the need for the meeting—what would be discussed.

The agenda, which is a list of topics to be discussed, should be carefully planned by the leader. Topics necessary to the purpose of the meeting should be listed in their proper sequence. In order to keep the meeting moving, a time limit can be established for the discussion of each topic.

Although the agenda establishes an outline and a time schedule, it should not be so rigid that it cannot be adjusted. Certain topics may take longer to discuss than anticipated, and some topics may arise that the leader had not foreseen. The agenda, therefore, should be planned with a degree of flexibility. The leader should use it to guide the discussion, as well as to point out to the group what remains to be covered. With practice, a leader will learn when the group has discussed a point sufficiently to move on to the next topic.

HOW DO YOU ACHIEVE GROUP PARTICIPATION?

The chairman's general attitude toward the group can do more to elicit group participation than any other single factor. After stating the purpose of the meeting and providing the group with the necessary background information, you should invite discussion from the floor. This is a critical spot. You should create the impression that what everyone says is important and that you want everyone to participate. To get things going, you may have to pose one or two controversial questions, followed by some of the "what, when, and where" questions. Or you may invite each member to express himself about one of the problems under consideration.

If the group is rather large and you want everyone to participate, it would be advisable to break it up into smaller groups. These small groups would then go off and meet separately to discuss and decide on an assigned topic. After a designated time, usually 20 minutes, the small groups report back to the entire meeting, stating their positions and why. This gives everyone a chance to speak and be heard. It also encourages those people who would hesitate to speak out in a large group to have their say in the smaller units.

SHOULD YOU TAKE A VOTE?

A lot of leaders think you should vote if a solution has been agreed upon, and a lot of participants think that a vote is the democratic way to do things. Taking a vote, however, has drawbacks. For one thing, it accentuates the differences between people. This makes some of the employees uncomfortable—especially the minority. Also, if a person has committed himself publicly to a position, it is difficult for him to later change his mind without looking as if he is weak or vacillating. And those in the minority who "lost" the vote cannot be expected to carry out the group decision with great enthusiasm. For all these reasons, therefore, it is better not to take a formal vote but to work toward a consensus instead. Try to get the sense of the group, and state to them, "If I understand what you've been saying, it is that we should not proceed with the incorporation of the new product at this time. Is this correct?" Hearing no objections, you should further indicate, "Hearing no objections, then, I'll inform top management of your decision." This technique gets agreement and puts no one on the spot.

WHEN DO YOU CALL A MEETING?

You don't need to call a meeting every time you have a decision to make. Supervisors are paid to make decisions and take action. Meetings and conferences are time-consuming, and unless you need to, don't call a meeting. You should solve the run-of-the-mill problem without any sweat. Only in situations where you need to involve other people to help solve or carry out solutions should you call a meeting.

WHAT ARE THE FINE POINTS TO SPEAKING AT MEETINGS?

The old saying, "Stand up so they can see you. Speak up so they can hear you. And shut up so they will like you," is pretty good advice. There are, however, some other points that you should consider.

If, for example, you are asked to brief your department on the advantages and disadvantages involved in the new machine-paced assembly, how will you go about it? Although there are no magic rules, several common-sense considerations, listed below, will make your job easier and better received.

1. Ask yourself what the objective of your speech is. Is your purpose to entertain, inform, persuade, get a decision, or get your audience to take some action? If you know what you will be trying to do, then you can "build" your meeting in a way that will achieve your objective.

2. Who will your audience be? Who are the key persons attending? Do they have any special quirks that you should be aware of? Do they have any major preferences or biases that you would be wise to avoid? If the big boss has a "thing" about slides and a darkened room, don't use slides.

3. Outline what you will need to tell the group in line with the objective of the meeting. Keep in mind what idea or central theme you will want the group to leave the meeting with. If you want them to remember that "the new machine is essential for low-cost production"—then build your speech around that idea.

Know your objective, your subject, and your audience

4. Remember that a read speech is a disaster. Don't read. Outline what you need to say, then *rehearse* your talk. Use your family, a friend, anyone as an audience for practice. Or practice your presentation by using a recorder and play it back to see what you said and how it

sounded. Keep rehearsing until you feel at ease with the material you have outlined. Don't try to memorize your speech. You might be like the high-school debater who memorized his speech and had to start all over every time he forgot a line.

5. If you think you will have audience participation or questions, try to predict what questions will be asked. Then prepare your answers in advance so that you can make a smooth presentation.

6. Tell your audience why the meeting was called. Then tell them what your part is—what you are going to talk about. Next, give your speech. Then summarize your remarks.

7. In your speech itself, use humor if it applies, but don't drag in an old joke that will break the trend of thought. Use everyday words in your speech. Don't try to impress your audience with long words. Speak clearly and enunciate each word clearly. A lot of words sound alike but can have very different meanings.

8. We think and comprehend at the rate of 500 to 600 words a minute, but to be understood you should speak no faster than about a 100 or 125 words per minute. Anything faster causes your audience to loose the sense of what you are saying, and they may therefore have difficulty following you. The rule, therefore, is to speak clearly, distinctly, and not too fast. Slow down.

9. Look at your audience—not at the floor, the ceiling, or out the window. Move your eyes slowly from one person to another, letting them rest momentarily on each individual as you talk. If you feel uncomfortable doing this, then pick out a spot in the back of the room and talk to that spot. This is better than looking up or down. When you look at your audience instead of away from them, you maintain contact with them. You can see whether they are "with you" or whether they themselves are gazing at the ceiling or looking out the window.

10. In closing your speech don't forget to summarize what you have told them. But be concise—not long-winded. Remember: If you want to give a good speech, keep in mind the "stand-up, speak-up, shut-up" rule!

A Case Study
PLANNING A MEETING

Assume that you are the manager of a large department in a retail store. You have just been informed of a major change in company policy that will affect your employees. You are faced with the problem of communicating and explaining this new change to your employees. You could write a letter or memo to them, but on second thought you decide to hold a meeting of your employees to tell them of the change and to get their suggestions about how the change can best be introduced.

1. What type of meeting would you hold for this purpose?
2. When would you hold your meeting?
3. Would you ask all employees to one big meeting, or would you hold two or three small meetings?
4. What kind of questions would you ask?
5. How would you conduct your meeting?
6. Are there any special things that you should be prepared for in your meeting?

A Case Study
HOLDING A MEETING

One of the best ways to learn is by doing, and one of the best ways to learn how to conduct a meeting is to hold one. For this case, therefore, select a person from your class to hold a "meeting" to explain to his "employees" how to perform a job. Have six or eight members of the class act as the "employees." You can choose any job or task you want to, but select one that the "supervisor" should know. For example, have the supervisor explain to the group how to tie a man's tie. Be sure to have some women in the group.

When this "meeting" is completed, choose one or two more "supervisors" and some other "employees" to hold other meetings to learn about other jobs.

When these "meetings" are over, choose a class member to lead the class in a discussion of how well the leaders did.

Rate the leaders on how well they conducted their meetings.

A Case Study
ELECTRIC COMPONENTS CORPORATION

As his first assignment with the Electric Components Corporation, Dick Parker was placed in charge of the company's storeroom. The company, a large nationally known manufacturer, engaged in the design, fabrication, and sale of many types of electronic products. Amplifiers, recorders, speakers, and transmitters were just a few of its products. Commonly used parts in these products were stocked and issued from one centralized storeroom. Over 10,000 different parts were stocked, including screws, nuts, bolts, resistors, condensers, grommets, and so on.

As a young graduate, Dick was anxious to "make good," and he incorporated several improvements. One of his problem areas was maintaining a sufficient stock of 72 different sizes and lengths of screws and nuts. He wondered at the necessity for the various sizes and decided to see what could be done to reduce the number.

Upon checking the product specifications, he found that the design engineers had specified for each product that a screw must extend beyond the nut exactly two threads. This, he discovered, accounted in part for the large variety of screw lengths he was required to stock. Furthermore, he found that each design engineer chose whatever diameter screw he felt appropriate for the product, thus accounting in part for the variety in the diameters of the screws. In general, the number of threads per inch was fairly well standardized.

After talking with a large number of design and product engineers, Dick believed that the variety of stocked screws could be considerably reduced. He reasoned that the length a screw extended beyond a nut, if it were a reasonable amount, was immaterial in the functioning of a product, and except for outside items where appearance was a factor, made no difference to the customer.

Accordingly, he prepared a report for top management showing the excess dollars tied up in "needless" varieties of screws. The plant manager was impressed with the report and decided that a meeting should be called to discuss its possibilities.

1. Around what theme should the meeting be organized?
2. Who should call the meeting?
3. Where should it be held?
4. Who should attend the meeting?

PART TWO
THE PROCESS OF SUPERVISION

8
HOW TO SUPERVISE OTHERS

This chapter explains—

- How to give orders
- Signals that indicate you are not doing a good job
- How age, sex, and professional status affect supervision

Your job as a supervisor is to get results through people. *How* you supervise determines the results you get. If you want to get employees involved in their work, if you want to get them going on their jobs, you've got to give them directions. Telling other people what you want them to do is the way you get your decisions and ideas implemented. It enables you to put your ideas into action. *How* you tell them what you want them to do—*how* you give directions—will determine how well the job will be done and whether or not you will succeed or fail as a supervisor.

Giving orders is so much a part of supervision that we sometimes take it for granted. Yet the act of giving an employee an order is a complicated and difficult task. It is more than simply saying, "Paint this red," because a supervisor's skill in understanding and motivating his employee is reflected in how he gives his order. The words he chooses, how he says them, his tone of voice—all of these factors help promote a climate in which work will be done. Because directing others is so important to a supervisor, let's look at how a supervisor should give an order.

HOW SHOULD YOU GIVE ORDERS?

There are six simple rules you should follow.

1. Create the Right Climate. Orders should be given in a climate and spirit of help and cooperation. Commands and brusque orders are the mark of an immature supervisor and seldom achieve more than a grudging compliance. As every supervisor knows, you will need all the cooperation and help your employees can give you, not just a reluctant compliance. You should, therefore, strive to create a climate of voluntary cooperation, respect, and understanding between you and your employees. This type of climate does not happen overnight but grows out of fair treatment, a just handling of differences, and firm supervision. Where employees willingly and enthusiastically accept a directive, you can be sure that a climate of helpful cooperation exists.

correct environment

Where employees do only what they are told, only what is expected of them, you will have a second-best climate of compliance, where work is completed without enthusiasm. Initiative, creativity, and suggestions from your employees will be lacking. Your employees will do only what you tell them. No more. No less.

The worst climate, of course, is one of open hostility. Orders are received with defiance, and the employee does only what he has to due to the authority you have over him. He constantly looks for an opportunity to foul up the process and to embarrass you.

The first rule for giving good orders, therefore, is to create a climate of mutual understanding, trust, and cooperation between you and your employees.

110

2. Make the Order Reasonable. A good order is a reasonable one. It is one that your employee can physically accomplish without danger to his life or limb. Remember, however, that an order that would be reasonable for one person might be unreasonable for another. It would be unreasonable, for example, to order an employee to drive a tractor-trailer to deliver a product if his only experience was driving pickups. The same order, however, would be reasonable to an experienced and licensed truck driver.

Sometimes orders are given that stretch an employee's capacities and make him learn something new. Reasonableness here is a matter of degree. Generally speaking, however, you should remember that any directive that you give should be capable of being accomplished by the employee to whom it is assigned.

appropriateness

3. Make the Order Understandable. Any order that cannot be understood cannot be executed. Be sure, therefore, that your order is understood by your employees. What we are talking about here is the process of communication that we discussed in Chapter 3. As we saw there, you can't overemphasize the importance of good communications.

clarity

How you communicate varies with the employee and the situation. For some employees you will need to "dot every i and cross every t" before they will understand what you want done. Other employees merely need a few

"Any order that cannot be understood cannot be executed."

key words to understand what you want them to do. Whatever the situation, be sure that the employee to whom you are talking understands your point of view and knows exactly what you want done. To be sure that he does, don't hesitate to repeat what you have said. Not everyone gets the same meaning from words—so give your employee an opportunity to ask questions if his understanding appears to be hazy. In fact, to make sure your employee understands you, it is a good idea to ask him to explain to you what you want done.

4. Choose the Right Words. When you give an order, choose the right words and say them in such a way that your employees enthusiastically accept your directions. Don't be like an army sergeant and issue commands. Instead, use suggestions or requests or instructions. Just because you say something like "Joe, how about giving me a hand with this new order?" it in no way lessens the force of your directive. But it does make it more palatable to your employee.

word choice

At times, of course, a direct command or order is needed. In case of danger, for example, you might shout to Joe, "Run for your life!" Or if the employee is one who only understands and responds to direct orders, you might say, "You're behind in your production, Ted, and I want you to complete twenty good units by five o'clock." Most employees, however, regard themselves as adults and want to be treated with consideration. As a result, direct commands are seldom needed. Instead you might say, "Ted, you're a little behind the rest of the gang. How about seeing if you can catch up by closing time today?" Or if Ted is a perceptive employee who only needs a suggestion to understand what you want, you might only need to say, "I see you're a little behind, Ted."

Remember that on most occasions you will fare better if you *request* your employees to do something. Commands and orders are words that kill willing cooperation. In fact, some employees backed by their unions will refuse to cooperate under such conditions. The thing to remember, therefore, is to choose words that will give your orders a pleasant ring. Your employees will cooperate more willingly, and you will get a higher rating as a supervisor.

5. Explain the "Why" of the Order. Always explain *why*. If there is the slightest chance that your employee will not understand why something needs to be done, be sure to tell him why. If you think about this for a moment, you will see why this is true. An employee who doesn't see why something should be done, who doesn't think it will help meet the goals of your department, will probably be reluctant to carry out your suggestion. And when he does do it, he may do it half-heartedly, without enthusiasm, and slowly. On the other hand if he understands why you gave him the order, he is more likely to pitch in and get the work accomplished with dispatch.

tell why

6. Be Prepared for Problems. No matter how carefully you have gone through the previous steps in giving directions, you are bound to have some problems. An employee, for example, may not be listening and may miss the message. You will, therefore, need to talk it over with him to "catch him up" on what you have said and what needs to be done. Another employee may not have understood your choice of words, even though you tried to use easy-to-understand language. In order to minimize your problems, therefore, don't give a directive and forget it. Follow it up with questions. Talk it over with employees who don't appear to understand. And be alert for actions that could signal a lack of understanding. Remember, your job is to get things done through the efforts of others, and they can't take the proper action unless they clearly understand your orders.

follow-up

WHAT SHOULD YOU DO WITH THE EMPLOYEE WHO REFUSES TO DO WHAT YOU SAY?

Suppose you have done everything that we have suggested so far and one of your employees still refuses to do what you request him to do. What should you do? First of all, don't blow your stack. Don't lose your temper. Take a walk and cool off if necessary, but don't blast your employee. Stay cool and calm and try to review in your mind what has happened.

Ask yourself questions like: Are you sure the employee can do what you want done? Are you sure he understands what you said? Is he willfully refusing to do the job for some reason that you are not aware of? If you cannot understand or see why he won't do what you say, the best thing for you to do is to approach him directly: "Well, John, what's your complaint? Why don't you want to go along with my suggestions?" Maybe he has a good reason for not doing what you requested. Maybe he didn't understand. Whatever his reason, your questioning approach will give him an opportunity to talk it out. Maybe something you said or the way he interpreted it "teed him off." Your questioning approach, therefore, might give him an opportunity to let off steam—to get it off his chest—and he will then go back to work in a better frame of mind.

However, if an employee absolutely refuses to follow your request, if he is stubborn and won't cooperate, if he won't calm down, what should you do? You can, of course, penalize him or suspend him on the spot if the union contract permits. This is punitive action, however, and is bound to cause ill will that might affect other employees, as well as be difficult for the penalized employee to overcome. If he is a good worker, your wiser course of action may be to modify your request to one that he will comply with. In this way, you will get him back to work, and later when he has calmed down, you can talk to him privately in a constructive manner. Remember that your job is to get work accomplished through the help of other people. You won't

steps to follow

get your work done by firing or punishing your employees or by creating ill will between yourself and your employees. Be firm in your talk, but be big enough to work *with* him, not *against* him. If, despite all this, he still shows evidence of resistance, you will need to let him know that appropriate disciplinary action or dismissal will result if he can't work with you. This is a last resort, however, and should be used only when everything else has failed.

WHAT DO YOU DO WHEN AN EMPLOYEE ASKS THE ANSWER TO A PROBLEM?

Do you give an employee the answer when he has a problem? Do you solve the problem for him? Most supervisors feel that this would be a poor supervisory approach to take. Solving a problem for an employee is not constructive because it doesn't place the employee in a position to make a sound decision the next time he faces a similar problem.

What you should do instead of giving him the answer is to lend the employee all the support and understanding you can. Do this by talking with him and getting him to see all the issues involved in the problem. Help him to come up with several alternative solutions to the problem. Then ask him to decide which alternative is best. In other words, don't *give* him the answer—help him to *discover* the answer for *himself*. If you do this, he will be in a better position to make a decision for himself next time, and you will have more freedom to do your own thing.

help employee discover answer

However, this is not to say that you should never help your employees—that you should never solve their problems for them. What is being said is, "Don't volunteer your total help until the employee specifically asks you for it." Then at that point help him solve the problem by asking questions that will encourage him to explore alternative solutions.

All this may seem like the long way around the barn—you could solve the problem yourself and give the employee the answer much quicker than you could get the employee to reason through it and come up with his own answer. This may be true in the one instance. But remember that you are training him to be a better employee—one who can make decisions on his own in the future. Of course, it may take more of your time in the short run to help him make a decision, but in the long run it will save you time because he will learn to decide for himself.

This process is like the answer the little boy gave to the teacher when she asked him if he bought a cart for $6.92 and sold it for $8.24, whether he would win or lose on the deal. He thought for a moment and then said he would win on the dollars but lose on the cents. In helping an employee solve his own problem you may lose on the cents (the short run), but you will win on the dollars (the long run).

Up to the time an employee is about 50 or 55 years old, his age has little bearing on how you supervise him. From about 50 on, however, age does enter into the picture. Older employees form a separate social group because their interests change and their physical capacities change. They should not, however, be made to feel socially isolated but should be accepted and respected for what they can do and for what they have to offer.

Older workers are important to industry. Not only do they provide about half of the needed labor force, they also bring skill, maturity, good judgment, and patience to many jobs. Older employees, both men and women, are much more stable than younger workers. They have gone through the period of changing jobs, usually have settled down, and are now prepared to stick to their jobs more than are younger employees. Older persons are usually work-oriented, have better attendance records, and are more loyal. For these reasons, they are valuable members of your work force.

Older employees do, however, have some drawbacks that you should recognize in supervising them. For one thing, their eyesight may be failing, which means that they may react more slowly or may require better light. Age also typically brings on some physical infirmities, which often slow down the older employee, reduce his strength, or cause him not to bounce back so quickly. You'll need to remember, however, that while the older employee may be slower, he typically makes fewer mistakes. Although his vision is weakening, it can be corrected by glasses and good light. And although his strength is fading, he typically works with greater skill and consistency to compensate.

CAN OLDER EMPLOYEES LEARN NEW JOBS?

Some older employees may not be as highly motivated to learn new jobs as are younger ones. As a consequence, new jobs requiring the employee to learn new skills should be assigned only to those employees, young or old, who have demonstrated that they want to learn. There are times, however, when an older employee who wants to learn a new job may still have trouble doing it. Suppose, for example, that you have two typists working for you, one 55 years old and the other 22, with the older a more consistent typist making fewer errors. Now suppose you purchase a new machine with mathematical symbols—one that requires that the operator relearn some of the major keys on the keyboard. In this instance, the older employee would probably have difficulty learning the new keyboard because of her thirty years of experience and skill on the old keyboard. This placement of the keys

age and supervision

115

on the new machine would be in conflict with a strong skill that she already has. She could learn the new machine and job, but it would probably be more difficult for her than for the younger employee whose skills are not set by years of experience. The wiser course of action would be not to change the older employee to the newer machine unless she expresses a desire to make the change. If you do make the change, you will need to be patient with the older employee, pointing out the similarities between the old and new machine, and giving her encouragement and praise for progress. Otherwise, leave the older employee where she is. If all your typewriters are not being changed, why disrupt a senior employee's work? Leave her job alone. Put the younger woman on the new machine. The older employee would be happier, and you would be smarter to keep her on a job where her thirty years of experience would not be wasted. Remember, however, that older employees should receive the same fair and equitable treatment that you give everyone else.

ARE OLDER EMPLOYEES HARD TO MOTIVATE?

As employees grow older, they tend to become complacent—satisfied with the way things are. They aren't motivated to venture to new jobs or to try to master new skills. They are satisfied with their way of doing things, with their skills, and with their job assignments. Because they are thus satisfied, they are good workers—loyal, consistent, always there. And it is difficult under these conditions to suggest to them that they should change their ways or improve the way a job is done. However, your job as a supervisor calls for you to try to motivate these older employees. Getting them to want to learn a new way to do a job better will depend on your skill in human relations and your salesmanship. It will require all the tact, skill, and persuasion that you can muster. You'll need to encourage them, praise them, overlook mistakes, and point out how others their age are using the new method. You'll need to show them that in time they can equal or exceed the production of even the younger employees.

To get an older employee to try a new way of performing his job, you should first talk with him in private about it, rather than in front of the other employees. If he agrees to change, you should if possible place him in an inconspicuous location—one that doesn't call attention to his mistakes. Work with him when you can. It will make him feel better to see that you aren't too skilled and that you too make mistakes. Once he has gotten the hang of it and has gained some skill in the new job, then you should begin to call his progress to the attention of other employees. By working with older employees in this manner, you will be able to "rehabilitate" them, so to speak, and make them more effective and up-to-date workers.

Yes. For one thing, women tend to react more positively to a clean and orderly work environment. In offices they are usually more interested in color harmony and furniture coordination than men are. And they frequently bring plants and flowers to their "office home." All these things tend to boost their morale. In this day of women's liberation, it pays to treat every woman as an individual, but treat every one equally, as you should all employees. Some *treat all employees* women tend to be more jealous than men, and they will probably look *fairly and equally* unfavorably upon any favoritism you might show another woman. Be as fair and equal as you can in making job assignments, in providing equipment, in assigning locations, and so on.

Women are excellent workers. They are loyal, diligent, and cooperative. They are especially good at doing intricate, fine work that is physically confining. But they cannot, of course, do all the kinds of work that men can. For one thing, they are usually not as strong physically as men are. Also, every state has laws limiting the day hours they can work, as well as night work. Work before and after childbirth is regulated in some states, and others have laws pertaining to rest rooms, or requiring chairs for alternate standing and sitting, or stipulating the amount of weight a woman can be expected to lift. Despite these limitations, women can and do hold down virtually every job that a man does. They are painters, plumbers, masons, welders, construction helpers, and so on.

Despite the fact that men and women hold many of the same jobs, they are different, and this difference may mean you will need to supervise them differently. For one thing, many women are more short-term oriented. They tend to look more at the immediate aspect, whereas men tend to view things more from a long-range aspect. Another difference is that men are not as socially oriented as women. Women typically need to like the people they work with if they are to do a good job, whereas men seem to have the ability to work effectively with people they don't necessarily like. This tends to affect job assignments, morale, and so on.

Men and women tend to have similar feelings, but women frequently show their feelings more readily than men. As a consequence, they need to be shown more consideration than men. They should not be criticized as thoughtlessly as men sometimes are. Women want to be known as individuals, and since women's lib is still not totally accepted, they may jealously guard their individuality. Like anyone else, they appreciate it if you take a special interest in them and their jobs. But treat all of them equally.

Women can demand more tact and courtesy in supervision than men. Be careful about how you criticize their work; women tend to take work criticism personally. You should, therefore, balance criticism with praise. If you point out a fault with one part of Mary's work, be sure to balance this with a good word for another part of her work.

In summary, women make excellent loyal employees. Because of their physical makeup, however, they may be limited in the type of work they can do. Because of their emotional makeup, you should be sure to supervise them impartially, treating everyone the same. This applies to the amount of personal attention you give each one, to where you physically locate them, to the equipment you assign to them, to the types of jobs you give them, and so on. Impartiality, equality, tact, and courtesy are the watchwords in supervising any group, but it is especially true with women workers.

SHOULD YOU TREAT PROFESSIONAL WORKERS DIFFERENTLY?

Yes. Professional employees are those with particular educational skills and training, such as doctors, engineers, scientists, nurses, and research workers. They are different from other employees and can cause you a ton of headaches if you don't understand these differences.

First of all, they feel that they are different from other employees and should, therefore, be treated differently. They typically know the technical aspects of their jobs much better than anyone else and resent being told how to do things. They are proud of their chosen field and are usually self-starters; that is, they are typically more highly motivated than the average employee. As a result, they don't need anyone to "crack the whip" over them. In fact, they resent it. As a general rule, the more professional an employee is and the higher his level of education, the more difficult he will be to supervise. His loyalty is not to you but to his profession. The company comes second. As a result, professional employees don't feel tied to the company and are usually more susceptible to offers from other companies. In fact, it is not at all unusual for a professional employee to change jobs more frequently than other employees. You can see, therefore, that they are more likely to be touchy employees, and supervising them will be more difficult.

Professional workers expect to be treated differently from the average employee. They want personal recognition for what they do, they want greater freedom and more liberties than the average employee, and they want better working conditions than those furnished the other employees. They want to be respected as a member of their chosen profession and be recognized as a doctor, or a research scientist, or a registered nurse—not as a company employee.

Inasmuch as they are self-starters, they are usually not clock watchers. They may get involved in problems and work long hours with no thought of *degrees of* extra compensation. They do, however, expect greater flexibility in rules *supervision* regarding when they start to work and time off for personal reasons. Generally, a work situation that calls for clock punching is rejected by them.

Inasmuch as professional workers regard themselves as different from the average employee, they resent doing any "average" work. They feel that anything routine that a clerk or technician can do should be done by a clerk and their talents should be used in a more productive way. They typically place emphasis on the chance for professional development above job security and money, so you can see why they are more independent and difficult to handle than the rank-and-file employee.

Professional workers are difficult to regiment, and almost all of them refuse to work by any time schedule. You can't tell a research scientist, for example, "I want you to invent a new method for making paper in two months." In like manner, you wouldn't tell a surgeon, "I'll give you fifteen minutes to take out my appendix." In both instances, you'd probably be told in no uncertain terms where to go.

HOW DO YOU SUPERVISE PROFESSIONAL WORKERS?

Recognizing all the above peculiarities, you may be wondering how you should supervise a professional person. There is no one right answer. In general, however, you should not supervise him too closely. Fortunately, since most of them are self-starters and are self-regulating, you won't have too many problems about a professional person "goofing off." You won't need to bear down on him; instead, you should try to act as an advisor, be a good listener, and serve as his link to higher management. Try to understand him and provide him with reasonable services and liberties. Insofar as you can, give a professional employee a challenging assignment and the opportunity to perform. When you have to say "no" to him, be sure to explain why. He will then gain a better understanding of you and your managerial problems and not view you as a person who thinks exclusively in terms of profits.

the link to higher management

Some individuals may think of themselves as professionals when in the strictest sense actually they are not. People in technical occupations such as draftsmen, surveyors, laboratory technicians, traffic managers, and purchasing agents, for example, frequently think of themselves as professionals. They should, therefore, be treated insofar as possible as professionals. You, however, will have to judge the degree of freedom they should be given and the difference with which they should be treated.

If you could use only two ideas to determine how best to supervise professional employees, these two ideas would probably be:

1. Give the professional employees as much freedom as you can.
2. Give them worthwhile and challenging assignments.

Remember, however, that both of these ideas should be used with moderation, they should be modified according to the individual you are supervising, and they should be in line with company policies.

Office workers have many of the same needs and desires that shop workers have, and supervising them is much the same. There are, however, some differences that you should be aware of. For one thing, office employees are often more status conscious than shop employees. Titles, locations, job assignments, and even their boss's status are more important to office workers than to shop employees. Office decor color schemes, and decorating harmony are also more important to office workers. The degree of importance of each of these factors varies with each employee. Your job, therefore, is to study each employee, try to understand his needs, and then deal with each of these needs according to what you know about him as an individual.

This is not to say that pay is unimportant to clerical workers. It is as important to them as it is to shop employees. You should, therefore, be sure that your clerical workers receive equal pay for equal work and that your salary scale is comparable to the wage level in the community for similar work.

Many of your office employees will be women, and the potential problems associated with female workers, which we have already discussed, apply here. Just remember to add to the list the additional problem of social status. Handle women office workers with tact and gentleness, but always be firm and fair. Women employees typically place great value on the social and *understand social* human aspects of the place where they work. They like to work with people *status* who are about their equals socially and educationally, who share similar likes and dislikes. A new female employee with good skills but not equal socially to the other employees may be shunned or rejected, causing her to be unhappy and eventually leave her job. Because of this, you will need to be especially careful in replacing and hiring new female employees, to be certain that the new worker will fit into the group.

You will probably run into the career woman versus the woman who regards the job only as a temporary experience until she can marry. These two types have to be handled differently. Both men and women who are career-oriented need stimulating jobs and good assignments where they have a chance to learn new skills and broaden their capacities. You should, therefore, try to broaden the job scope of career-oriented women. Give them additional duties. Assign them jobs typically performed by men. Let them try their hand at a more difficult or skilled job. And move them ahead when their skills fit new job opportunities. Be careful, however, not to shower this type of worker with too much attention. If you do, your other female employees will become jealous of "teacher's pet," and office morale could suffer.

ARE THERE SIGNALS YOU AREN'T DOING A GOOD SUPERVISING JOB?

No one signal will clearly indicate that you are doing a poor job of supervising. However, several factors combined might be telling you that something is wrong. Look at the following checklist. If two or more of these items apply to you, then it may be a signal that you are not doing your best.

1. Do you get complaints from your customers (other departments) about the quality and delivery of your work?
2. Are costs increasing in your department that you can't justify?
3. Is the production output per employee decreasing?
4. Have you suffered any increase in the number of complaints or any unusual number of grievances within the past year?
5. Have you had to reprimand several of your employees during the past year for conflicts, hostility, and unjustified actions?
6. Do you find that you have to watch your employees more closely than you used to? That they are no longer self-starters?
7. Is there a general indication of apathy and disinterest among your employees about their jobs and the company?
8. When you hold employee meetings, do you find that attendance is perfunctory with little real interest shown in the topic being discussed?
9. Do your employees misunderstand your instructions and not follow through on what you tell them to do?
10. Do you have any noticeable increase in absences, lateness, requests for transfers, or turnover?

SHOULD YOU COUNSEL EMPLOYEES WITH SPECIAL PROBLEMS?

From time to time, everyone has problems that affect his work. In such instances, an understanding and cooperative supervisor who recognizes these problems can do much to help his employees get over this difficult time.

What the supervisor should be concerned with in such cases is helping worried and unhappy employees get over their problems and thus be better workers. There are lots of things that worried employees do that may signal their state of unhappiness. A sudden change in behavior is a prime indication. For example, Tom used to smile and say, "Howdy" to everyone. Now he seldom speaks or smiles; something is wrong. Increases in an employee's absences and accidents may point to a state of worry. When these and other *listen carefully* signals tell you that an employee is worried, you should try to help him get himself straightened out by listening to him talk in some counseling sessions.

A counseling session is nothing more than a talk in private wherein you listen to everything your employee has to say before you make a comment. In these sessions, always listen carefully. Don't argue with what he has to say, and don't criticize him. Instead, try to understand what he is trying to tell you. Like an iceberg, only 10% of an employee's feelings show. The other 90% are below the surface. A conscientious supervisor tries to discover these hidden feelings through a detailed talk with his employee.

By listening to what an employee has to say, you may discover, for example, that although he is complaining about his pay (the 10% that shows), his real concern is about the machine you have assigned him (the hidden 90%). In counseling sessions, you discuss items that may be bothering employees with the objective being to understand and decrease the resulting emotional problems. A good counseling session may provide the employee with sound advice or with hope and reassurance. Or it may enable him to clarify his own thinking and thus become a better employee. Such sessions can provide the employee with a means to release his emotional tensions, or supply a communications bridge between him and management, or simply serve to help him regain and clarify his perspective about his work, the other employees, and so on.

In beginning a counseling session with an employee, it is a good idea to try to put him at ease. Don't jump in and start asking questions. This will confuse the employee, put him on the defensive, and perhaps cause him to shut up. Instead, try to say something that will open up the conversation and allow him to talk freely. Ask questions you know he can answer. Ask about problems you know he will feel comfortable talking about. Get him to open up by asking a question like, "What kind of dog is best for hunting quail—a pointer or a setter?" He knows hunting, and this type of question will open the way for him to talk freely about it. And he may relax and tell you some of his other problems, too. The session won't be brief. In fact, you should be prepared to spend 30 or 40 minutes. Anything less than that won't give you time to accomplish very much.

In these sessions, your job is to serve as a fact finder and listening post. Let your employee talk out his own problem and find some answers he can live with. Be careful, however, not to get in over your head. If the employee has a real problem that is beyond your experience, don't hesitate to get him to a competent professional counselor. In most communities of any size you will usually find a fair number of psychiatrists, social workers, or clinical psychologists who can give your employee help. If you don't know of any, start by asking the company physician, the employee's physician, or your own personal physician whom he would recommend.

seek outside help

Generally, the most difficult problems to identify and correct are personal problems. These range from money and family problems to problems with law-enforcement officials. Whatever these problems are, they bother the employees. For example, if Janie's mother has to go to the hospital for a serious operation, it may cause her to be absent or late, or it may result in an increase in posting and typing errors. Or if Joe is worried that his creditors are going to repossess his motorcycle, the quality of his work may suffer. This affects the work of your department as well as the work of other employees.

Personal problems may be interrelated with all sorts of other problems—all of which may have some negative effect on an employee's work pattern. Even though you may dislike it, it is a supervisor's job to try to help employees with such problems. It may be unpleasant, but remember that problem employees can do more harm than good if they are not helped. They are expensive to keep on the payroll. They are difficult to motivate.

They may be demoralizing to other workers. And they are the most difficult to supervise. When you help such a person solve his problem through counseling, you will be doing him a favor as well as making your own work easier and more rewarding.

Sometimes an employee's problems are so severe that the employee is a disruptive influence at work, he is difficult to supervise, and morale for the whole department is suffering. If you know a person is that type before you hire him, you should avoid putting him on the payroll. If he already works for you, however, your job is to help him or see that he gets professional attention.

After you have had two or three sessions with a troubled employee and do not seem to be making any progress, the best thing is to send him to a professional for help. Sometimes, of course, it is difficult to know when you should try to help an employee and when you should suggest that he see a psychiatrist or professional counselor. If you have any question about how to handle the situation, it is better to err on the side of caution. Therefore, if there is any reasonable doubt in your mind, *send him to a professional counselor.* The employee may be emotionally disturbed or psychotic and beyond your friendly help.

A Case Study
THE CASE OF MARJ BURNS

Marj Burns supervised 37 women employees who were assigned to typing pools in five different locations throughout the central agency's five-story home-office building. Inasmuch as she couldn't closely supervise the employees in every location, Marj had appointed a "lead worker" for each of the five locations to give out the work and answer questions.

Anita, the lead worker in the premium accounts pool, was one of the company's senior employees with over twenty-six years of experience. A career employee, Anita had always spoken up for the company. Her girls had always taken their coffee breaks and lunch periods promptly, were virtually never late, and had always worked overtime when required.

Six months ago, the company hired six new women to do publicity and publication work: two were commercial artists, one a layout expert, one a skilled copy editor, and two were communications specialists. Their job was to prepare and supervise publication of all company reports, as well as give publicity to company news through the newspapers, TV, and other media. The work required a great deal of outside contact and work, with the women visiting outside suppliers, editors, and so on. Marj appointed the copy editor, Elizabeth Ware, to be the lead worker for the group.

From the very beginning, Elizabeth Ware's group seemed to feel that they were different from the other women employees. Although work hours were from 8:00 A.M. to 5:00 P.M., it was not unusual for individuals in the publicity group to start work anywhere between 8:00 and 8:45 A.M. They were equally lax about lunch periods. Their work, however, was excellent and had received good reviews by local publicity experts. As a result, the group was a highly cohesive one and worked well as a unit. It was not at all unusual to see their lights burning long after everyone had left the building.

The work of the publicity group, however, had not gone unnoticed by the other women employees. In fact, several of the lead workers reported to Marj Burns that their girls wanted to know how that "special group got by, coming in at all hours and taking any amount of time they wanted to for lunch." To cite another problem, just this week one of Anita's girls had refused to work past 5:00 P.M. to get a report out, stating that her workday was from 8:00 A.M. to 5:00 P.M. and she didn't see why she should break her back working past 5:00 P.M. when others in the company came in 30 or 45 minutes late with no punishment. As time passed, more and more women came in late in various groups, and the lead workers always gave Marj the same answer: The girls felt that if the publicity group could come in late, they could, too. Marj recognized that things were getting out of hand.

1. What caused the trouble for Marj Burns?
2. What do you think she should do? What steps should she take? Why?

A Case Study
WHITSET HOSIERY MILLS

Whitset Hosiery Mills manufactures one of the nationally known brands of high-quality ladies' hosiery. It is an aggressive and progressive company that is proud of its good employee relationships. In fact, it is not unusual to find two or three generations of a family working with Whitset Mills.

Inspecting women's nylon hosiery for flaws has traditionally been performed by women. The process consists of visually inspecting the hose for snags, runs, poor-quality seams, picked threads, and the like, by "boarding" or placing the hose on a leg-shaped form and revolving it so that all sides of the hose can be seen. This is basically the inspection process employed by Whitset Hosiery Mills, and it is the one that has given them some recent trouble.

Actually, the women in Whitset Mills inspection room #4 have a thorough knowledge of hosiery inspection procedures. Most of them are between 50 and 60 years old and have been with the company for twenty or more years. Because of their long experience, they know what to look for and where flaws will probably occur. Output for the department formerly averaged about 200–250 pairs of hose per hour, with the better operators averaging 300–325 pairs per hour. During the past eight years, however, their inspection output has gradually decreased to a point where the inspectors are now producing an average of 150–200 pairs per hour. During this eight-year period, the company has tried a series of installations and adjustments to get the output back up to the old level. They changed the layout of the room; they designed and installed new "boards" on which the hose were examined; they installed a loud-speaking system and played any music the women wanted; they changed the color scheme of the room. In each of these instances, output was increased slightly but quickly fell back to the old level in several days.

A member of the plant's engineering team suggested the installation of a new-type fluorescent light. This was done and proved to be no more effective than the other changes. A check of the intensity of light at the time of the installation showed the level of intensity was equal to the minimum recommendations for this type of work.

After doing everything of this nature that they could think of, the plant officials were becoming discouraged. They talked to the employees who indicated that they were going as fast as they could while still doing a thorough inspection job. The employees were aware that management wanted to raise output to the old level, but they claimed that with the new shades and deniers of nylon, seeing was more difficult, and it took longer to inspect. Management, however, discounted the idea because the same basic shades were being used and the denier had not decreased an appreciable amount. Nevertheless the employees stated that the stockings were more difficult to see and took longer, therefore, to inspect.

1. If you were on the staff of Whitset Mills, what supervisory action would you take? Why?
2. Are there any signs that supervision has not been as good as it might be?

9
HOW TO MOTIVATE YOUR EMPLOYEES

This chapter explains—

- What employees look for and need in their work
- How you can recognize the important areas of motivation
- The characteristics of the supervisor who motivates best

Your job as a supervisor is to motivate others to work—to make them want to do their jobs. The main problem you face, however, is actually discovering *how to motivate your employees*. Let's look at this problem.

When you go to work, you take with you certain needs or wants that affect how well you do your job. For example, you want to be treated courteously and fairly, and you want to do interesting work. You also want good working conditions and fair pay. These wants are called *motives*. They are the things that make you want to do what you do. In fact, virtually everything you do is to satisfy some need or motive. If you don't do something, it's because you see no personal advantage in doing it. It doesn't satisfy some want.

WHAT KINDS OF NEEDS DO PEOPLE HAVE?

All of us have different needs or wants. Jim, for example, might work hard because he gets a feeling of accomplishment from what he is doing. Tillie might work hard because doing her job well makes her feel important. And Dick might work hard because he enjoys being with a gang of people. Psychologists have classified these wants or needs into five groups.[1] If we look at these five classifications briefly, we will understand better why we want to do the things we do.

Basic Physical Needs.   The basic necessities of life—food, shelter, clothing, rest, reproduction, and the other physical needs—are instilled in us that we might survive.

individual needs

Safety Needs.   Once our basic physical needs are somewhat satisfied, our thoughts turn to the need to protect ourselves from danger, to be secure. We want freedom from worry about our future welfare, and normally this means job security to most of us. We want to feel that our jobs are secure and that we will have an income until we retire.

Social Needs.   All of us want to feel that we are "in"—that we are a member of or belong to a certain group. This need is the social need. This need to belong, to be a part of the group, and to be accepted and respected by other members of the group is a strong urge in all of us.

Esteem Needs.   Closely related to the social need is the need for self-respect. All of us feel this need when we want recognition, status, achievement, or a sense of accomplishment. It is basically respect for yourself. You

[1]A. H. Maslow, *Motivation and Personality* (New York: Harper & Row, 1954), Chapter 5.

"The main problem you face as a supervisor is discovering how to motivate your employees."

feel that you are doing what you were put here to do. Esteem needs are very powerful needs because they relate to our feelings of worth and importance.

Self-Realization Needs. Self-realization needs are what the psychologists call the highest order of needs. After the first four needs have been somewhat satisfied, then we experience the need for self-realization. We want to feel that we have accomplished things to the best of our abilities—our potentialities. When we have met this need, we say to ourselves that we have become all that we are capable of becoming. When we have met this need, we have been fully creative and are occupied in performing to the limits of our capacities. Not many of us turn to this need because we are so busy trying to satisfy *social* and *esteem* needs.

All five of these different needs, however, are active to some degree at all times. We don't, for example, satisfy social needs and then move on to esteem. Frequently we are striving to satisfy both of these, along with satisfying our basic physical and safety needs.

WHY ARE WE AS WE ARE?

Every person is different. You are different from any other person anywhere in the world. As the saying goes, "They broke the mold when they made you." What causes us to be different? Several things.

A major influence is our *biological makeup.* Age, sex, weight, height, race, and physique are factors that have an important bearing on our personality and makeup. If a man is large and strong, he will probably be a mild-mannered individual. He doesn't have to tell people he can lick them. It's obvious. If he is small in stature, he may need to compensate and may be "touchy." People can't run over him. He may be the cocky, belligerent, "bantam rooster" type, always ready to pick a fight. Most physical characteristics are hereditary in nature.

individual differences

Psychologists also tell us that our *childhood* plays a large part in determining our later adjustment and personality. Such factors as feeding patterns, environmental conditions, family units, and training patterns are things that affect our personality and adjustment.

Finally, the broad *culture* in which we grow up has a profound influence on making us the way we are. Our American culture, for example, stresses freedom of choice, competition, equal opportunity, and rewards for accomplishment. We are born and brought up to think and act in many ways different from people brought up in other cultures. In America, for example, we have a strong regard for a good day's work, whereas in other cultures work is looked upon as something to be avoided whenever possible.

We are a product, therefore, of our inherited physical makeup, our early childhood, and our culture. These factors make us what we are, and supervisors should recognize that these are a part of our personalities and should be employed to the best advantage.

HOW DO YOU GET OTHERS TO WANT TO WORK FOR YOU?

The job of a supervisor is to get others to do things *because they want to do them.* In other words, the successful supervisor is one who provides his employees with the opportunity to satisfy their own needs. They will work because they see that by doing so they will satisfy certain needs.

Most everything you do is directed toward satisfying some need. Getting a drink of water as you pass a fountain, for example, satisfies a physical need. You might not be very thirsty and, therefore, your need for water isn't strong—but you still have the need. If you go without water for twenty-four hours, then your need for water is strong, and it exerts a powerful influence on what you will do to get a drink of water. This illustrates a point about needs and supervision. A need that has been satisfied remains relatively quiet, but if you withhold or deny the satisfaction of a need, it will eventually dominate your behavior.

opportunity to satisfy needs

Although you can readily see and understand the water need, which is a first-level or physical need, it is not so easy to see and understand social and esteem needs, which are third- and fourth-level needs. Like the water need, however, if these social and esteem needs are completely unsatisfied, they may well dominate the behavior of an employee. The supervisor, therefore, needs to provide his employees with the opportunity to satisfy their needs. But before he can provide this opportunity to his employees, the supervisor must first of all be aware of the types of things that motivate his workers.

WHAT HAPPENS WHEN NEEDS ARE NOT SATISFIED BY JOBS?

When employees' needs are not satisfied on the job, then many workers may try to overcome this lack by doing things that have a bad effect on their job performance. For example, a frustrated employee who cannot satisfy some of his needs on the job may say to himself, "What the heck. Why beat my brains out doing this job?" and then simply resign himself to doing just a passable job. He will only do enough to draw his paycheck and will seek the opportunity to satisfy his needs off the job. Or the employee might react in the opposite manner. Instead of resigning himself to the situation, he might react in an aggressive manner with outbursts of temper, negative attitudes, or even fighting. In either instance, poor job performance results and may mean that the employee will quit or be fired.

*poor job
performance*

DOES JOB PLACEMENT HELP SATISFY NEEDS?

Yes. To get others to want to work for you you will have to place them in jobs that will allow them to satisfy some of their strongest needs. This may mean reworking jobs to make them more complex, more challenging, and perhaps more satisfying to the employee. It may mean changing an employee from an independent job where a need, such as the need to belong, cannot be satisfied, to a job working with a group of people where this need to belong can be satisfied. Matching employee needs with jobs is a very difficult process. Once you've come to understand what an employee's basic needs are, however, you can teach yourself to be more sensitive to these needs and try to match the employee with jobs that offer him the opportunity to satisfy his needs. If you do this, you will have made a giant step in the process of getting others to want to work for you.

*matching jobs and
needs*

WHAT DO EMPLOYEES WANT FROM WORK?

A lot of time and money have been spent trying to determine what employees want from their work. Some people say that money is the first need. Others say that working conditions come first. If you ask the employee what is most important, you get one answer. If you ask his supervisor what he thinks is most important to the employee, you probably get another answer. To show you how different the answers are, look at the results of the follow-

Employee Ranking	Item Being Rated	Supervisor Ranking
1	Appreciation of work well done	8
2	Feeling of being "in on things"	10
3	Sympathetic help on personal problems	9
4	Job security	2
5	Good wages	1
6	Interesting work	5
7	Promotion and growth in company	3
8	Personal loyalty to employees	6
9	Good working conditions	4
10	Tactful disciplining	7

importance of job factor

ing survey of thousands of employees in many different industries.[2] In this survey, the foremen were asked to rank ten job factors in the same way they thought their employees would. Then the employees were asked to rank these same ten factors in order of their importance to them. The results show that many foremen didn't understand what workers wanted out of their jobs.

You shouldn't look at this report and say that money, good working conditions, and loyalty to employees are unimportant. These factors are extremely important, as you well know, and companies must continually strive to be competitive in these areas. In fact, all ten factors are important needs to every employee. Most of the time, however, employees expect a company to provide good working conditions, fair pay, opportunity for growth, and interesting work. Since most companies do attempt to provide these needs and since the employees have been somewhat satisfied in these areas, they ranked them on the lower end of the scale. The low ranking needs are very important, however, and if they aren't satisfied (like the drink of water), they will surface and dominate the behavior of the employee. The interesting part of the survey—and what is important to you—is that inasmuch as the employee expects and usually gets his basic needs satisfied, his important wants are in the areas of social and esteem needs. This should tell you that these are the areas to which supervisors should pay most attention.

WHAT ARE THE IMPORTANT MOTIVATION AREAS?

Supervisors should recognize that employees need and expect good working conditions and fair pay. Government regulations set minimum wage standards, and competition usually forces employers to establish acceptable working conditions and competitive wages. Therefore, since these lower-

[2]W. C. Menninger and H. Levinson, *Human Understanding in Industry* (Chicago: Science Research Associates, 1956), p. 12.

level needs are usually satisfied, supervisors should turn their attention to satisfying their employees' other needs. These needs include the following:

Treat Employees as Individuals. All of us like to be treated as individuals—not as numbers or cogs in a wheel. You like to have people show personal interest in you. A supervisor, therefore, should not get so wrapped up in his other duties that he neglects his employees, forgetting that they are individuals with feelings and opinions who want to talk about them. Most employees welcome the opportunity to talk over their ideas and opinions with their supervisor. The smart foreman, therefore, is the one who finds time to listen to his employees. It makes them feel good to tell some-one, "I was talking to the boss the other day, and I told him exactly what I thought he should do about our office layout." The employee likes to be thus identified with the firm's leadership, thereby satisfying his need to feel important. During these talking sessions, the supervisor can also point out the importance of the individual to the company, and what he is doing to help the company make progress. It makes the employee feel he is more than a cog. It helps raise his self-esteem.

higher-level needs

Be Sincere with Praise. Genuine praise and recognition for a job well done are always appreciated. What we don't like is the routine remark, "Thank you for your effort," though this is better than no thanks at all. Consider, instead, your reaction to the following: "Hank, I really appreciate the outstanding job you did in pushing the Grayblock order through. You were great in the way you handled your gang, and I still don't see how you got those presses running so well. Keep up the good work."

Be sure the praise is justified, however. An employee knows when he's done a good job or a mediocre job. If you praise him for mediocre or poor work, your flattery will have a hollow ring, and he'll regard it as so much applesauce. The rule is *be genuine and sincere in your praise and recognition of individuals.* This will help satisfy their esteem needs.

Promote Participation. All of us want to be "in" on what is happening, and nothing helps boost our social and esteem needs like having a part in making a decision. Good supervision, therefore, calls for us to invite employees to help set goals and standards. Employees who have a part in setting up a goal or a program work harder to bring about its success because it is their own program. It is one that they helped develop. They helped set it up, and you don't have to "sell" them on it or push them to meet quotas.

Satisfying the need to be in on things is why this approach, called *management by objectives,* is so successful.

Make the Work Interesting. Many jobs in government and industry are monotonous and boring. As a consequence, employees in these jobs lack interest in their work—though they like their surroundings, their fellow workers, and the company. Lack of interest coupled with boredom and monotony can lead to all sorts of problems. The supervisor, therefore, should identify these boring jobs and work to make them more acceptable. One approach is job enlargement, where interest is created by increasing the number of tasks performed by the employee on the job.

Job rotation is another possibility, where the employee swaps jobs with someone else for, say, a couple of hours and then goes back to his old job for two hours, then swaps again, and so on. Like job enlargement, job rotation helps relieve monotony and makes the work more interesting. These and other ways you can think of indicate the approach you can use to relieve job monotony and make the work more interesting.

Promote Cooperation and Teamwork.   Promoting teamwork and cooperation helps satisfy our social needs. The basic buddy system is an example of a system used extensively in youth organizations to encourage one person or buddy to help the other. The buddy is always with his partner, willingly helping and making mutual sacrifices. This same sort of teamwork needs to be promoted in business, where we have groups of employees dealing with each other in frequent face-to-face communication. If encouraged by supervisors, these groups can promote social bonds of friendship and team spirit, and this will enable them to get the job done in a better way. When an employee knows that he belongs to and is a vital member of a team, it does much to help satisfy his social needs.

This type of cooperation and teamwork is best promoted by the supervisor who can be freely approached by his employees, who listens carefully to their problems and ideas, who remains calm and stable under trying conditions, who is always willing to help his employees, and who tries to build up his employees' egos and security needs. This is a good prescription that is hard to follow, but you will find it well worth your effort.

Provide Growth Opportunities.   The opportunity to grow promotes self-esteem, and the alert supervisor can usually find ways to provide this opportunity. It may mean letting an employee learn a more difficult job while he is doing his regular work. It could be encouraging the employee to go to night school to enlarge his skill and thus qualify for a better job. Or it could come about by delegating to an employee the authority to do some job. The delegation would give him a chance to "show his stuff." It should broaden his capacities and make him a more valuable employee, thereby strengthening the whole work team. When an employee is growing in a job, he is typically a motivated and happy employee.

IS THERE A FORMULA FOR MOTIVATING PEOPLE?

motivational needs

No. Despite all that we know about motivational areas and why we are what we are, we still don't have a magic formula to motivate people to work. There are no shortcuts, no gimmicks, to securing employee cooperation. One of the best approaches to getting people to work with you, however, is to re-member the following:

1. Communicate with your employees and praise them.
2. Consult with your employees about their work.
3. Encourage your employees to participate in setting goals and jobs.
4. Counsel your employees about teamwork, opportunity, and so on.

Make these four concepts so much a part of you that they become second nature. Be sensitive to people and their needs. Use empathy to try to under-stand the other fellow's point of view before you act. Talk with and listen to the other fellow. Remember, you only learn when you aren't talking. Try to get others to participate in some of the decision-making processes. Try to know and understand people because only then will you be in a position to help them with their personal problems. Making some of these simple ideas a part of you will do much to help you get others to work for you.

WHAT ARE THE CHARACTERISTICS OF THE SUPERVISOR WHO BEST MOTIVATES HIS EMPLOYEES?

The supervisor who motivates best is not the bull-of-the-woods tough guy or the one who uses fear. Both of these types tend to make employees resentful and may even make them unconsciously reduce their work pace. The best motivator is not the one who constantly harps on production and output. Instead, higher production usually results when less emphasis is placed on output and more emphasis is placed on the individual. The boss who motivates best is not the one who plays his cards close to his chest and makes all the decisions himself. This type of supervisor usually gets the least coop-eration from his employees.

The supervisor who motivates his employees best is the one who—

1. *Establishes realistic goals* for himself and others—goals that are worth-while, challenging, and attainable.
2. *Makes decisions after relevant participation* by his subordinates. He seeks and is seriously interested in their thoughts and ideas. As a result, his employees don't hesitate to offer suggestions and work with him fully to get the best possible outcome.
3. *Seeks and gives feedback* to his employees about how they are doing, the progress they are making, and the problems that are coming up. Because of his open communication and feedback, his employees are motivated to perform well. They openly evaluate their progress, and they do not hesitate to seek changes when they think they are needed.

*supervisory
motivation*

4. *Resolves conflicts* with good judgment, understanding, and openness. He focuses on solving the conflict rather than placing the blame. He attempts to understand the problem and determine the best solution. He approaches his employees with the spirit of, "Let's see what we can do to straighten out this problem." This approach and his fairness promote a more relaxed and trusting relationship between the supervisor and his employees.

5. *Always communicates* to his employees, explaining what is being done and why it is being done. He talks honestly and openly about how he feels about things. This process of open and continuous communication lets the employees know what's going on inside him. They feel they know and understand him better, thus promoting trust and confidence.

6. *Always listens* to what his employees tell him, tries to understand what they are saying, and makes good comments about their ideas. He doesn't hesitate to question them and ask them, "How about explaining that again to me?" Being listened to makes the employee feel important and also makes him more willing to listen to what the boss says.

7. *Is genuinely interested* in his employees as individuals. He is interested in their growth and future progress. He talks this over with them and offers suggestions where appropriate.

8. *Is open and sincere in his praise*, reprimands in private, and praises in public.

9. *Controls his temper.* When he is angry he doesn't brood but openly approaches the person he is mad with and tells him, "Jack, I didn't like the way you handled that problem. Tell me why you handled it as you did instead of following our regulations." This gets the two talking, and what could have been a major crisis can be disposed of as a minor problem.

10. *Is open-minded,* always willing to listen to new ideas—even those that are different from his own. He doesn't mind criticism and readily admits his mistakes. He is the type of guy you'd like to have as a personal friend.

11. *Uses reprimands only when necessary,* and even then delivers them in private. He uses them to educate and correct—never to punish an employee.

12. *Makes jobs as interesting and desirable as possible.*

13. *Is not afraid to delegate* and willingly gives credit to his employees for a job.

14. *Doesn't try to get work out of his employees by threatening them.*

15. *Is not afraid to admit he is wrong* and his employee is right.

16. *Actively seeks the opportunity to promote his employees*—even if it means losing them.

17. *Tries to run an orderly department,* bringing system to an otherwise confused situation.

18. *Is big enough not to compete* with his employees for credit. He lets his employees bask in the spotlight for a job well done.

19. *Is not condescending.*

20. *Is not a know-it-all.*

WHICH APPROACH TO SUPERVISION IS BEST?

From all that we have said, which approach to supervision is best?

1. To appeal to the lower-level needs (physical and safety needs)?
2. To appeal to the higher-level needs (social and esteem needs)?
3. Some combination of the two?

Probably you shouldn't appeal to one level entirely and ignore the other. You could, of course, emphasize the lower-level needs. Or you could emphasize the higher-level needs. The question we need to answer is, "Which ones should you emphasize?"

A number of years ago Professor Douglas McGregor wrote *The Human Side of Enterprise,* in which he stated that supervisors appealed either to their employees' lower- or their higher-level needs, depending on what the supervisor visualized his employees' needs to be.[3] For example, if a supervisor thought that everyone was primarily concerned over pay, job security, etc., then he supervised in a way that would appeal to their lower-level needs. But if he thought most employees were more concerned over the higher-level needs, then he supervised in a way to appeal to their social and esteem needs.

lower- vs. higher-level needs

To illustrate his ideas, McGregor listed the two extreme ways supervisors could think about people. He called these Theory X and Theory Y. At one extreme is the Theory X supervisor who appeals to employees through their lower-level needs. The Theory X supervisor believes the following about people:

Theory X

1. The average human being dislikes work and will avoid it if he can do so.
2. Because people dislike work, they have to be coerced, or directed, or made to work by threat of punishment in order to get them to do what is needed for the organization.
3. The average person would rather be told what to do, wants to avoid responsibility, has relatively little ambition, and wants security above all.

[3]Douglas McGregor, *The Human Side of Enterprise* (New York: McGraw-Hill Book Company, 1960), pp. 33–43 and 45–57.

At the other extreme is the supervisor who appeals to employees through their higher-level needs. In contrast to Theory X, above, this supervisor believes the following:

Theory Y

1. It is as natural for people to exert themselves physically and mentally at work as it is for them to play and rest.
2. The threat of punishment and external controls are not the only ways to get employees to do what is needed by the organization. A man will exercise self-direction and self-control to achieve objectives he believes in and wants to achieve.
3. The degree to which employees are committed to objectives depends on the rewards associated with achieving them.
4. The average employee under proper conditions not only accepts responsibility, he also seeks it.
5. Using imagination and creativity to solve problems is not something that just a few bright people can do; instead, most of us have that ability.
6. Most employees' mental capacities are only partially used in business.

We recognize that Theory X and Theory Y are two extreme positions and that very few supervisors will exactly fit either one mold or the other. Therefore, instead of trying to motivate their employees by using only Theory X or only Theory Y, supervisors will probably take a middle approach but will *lean* in the direction of either Theory X or Theory Y. In other words, they will use some of the ideas from both theories, but they will emphasize one approach to supervision (one theory) more than they will the other. The question is, What type of supervision motivates employees best? Do workers respond best to the supervisor who leans in the direction of Theory X or to the one who leans in the direction of Theory Y?

The supervisor who leans towards Theory X and tries to motivate using the Theory X approach may be letting himself in for trouble. He thinks he's got to strictly control and supervise his employees, and believes the best way to motivate them is through money, discipline, and the exercise of authority—appealing to lower-level needs. This may be the case in some situations, but it rarely holds true in our society today.

The supervisor who motivates using the Theory Y approach has a much higher regard for his employees. He trusts them and believes that they will do what is necessary to get the job done with efficiency and dispatch. He doesn't think he has to stand over them to get them to work. Given the proper conditions and understanding, he thinks employees will respond to the type of treatment that appeals to their higher-level needs.

Most modern managers agree that Theory Y has much to offer. In fact, most of the evidence indicates that if you use this approach, you will accomplish the greatest good. Thus, if you want to be a better supervisor, you should lean in the direction of Theory Y. It's not a magic answer, but if you lean toward the Theory Y approach, you will probably get the best in quality and performance that could reasonably be expected in the long run.

From all that we have said, you can see that there is no *one* how-to-do-it approach to motivation. People are much too complex to have some formula applied across the board. Instead, supervisors are advised to study, talk with, and know their employees. Only by taking this approach can the proper atmosphere be generated for the most positive long-run motivation.

A Case Study
BEN BROWN AND HIS SUPERVISORY STYLE

Ben Brown was sure he was right. His approach to supervising his employees had always been a no-nonsense, tough-but-fair, close-to-the-chest approach to supervision. His output had been consistently good over the years, and he firmly believed that the best way to motivate a worker was through his pocketbook.

A recent company survey, however, showed Ben's department was way below the company average on such things as appreciation for work performed, ease of communication with supervision, job status, loyalty, personal help and understanding by the supervisor, and feeling of belonging. Privately, Ben was somewhat concerned over his low ranking, but publicly he passed it off as just another "screwball personnel popularity contest."

He wanted to be liked and accepted by his men, but he knew what he had to do to get the work out, and productivity came first. He set high output standards and closely supervised every one of his fourteen men, pushing the work through his department at top speed. Of course, training was a problem for him. As he explained it, "You can't get decent help these days. They're never satisfied—always leaving to look for greener fields." He often complained that if he didn't have to train so many new employees, he could increase production by 30%.

Last week, Ben's supervisor, Mr. Gilmore, had talked with him about his low rating and had given him an article to read that explained the Theory Y approach to supervision. Today, Mr. Gilmore talked with Ben again about Theory Y management. But Ben expressed doubts that the Theory Y supervision would work. It was overly permissive, too democratic, and gave the employees too much of a voice in their work. Ben strongly believed that his employees were supposed to do what he told them without back talk. His attitude was that they were to work and try but never question or reason why.

Mr. Gilmore didn't push Ben, who was too good and loyal an employee; during his 32 years with the company he had turned in a consistently good work record. Yet he wanted in some way to reach Ben and get him to approach Theory Y management with an open mind. After leaving Ben, Mr. Gilmore wondered if he should attempt to change him, and if so, how he should approach the job.

1. Do you think Ben was a good supervisor? Why?
2. Do you think Mr. Gilmore should try to motivate Ben to incorporate some of the Theory Y approach in his supervision? How?
3. Despite his good record of output, are there any signs other than those in the survey that indicate that Ben's employees are not too happy with his supervision?

A Case Study
ROUGEMONT COMPANY (A)

The Rougemont Company owned and operated eighteen textile plants employing a total of 5,400 employees. Many of these plants engaged in the same types of textile operations, such as spinning, throwing, dyeing, weaving, etc.

The company was founded in 1938 and got its real start during World War II. During and immediately after the war, the management in an effort to round out and complement their activities acquired a series of small mills scattered over a radius of 300 miles from the home office. In acquiring these plants, the Rougemont Company maintained, insofar as possible, the same local administrative and operative officials, the same policies, the same labor, and in every way attempted to make the local unit autonomous. Each plant was considered as a profit center, and each plant manager operated his plant in the way that he thought best for sound business operation and maximum profits. This practice was apparently successful, and the company continued to grow.

Sixteen months ago, however, a textile union began a campaign to organize the company's eighteen plants. The union has not, to date, been successful in their mission. Many of the employees expressed the feeling that they would wait and see what the management of the Rougemont Company planned for them before they definitely decided on union representation. Even though the union has not succeeded in its drive, it has planted some seeds of doubt and distrust in the employees' minds. For example, it has demonstrated to the employees that no consistent wage scale has been adhered to by the company. The union showed that employees performing the same work but in different plants received wage differentials as great as 26% in some situations. Even within some plants, it was pointed out that no systematic attempt had been made by the company to establish fair and just relative wages. In one plant, for example, the union representatives pointed out that the plant janitor was making 3 cents per hour more than employees who were doffing (doffing is a job requiring manual dexterity in removing and placing bobbins on textile machines).

Many of these wage ills, of course, were acquired with the various plants. And some of them were brought about because the several plants were brought together under one common owner. How the company acquired the troubles, however, was of no interest to the union. But what the company did about them was vital to organized labor.

1. What steps do you think the Rougemont Company should take to answer the union charges?
2. Would correcting the inequities motivate the employees in any way? How?

10
HOW TO USE YOUR PERSONNEL DEPARTMENT

This chapter explains—

- What the function of the personnel department is
- How the personnel department can help you

In every business, regardless of size, someone has to recruit and hire people to work for the company. In small firms, this work is frequently done by the owner-manager. He hires, promotes, and discharges workers in accordance with their capacities and his needs. He plans for, recruits, and trains his employees. In fact, he performs all the functions we normally think of as necessary to securing and maintaining an adequate work force.

As his business grows and he hires more and more employees, however, the owner-manager reaches a point where he does not have enough time to make sure that he complies with all federal, state, and local laws pertaining to employees, as well as to keep track of such personnel records as application blanks, letters of recommendation, records of jobs held in the company by each employee, records of promotion, accounts of disciplinary action, changes in pay grade, and so on. As a result, the personnel work in larger firms is usually done by a separate department called the Personnel Department or the Industrial Relations Department. Its job is to secure and keep on hand an adequate, healthy work force.

WHAT DOES THE PERSONNEL DEPARTMENT DO?

The personnel department tries to help supervisors with their personnel work in every way that it can, by providing service, advice, and coordination between departments. Specifically, the personnel department's job is to help the company reach its objective by assisting you as a supervisor with the management of the persons employed by the company and working in your department. In lending this assistance, the personnel department recruits, hires, trains, places, and maintains an effective work force. However, although the personnel department helps you as a supervisor to do a better job, it cannot do everything for you. The responsibility for managing person-

effective work force

nel does not belong to the personnel department alone. On the contrary, the responsibility for good personnel administration rests on you and on every other supervisor working for the firm. It is a *total, cooperative endeavor* that comes from a common feeling of responsibility and cooperation. All that the personnel department can do to bring this about is to offer every supervisor every ounce of help that it can in recruiting and training employees; to offer him any suggestions that it can in how personnel matters should be handled; and to offer any service that it can, such as record keeping. Thus, the personnel department is essentially a service department in nature. It aids in the performance of personnel services for the entire company.

WHAT ARE PERSONNEL POLICIES?

A personnel policy is a rule, usually written, that guides the personnel department and the company in its personnel relations. It tells how things are to be done, like recipes in a cookbook. Thus, it helps the personnel department and supervisors get their jobs done by providing directions. Personnel policies are usually made up by management in consultation with the personnel department. In large firms, these policies can get complex. One of the personnel department's jobs, therefore, is to keep up with these policies and interpret and explain them to supervisors. Personnel policies cover a lot of different topics and discuss items such as: *interpreting personnel policies*

1. Hiring employees.
2. Employee absences.
3. Physical examinations.
4. Conditions of employment.
5. Employee dismissal.
6. Safety practices.
7. The employee suggestion system.
8. The grievance procedure.
9. Improving the employees' education with company help.
10. Promotions and transfers.
11. Conditions for financial aid.
12. Separation (resignation) of employees.

Although the responsibility for deciding what the company policy should be on these and similar matters rests with top management, it is the personnel department's responsibility to see that all such policies are applied uniformly throughout the company. As a result, the personnel department can be a big help to the line supervisor who is often so busy with the problems of his department that he frequently does not have time to keep up with all the details of how something should be done. He can, therefore, turn to the personnel department for information, advice, or help regarding any personnel action that he needs to take.

WHAT ARE THE PERSONNEL DEPARTMENT'S DUTIES?

The duties of the personnel department vary with the size and type of company, but the first duty of the personnel department regardless of company size is to keep enough workers on hand at all times to get the job done. To do this, personnel departments typically—

1. Estimate the labor requirements for the future.
2. Set up job descriptions.
3. Set up job specifications.
4. Establish labor sources and recruit workers.

5. Interview, select, and place employees.
6. Develop educational and training programs for workers.
7. Coordinate and process promotions and transfers within the company.
8. Conduct separation procedures for all employees.
9. Set up and keep adequate records on all of the above.

adequate supply of workers

Let's examine these activities briefly to see how they help supervisors do their jobs more effectively.

How Do You Estimate Labor Requirements?   In a lot of companies, labor requirements are not estimated. Instead, a new person is hired whenever an old one quits or retires. If the company operates on a regular basis and the number of workers it needs is constant, this might work all right. In most companies, however, this approach does not work well because waiting until an employee quits to hire another might make for a poor selection—or even worse, applicants with the necessary qualifications might not be available at the time the job is open. Thus, instead of waiting for an opening before hiring someone, plans need to be made ahead of time for future personnel requirements.

With fluctuations in business activity such as we have in this country, someone needs to plan how many employees will be needed to work in a company and when they will be required. For example, if a company's customers require 10,000 units each month for the next two months, 6,000 units monthly for the next three months, and 22,000 units monthly for the balance of the year, someone has to give some thought to determining how many employees will be required to produce the units the customers need. Each supervisor, of course, could do this for his own department, but in a large company, it might happen that one supervisor was reducing the number of employees by *discharging* them, while another supervisor in another department was *hiring* new employees. Obviously, this is bad for morale and uneconomical, because the employees are not being transferred from the departments where they are surplus to the departments where they are needed. This won't happen, however, if you use the personnel department to estimate the labor requirements for the whole company. With the personnel department in charge, the needs of every department can be coordinated so that surplus workers in one department can be transferred to open jobs in other departments.

figuring labor requirements

The best way to estimate labor requirements is:

1. Find out what has to be produced in the future—next week, next month, next quarter, or next year—as far ahead as you can. You can usually get this information from sales forecasts. Assume, for example, that you do this and find you will need to produce 12,800 units per week for the next six months.
2. Next, calculate how many man-hours of certain skills you will need to produce the 12,800 units per week. You do this by multiplying the

number of units you need to produce per week by the man-hours it takes of each skill to manufacture each unit of product. You can usually get this figure from the time-study department, or you might have to use your best estimate. You might find, for example, that to produce one unit you will need 30 minutes of work by a skilled carpenter. Thus, if you are producing 12,800 units per week, you will need 6,400 hours of work per week by skilled carpenters.

3. Now you can determine the number of workers that you will need by dividing the number of man-hours you will need per week for each skill (which you figured in step 2 above) by the number of work hours in a week. This would be 6,400 hours divided by 40 hours, giving an answer of 160 carpenters needed to produce 12,800 units per week.

4. If you think you need to, you can now throw in a factor for sickness and other absences. For example, if each of your carpenters averages about ½ hour of absences per week, then you will multiply the number of carpenters (160) by ½ hour to get the number of extra hours of work you will need per week to cover these absences. Thus, 160 men times ½ hour of absences per week equals 80 hours absent per week for these 160 men. This means that you might want to hire a couple of extra carpenters to cover the absences each week for the 160 carpenters.

5. Finally, add any other personnel (such as maintenance men, cafeteria workers, material handlers, clean-up men, secretarial help, and so on) that you think you will require. Don't forget to throw in an absence factor (discussed in step 4 above) for these service personnel if you think it will apply.

As you can see, estimating labor requirements for any specific future period is not hard to do if you translate sales forecasts into manpower requirements for each skill, and then follow the steps indicated above.

What Are Job Descriptions? After the personnel department determines the number and kind of employees needed for each department, the next step is to find out what the work of each job is. Thus for every individual job in the department, you'll want to know what the duties and responsibilities are. This is called a *job description*. It describes the job—not the man doing the job. The personnel department can be called on to do this work, or it can assist the supervisor in doing it. Inasmuch as the supervisor is in charge of each job in his department, he should know what makes up each job better than anyone else. He should, therefore, work with the personnel department to get the information necessary to write the job description, with the actual preparation of the job description under the control of the personnel department.

Job descriptions are needed in order to better match individual employees with appropriate job openings. A job description for a clerk typist, for example, might show that the employee performing the job has to operate an electric typewriter with special type in the preparation of reports. One of the employee qualifications for the job, therefore, would be that the employee be able to type.

Job descriptions should be reviewed periodically to be sure that they actually show what the job consists of. Jobs change over time, and job descriptions, therefore, get out of date unless they are periodically reviewed and changed. The personnel department can be of help in keeping these up to date.

Once the contents of jobs have been determined, the next requirement is for the supervisor to specify the knowledge and skills that employees should have in order to qualify for these jobs. This is called a *job specification*.

Why Do You Need Job Specifications? In a very small company, the personnel department might not have any problem knowing the skills that a new employee should have. In a large company, however, there are so many different jobs and men that some sort of written specification is needed by the personnel department in order for it to know what type of person is required. You can't say, "I need an electrician's helper." Instead, you have to spell out what an electrician's helper should be able to do. You might want him to be able to read blueprints, follow wiring diagrams, understand the local wiring code, and so on. Therefore a job specification is set up for an electrician's helper showing what the job consists of and what abilities you would want a new employee to have. A job specification, sometimes called a

job descriptions and specifications

"Job specifications list only the minimum capacities you expect any employee to have."

man specification, is, therefore, a written record of what qualities you need in a person to fill a particular job. It indicates such things as job knowledge, skill, experience, aptitudes, speaking or writing ability, and physical strength. These job specifications are short and list only the *minimum* capacities that you expect a person to have.

The personnel department is responsible for making the job specifications and keeping them up to date, and each supervisor should take care that his job specifications are not set too high. If they are set too high, he might not be able to find employees who can qualify, or if he does, the employees may be too costly. Also, if he specifies an overly qualified employee for a routine job, the employee is likely to have capacities far in excess of the job requirements and therefore may become bored. The reverse is also true. You don't want to have a mediocre employee in a job calling for an expert because such an employee couldn't do the job, wouldn't be satisfactory, and would have to be fired. The supervisor, therefore, should carefully analyze what each job consists of and then with equal care specify the knowledge and skills required of a person to fill the job.

Job descriptions and job specifications should be maintained by the personnel department, with copies furnished to the supervisors. In this way, whenever the supervisor needs an employee to fill a certain job, he can notify the personnel department that the job is open, and the personnel department by using the job description and job specification can set the machinery in motion to recruit a qualified employee. After screening out the applicants who do not have the necessary qualifications, the personnel department can send the remaining applicants to the supervisor for him to interview and accept or reject as he may decide.

How Do You Establish Labor Sources and Recruit Workers? Once you determine the type of employee you need, the next problem is finding him. A good practice that many personnel departments follow is to fill a vacancy from within the company. "Inside" employees already know the company and its rules and apparently want to work there. Also, when workers are given a chance for a new job in the company, it improves their morale because you are showing an interest in them— giving them an opportunity to improve themselves. Another advantage of inside employees is that when you promote one worker, several more are often upgraded, and then an unskilled man can be hired at the bottom. Job specifications are a big help to the personnel department in making such transfers and filling vacancies from within the company.

*finding
and
selecting
employees*

Other sources used by the personnel department to get new employees include former workers (if their records with the company were good), employment agencies, high schools, technical schools, and colleges. Handicapped workers also make good employees. Once an employee has been recruited, a lot of care has to be used by the personnel department in placing him in a proper job in the company. Placing the right man in the right job is good for morale and costs less. To do the best job it can, the personnel department uses application blanks, interviews, tests, references, and physical exams to select and place employees.

How Are Employees Selected and Placed?   The method used by most personnel departments to screen and select job applicants is the *application blank*. This should be a simple blank that asks only for information such as name, address, physical characteristics, education, experience, necessary personal information, and references. Application blanks are used to screen out applicants who don't meet some requirement, such as education. They are not, however, used to hire a person. Instead, a person should be *interviewed* in order to learn about him and let him learn about the company. An interview is the place where you can determine whether or not you think the applicant would make a good employee. If the job requires some special skill, typing for example, a *test* might be given. Also, most personnel departments *contact previous employers* to find out what kind of worker the applicant was and why he left his previous job. Finally, an employee should be given a *physical examination* to determine any major defects that would cause him to be unsuited for the job.

hiring new workers If the applicant passes all the tests and you tell the personnel department to hire him, the next thing that you need to do is *to introduce the new employee to the job*. This is a very important step that some personnel departments omit. Instead, they expect the new employee to "find his way around" by talking with other employees. This is not a good practice. A new employee is a valuable person, and the personnel department should carefully introduce him to the company and to his job. He should be told something about the company's history, what products are made, employee benefits and activities, the way the company is organized, where he fits in the organization structure, company rules and regulations, and any special duties and responsibilities involved in the job. A good deal of time and money have been spent up to this point to hire a new employee, and a haphazard, poor introduction to his job can do much to dampen his spirits, lower his morale, and get him off to a bad start. In contrast, a good introduction to the job may make an employee enthusiastic in his approach to learning his new work as well as give him a good opinion of the company.

Why Develop Training and Education Programs?   After a person has been hired, the personnel department's next job is to provide the opportunity for the employee to improve himself and his skills so as to prepare himself for advancement and further responsibility. Some training is basic to the job and is done while the employee is working. It is called *on-the-job training*. In this type of training, the employee is put on a new job and told what to do. Frequently, a skilled worker serves as his coach and gives him tips on how to get the job done. At other times, an employee is trained in a special area

training employees or room on a machine that has been set up for him to learn on. This is usually similar to a school with a skilled instructor to teach the workers correct work procedures. This will be discussed in more detail in Chapter 11.

In addition to these job-related skills, many companies today are helping to train their employees for larger responsibilities through educational courses given by the company in the evenings. Courses are offered in such things as letter writing, stenography, mathematics, blueprint reading, drafting, selling, speech, and so on. If technical institutes or evening colleges are in the community, many companies pay tuition for their employees to attend these night courses.

All of this is an attempt by the company to make the employee a healthier and happier worker. Training and general education exert a positive influence on the employee and may result in an improvement in morale and a decrease in turnover, absenteeism, accidents, and so on. Educational activities are expensive, but their worth is well recognized in growing concerns.

Who Coordinates Promotions and Transfers?   In small companies, employees can be transferred between departments because vacancies are generally known by supervisors, and transfers can be arranged. Not so in the large complex firms. They are usually so big that their size makes informal communication about job openings impossible. In these big companies, therefore, the personnel department has the responsibility of notifying all persons qualified for the job and their supervisors that an opening exists. As we all know, such inside promotions and transfers can do much for employee morale. In fact, even when a new job is on the same pay level as an old one, it might be considered a promotion because of a change in shifts or a move from a hot, undesirable location to a cooler, cleaner part of the plant.

Are Exit Interviews Necessary?   Whenever a person quits his job and leaves the company, we should know why and under what conditions. This is determined by what is called an *exit interview.* Conducting this interview is the responsibility of the personnel department because it can give an unbiased judgment as to why the employee left. Also, the employee may not mind telling a disinterested personnel employee why he quit his job—but he would hesitate to tell his supervisor why he quit. If the employee is leaving the company on his own accord, this interview gives the company the chance to find out why he is dissatisfied and perhaps take action to prevent this from happening in the future. If the employee is being fired, the interview gives him the opportunity to vent his feelings before leaving and also provides the company the opportunity to correct any misunderstandings that he might have. The interviewer might even find out that an employee has been unfairly discharged and corrections can be made. Finally, from a legal point of view, the separation interview is a must. Employees leaving the company may institute union proceedings to be reinstated with back pay, and accurate records of the separation may be invaluable before a mediator or the National Labor Relations Board (NLRB).

other duties of the personnel department

Who Is Responsible for Keeping Records?   The personnel department has the big job of keeping straight all of the countless records and details relating to every employee and his employment, including complete and accurate records pertaining to his hiring, performance evaluations by his supervisor, promotions, transfers, merit increases, educational advances, grievances, suspensions, and so on. In union cases, these records are essential to determining what should be done under the terms of the union agreement.

In addition to records about individual employees, the personnel department also keeps general records of such things as labor turnover, absenteeism, number of people applying for jobs, average level of pay, and so on. Along with other varied and time-consuming activities, keeping records is an important part of the personnel department's job. The purpose of keeping records, as with all the other duties of the personnel department, is to help the supervisor do a better job of supervising and managing his employees.

WHAT ELSE DOES THE PERSONNEL DEPARTMENT DO?

Up to this point we've talked about the typical or average duties that personnel departments perform in order to help supervisors. A lot of personnel departments, however, are helping supervisors in other special ways. They are, for example, making sure that equal opportunity laws are being followed and that women and minority groups are represented in the right ratio on the work staff.

Many personnel departments are also adding electronic data processing of personnel records to their list of duties. Instead of the typical folder containing $8\frac{1}{2}'' \times 11''$ information sheets on each employee, their records are on magnetic tape in a data bank of a computer. Application data, performance ratings, job histories, test results, promotions, payroll data, and the

records and reports

like are now on the computer and are maintained by the personnel department. With the information thus recorded, personnel can prepare and distribute to supervisors all types of reports showing employment trends, types of employees hired, absences classified by type of employee, and so on. All of these things can be helpful in estimating future employee requirements as discussed on pages 148–9.

More and more personnel departments are making employee attitude surveys, rather than having outside firms do the work. Computerizing these surveys enables the personnel department to prepare different kinds of reports showing employees' feelings and opinions. Supervisors use these reports, of course, to learn more about their employees' ideas and feelings so that changes can be made and supervision can be improved.

There is almost no end of ways in which a personnel department can help you as a supervisor do a better job. The factor that limits how much it does is the cost of doing the work versus its usefulness to you.

With all of this, however, there is one fact that you as a supervisor should not forget: staffing is a fundamental managerial activity for which you are responsible. And staffing includes such areas as recruiting, hiring, training, evaluating, testing, promoting, and compensating employees. Because of the time and complexity involved in doing a good job in each of these, however, you should feel free to turn to the personnel department for substantial help and guidance in any of these areas. This does not relieve you of the responsibility; it simply gives you help when and where you need it.

A Case Study
JACK NELSON'S PROBLEM

As a new man on the board of directors for a local savings and loan association, Jack Nelson was being introduced to all the employees in the home office. When he was introduced to Ruth, he was curious about her work and asked her what her machine did. Ruth replied that she really did not know what the machine was called or what it did. She explained that she had only been working there for two months. She did, however, know precisely how to operate the machine and according to her supervisor, she was an excellent employee.

At one of the branch offices, the supervisor in charge spoke to Mr. Nelson quite confidentially, telling him that "something was wrong," but he didn't know what. For one thing, the supervisor explained, employee turnover was too high and no sooner had one girl been put on a job, when another one resigned. With customers to see and loans to be made, he explained that he had little time to work with the new employees as they came and went.

Each branch supervisor hired his own employees with no communications with the home office or other branches. When an opening developed, he did the best he could to find a suitable employee to replace the worker who quit.

After touring the twenty-two branches and finding similar problems in many of them, Mr. Nelson wondered what the home office should do or what action he should take. The savings and loan firm was generally regarded as a well-run institution that had grown from 27 to 191 employees during the past eight years. The more he thought about the matter, the more puzzled Mr. Nelson became. He couldn't quite put his finger on the problem, and he didn't know whether or not to report his findings to the president.

1. What do you think was causing some of the problems in the savings and loan home office and branches?
2. What do you think should be done to help solve the problem?

A Case Study
ADVANCE MANUFACTURING

It was one of those rush jobs. Sid Thompson, maintenance foreman for the Advance Manufacturing Company, called the Personnel Department and requested that they get him a painter right away. One of his painting crew, he explained, was moving to another state, and he needed a replacement as quickly as possible.

With a rush request like this, the Personnel Department got on the phone right away and started making contacts. Within three days they found a man who was a painter, and sent him around to see Sid. After talking for a few minutes, Sid hired the man and put him to work that afternoon.

Within two weeks, Sid was back at the Personnel Department again, asking for a painter—explaining that the last man they sent him didn't know which end of a brush to dip in the paint, so he let him go. Personnel again tried to get a man for Sid, and within a week located another experienced painter. Sid quickly hired him and put him on the job. But again, within a few days, Sid was back in the Personnel Department asking for another painter. This time, he explained, the man didn't understand colors, color coordination, and how to mix tints and shades to match existing paint. With that, Jim Boles, the supervisor of Personnel threw up his hands in despair, asking, "What do you want in a painter, Sid? A Michelangelo? We've sent you two good painters within a month and you let both of them go. What's the problem? What did the men have to say for themselves? What do you expect us to do? We aren't mind readers. We don't know precisely what kind of man you want. We'll try again, but for gosh sakes, use some judgment in hiring and keeping another man—if we can find one."

1. What do you see lacking in the operation of the Personnel Department?
2. What normal or typical practices appear to be violated?
3. What changes would you instigate if you were Jim Boles?

11
INTERVIEWING, ORIENTING, AND TRAINING EMPLOYEES

This chapter explains—

- How you should conduct an interview
- Why you should orient new employees
- The most effective types of training to use

No one wants to hire a person without talking with him first. Likewise, most employees wouldn't take a job until they had first talked with a representative of the firm. The employment interview satisfies both of these needs: the employer can size up the employee, and the employee can find out about the job and the company.

Job interviews, therefore, are the most universally used method of employee selection. Some firms even use three interviews:

1. A preliminary interview to weed out those applicants obviously disqualified.
2. A main employment office interview to select several candidates for the job.
3. A final interview by the prospective supervisor who will make the decision about who will get the job.

WHAT DOES AN INTERVIEWER LOOK FOR?

Whether you are a personnel director or a first-line supervisor, you should look at a lot of things in interviewing and sizing up a job applicant. You should try to assess the applicant's emotional stability, his maturity, interests, motivation, judgment, attitudes, and ability to express himself. In addition, you should look for such attributes as self-confidence, personal appearance, and openness. By the way the applicant answers questions, you should

a satisfactory employee

be able to tell how well he will probably fit into the work and how well he will fit into the social situation existing in the area where you have a job opening. In fact, through well-directed interviews, you can even learn a lot about the applicant's home and family background, previous work experience, education, hobbies, and the like.

The major purpose of the employment interview is to determine whether or not the applicant's education and experience will make him a satisfactory employee in a particular job. In addition to work skills, you will also want to find out whether the applicant's personal attributes would make him happy working with the people in your department. For example, does he have hobbies and interests that would make him congenial with the other workers? If he likes to talk art and antiques and doesn't care about bowling and fishing, while everyone else likes bowling and fishing, he might get bored and find little in common with the other men. As a consequence, he probably would not be happy working with the group for a long period of time.

Does he have any special capacities or achievements that will make him a better employee? Is this job a complete switch from his previous work? For example, if he has always been an outside maintenance man, why does he now want to switch to an assembly operator?

To summarize, you should try to find out everything you can in a tactful way that will help you decide whether or not the applicant would make a good employee and would be happy working with you and your company.

WHAT SHOULD YOU TELL AN APPLICANT ABOUT THE JOB?

The applicant is interested in the job or else he would not be there. So, tell him everything about the job, covering such points as:

1. Duties and responsibilities of the job.
2. Activities involved in doing the job, like standing, walking, or sitting.
3. Job title and relationship with other jobs.
4. Promotion possibilities.
5. What kind of equipment and materials he will handle.
6. The environment or working conditions where the job will be performed.
7. Pay and all related factors.

job information

You should be as honest and factual as you can. If the job is a dirty one performed in a hot room, you should tell him. Don't paint a dark picture that will scare him off, but be sure he knows what to expect.

The applicant is also interested in the company in general, so tell him about how the company is as an employer. Cover such things as fringe benefits, free health examinations, opportunities to learn new jobs, and the like.

HOW SHOULD YOU HANDLE THE INTERVIEW?

First of all, don't be formal or stuffy in an interview. Put the person seeking the job at ease. Talk about some current topic, like who's going to win the series or the latest equipment used for bass fishing.

After the prospective employee has relaxed somewhat, you might ask him questions about his previous employment. Questions dealing with his work, such as the things he did and what his responsibilities were, are good ones to use. Such questions cover things he is familiar with and should encourage him to express himself. Whenever you want to get the other fellow talking—whether it is for a job interview or over a card game— remember to ask questions that demand more than a yes or no reply. In other words, keep your questions open-ended. Questions that cause us to talk are usually those that start with *what, how, when, why, and who.*

take time, listen, use open-end questions

If, for example, you ask a person, "Do you like to fish?" he may say either "yes" or "no"—depending on his likes. But if you ask him, "How do you manage to always catch bass?" he'll probably get involved in a longer response. In a similar way, when you are talking about the job the person is seeking, you might ask questions like, "How did you learn about this job?" "What was the problem with your old job?" After you ask such questions, however, be sure to give the applicant enough time to think and make an adequate response. Remember that everyone is not as quick to respond as you are.

Always give the person you are interviewing your complete attention. This is an important step for both of you. You want to find out if he'll be a good employee, and he wants to know if you'll be a good boss. So talk *to him*—not to the ceiling or the floor. And *listen* to what he says, and ask questions if needed.

Don't clutter up an interview with distractions such as shuffling papers, jotting down ideas, or taking telephone calls. These will serve to disrupt a trend of thought, as well as tell the employee that you don't think he's important enough for you to give him your undivided attention. When he feels this, he'll shut up and you'll fail to get the information you need. Don't give your true feelings away by scowls, frowns, or grunts. If you do, the prospect will get the message and you won't get the full picture.

Don't drum your fingers on the table or tap your pencil or your shoe. Such things tell him you are impatient and want to get the interview over with. Instead, keep quiet, be pleasant, and let the applicant talk. Remember, you can't learn about a prospect while you are talking. Let him talk—and listen to what he is saying to you.

Always be as honest and factual as you can when you answer questions.

Don't either oversell or undersell the company or the job. An oversell may mean a dissatisfied employee within a few days. An undersell may mean that you will lose a potentially excellent employee. Above all, make sure that the employee fits the job. Don't put a Cadillac man on a Chevette job. If you aren't thoroughly familiar with the job, look for and use the job specification and job description that have been prepared.

be patient and honest

Don't let a single negative trait of the applicant influence your judgment on all other traits. For example, if he won't look you in the eye but always looks down or away when talking to you (and you don't like this trait), don't let it influence you negatively in evaluating his other traits. Or if the applicant wears a hat and you are against men who wear hats, don't let this negatively influence you. Instead, try to determine whether or not the quality or trait will have any effect on the employee's future job performance. Don't jump to the conclusion that he has a hot temper because he has red hair, or that he smokes pot because he has long hair, or that his short fingernails mean he is stupid. These and similar "old wives' tales" are completely lacking any valid foundation and can easily hamper your sound judgment. Be on guard to avoid them.

Believe it or not, you have to make careful plans about how you should close an interview. Don't close the interview by saying to the applicant, "I'm sorry, sir, but your negative attitude (or general unreliability, or poor personality) makes you unqualified for this job." Such frankness may offend the applicant and leave a bad taste in his mouth concerning the company and its employees.

Instead, the interview should be concluded in a friendly manner, avoiding any generalizations or evaluations that might be open to question and perhaps develop into a long and fruitless discussion. Say something like, "I appreciate your interest in our company and in this job. As you know, we are interviewing several other applicants before making a decision. Thank you again for your interest. We'll let you know our decision within a couple of days." If he doesn't get the job, the least you can do is see that he gets a courteous letter explaining that another person with more experience was chosen to fill the position.

a friendly manner

If the applicant makes no move to leave after you have finished your closing speech, then the best thing to do is stand up, open the door, and say, "Thank you again for your interest in us. As soon as we make a decision, you'll be notified." Most people will get the hint and will rise and leave with you.

WHAT DOES IT TAKE TO BE A GOOD INTERVIEWER?

Just because you are a supervisor doesn't mean that you automatically possess the knowledge and skills necessary to be a successful interviewer. Competence in the area of interviewing comes from practice, experience, and sound training in conducting interviews.

To be a good interviewer, you will need to have a good understanding about your company and the relationships that exist between departments and divisions. You'll also need to know how jobs in your division relate to each other, the route and opportunities for promotion from one job to the next, and what is required to be qualified for the particular job that is open. You'll need to be able to size up from long experience or formal study an applicant's abilities, personality traits, motivations, frustrations, attitudes, and individual differences. You must be objective in sizing up people. You can't let your personal biases or prejudices influence you if these have no bearing on the matter.

sizing up a prospect

You must be a good listener. Don't take advantage of your captive audience by expounding at length about the virtues of the company, the advantages of the job, and your personal experiences while working for the company.

You'll need to be alert and perceptive to anything that the applicant does that might throw a new light on how he feels. Such things as a change in his tone of voice, a shift in his expression, a pause or hesitation at a critical point, and any show of emotion about certain topics might give away an applicant's true feelings.

Give encouragement and support to the applicant by nodding your head, by a reassuring gesture, or by saying such things as, "That's interesting," or "Tell me more," or, "Oh, I see." Remember when we talked about empathy in Chapter 4? Well here is a place to use it. Empathize with the applicant. Try to see what he is trying to say from his point of view. Many applicants have difficulty in expressing their ideas. Help the applicant by restating his ideas in better organized, simpler ways. Ask questions like, "Did you mean to say you hated your boss—or that you disliked the job you were doing?" This will give the applicant a chance to reflect and clarify his true meaning.

Not all of us are capable of being good interviewers. It is an art more than a science. Yet it can be learned through reading, educational courses, role playing, and experience. You can also benefit by working with and observing experienced interviewers, learning from them how to develop your perceptiveness and skills.

HOW DO YOU ORIENT THE NEW EMPLOYEE?

When a new employee has been hired, the next step is to introduce him to his new job. In some companies, the personnel officer is responsible for introducing the employee to the company and its rules and regulations. In other companies, this responsibility falls to the supervisor in whose department the new employee will work. Regardless of who is responsible, that person should fully inform the employee about all aspects of his job and should start him out on the right foot. A haphazard, ineffective introduction of a new worker to his job and to his associates and his work facilities is both wasteful and inexcusable. However, despite the importance of a good introduction, probably no supervisory skill is more poorly handled than introducing the new employee. A good deal of money and effort have been spent up to this point in locating and hiring this individual, and though first impressions are not always lasting ones, they can do much to make an employee enthusiastic in his approach to his new job as well as prepare him to react positively to future conditions. Remember that the employee is the most important possession that your company has, and he should be treated as such. A good job introduction serves as an excellent starting place to sell the company to the new employee and engender confidence in him.

introducing the employee to the job

Proper job orientation also reduces employee dissatisfaction and turnover because it gives you, the supervisor, the opportunity to explain the employee's job in relation to other parts of the company before the employee

"One of the most important first steps
is to properly introduce a new employee
to the job."

can be misinformed by rumor. While the employee is new and impressionable, company rules and regulations can be explained carefully, thereby minimizing subsequent disciplinary action, misunderstandings, and possible dismissal because the employee did not understand and follow company rules and regulations. And perhaps one of the biggest plusses of all is that a job orientation will serve to brush away the fear of the unknown that all employees have in going to a new place of employment. As you know from experience, the first few days in new surroundings are always disturbing and anxious ones for most new employees.

WHAT SHOULD A NEW EMPLOYEE BE TOLD?

It's a good idea for the supervisor to sit down with the new employee in some quiet place and talk with him about the department, his job, company regulations, and so on. Among many other things, the supervisor should be sure to cover such topics as:

1. *Pay*—how and when the employee is paid, pay rates, deductions, the first day the new employee will be paid, shift premium pay, savings opportunities, pay for overtime, and so on.
2. *Hours of work*—when to come to work, breaks, lunch period, wash-up time, quitting time, and what to do if the employee is late.
3. *Time clocks*—when to punch in and out, where clocks and time cards are located, what to do if the employee has to leave early, etc.

4. *Sickness*—when and where to call in, how to report to the company doctor, the location of first-aid and nursing facilities, how to report injuries, and so on.

5. *Everything about his work*—where he will be working; with whom he will be working; what tools, equipment, and supplies he will be using; layout of the department and plant so that he will know his way around; where the cafeteria is; where the washroom and rest facilities are; safety precautions; use of special clothing; fire regulations; housekeeping; and so on.

It is basically up to you as a supervisor to choose what method you will use or how you will do the job. What you do and how you do it, however, are critical. If you convey the idea that you are interested in the new employee and want to make his transition to a new job a smooth one, this will help minimize the employee's fears and make him receptive to suggestions and instructions. You should also assure the employee that you will work with him during the coming weeks to explain the details of his job and company policies, and will answer any questions that might arise.

WHY DO YOU NEED TO TRAIN EMPLOYEES?

Training employees makes good sense for many reasons. For one thing, it reduces the length of time it takes to reach an acceptable level of performance. Good instructions in carefully controlled learning situations can save a lot of money by shortening the learning periods. For example, prior to World War II, one machine tool company usually taught a new employee a certain skill by having him work as an apprentice with an old hand for four years. During the war, however, a rapid expansion of operations forced such companies to try a formal classroom approach to speed up the learning process. Using this new approach, they found that new men were able to reach acceptable performance levels within a year or less.

In addition to preparing employees for new jobs, training frequently improves job performance of employees in old jobs, through such things as cutting down on waste, reducing accidents, minimizing customer complaints, and the like.

Training frequently gives us an unexpected bonus by making employees feel that you are concerned for them and their welfare. As a result, their attitudes and feelings about the company may improve. As this happens, tardiness, absenteeism, and turnover are also reduced. Thus, when you train an employee to do a better job, you may also get unexpected bonuses in the way of improved morale and reduced turnover.

motivation, morale, and skill

When a firm moves into a town, it may not find workers who are skilled in jobs that it requires. Employee training in this case enables the company to fill its manpower needs. Thus, the company recruits unskilled, "green" employees and trains them to perform the work that the company requires. For example, one North Carolina firm manufacturing women's sleepwear maintains a constant training program teaching new employees how to operate special sewing machines that stitch light and lacy material.

Another important reason to train employees is that it helps them personally. They develop new skills, new abilities, and new concepts that upgrade their earning ability. They are more valuable to the company, frequently have more opportunities for jobs with other firms, and as a consequence find themselves more secure in their jobs because of these increased job opportunities.

Finally, training is also for supervisory personnel, particularly in such areas as human relations, grievance handling, and leadership. Training supervisors to do better jobs of supervising frequently eliminates the cause of many employee complaints and grievances.

HOW CAN EMPLOYEES BE TRAINED?

There are a lot of ways in which employees can be trained. The choice of method depends a great deal on how much time is available, the type of training needed, the number of people to be trained, the cost, the amount of training required, and so on. Most business firms, however, use one of three major methods to train people. (1) on-the-job, (2) vestibule, and (3) classroom.

1. *On-the-job* training is by far the most frequently used method, and as the name implies, the training is done at the work place. In this type of training, the departmental supervisor is responsible, and either he or an employee appointed by him does the training. Teaching another person how to perform a job is not easy, and the instructor needs to know how to break the job down, how to teach it step by step, and how to guide and encourage the trainee as he learns the job. On-the-job training is most appropriately used to teach knowledge and skills that can be learned in a relatively short time—no more than two or three weeks—and where only a few employees are involved. Sales jobs, clerical skills, and simple machine operations are examples of skills that can be learned on the job. *types of training*

2. *Vestibule* training takes place in a classroom (or vestibule) to train employees in clerical and semiskilled jobs. An attempt is made in the class to duplicate work conditions, with machines and other equipment set up if needed. A common example of vestibule training found outside of industry is the typical classroom found in high schools and technical schools where people are taught to use the typewriter. The

emphasis in vestibule training is on learning rather than speed. And usually the instructors are much better qualified than those in on-the-job training programs. You'll find vestibule training used most frequently where a large number of employees need to be trained as machine operators, typists, office clerks, bank tellers, inspectors, and so on.

3. *Classroom* training is most frequently used where mental abilities such as problem solving, theories, and new concepts are emphasized rather than manual skills. Some portions of orientation programs may take place in classrooms, but most frequently we think of classroom training in connection with in-depth knowledge of a field where a person needs to be well grounded in principles and theory.

The classroom lends itself to all sorts of teaching and learning techniques. Lectures or formal talks by the instructor to the students can be boring and dull and can lull the student rather than excite his interest. As a result, most experienced teachers combine lectures with other techniques such as case study and role playing.

Case study involves the use of a realistic case or problem that makes the material come alive and shows why and how it is used. In your study of multiplication and division, for example, you were probably given short cases or problems to solve rather than tables to fill out. In this way, you could see how multiplication and division could be used and why you needed to learn them. It made the subject seem alive and useful. Thus, when using cases, you learn by doing rather than by reading about it. Cases are good learning devices for problems in such

lectures, cases, role playing

areas as organization, human relations, labor negotiations, policy, business ethics, law, and personnel management.

Role playing is typically used along with the lecture method in classes. In role playing, two or more employees are given roles to play before the group. There are no lines to memorize, but the employees must act out a situation that has been described to them. For example, one employee might act as the supervisor and the other as a worker who has a grievance. How the "worker" presents the grievance to the "supervisor" and how the "supervisor" handles the "worker's" grievance are observed and criticized by the other employees. They learn from watching, and the role players learn from doing and from class criticism. Role playing is a good learning technique because it allows you to put into practice what you have learned from texts and lectures.

Role playing is particularly useful in making us more sensitive to how others feel and how our behavior affects others. The best use of role playing, therefore, is in such situations as a salesman selling a product to a customer, a foreman interviewing an applicant for a job, a supervisor conducting an exit interview, or a union representative negotiating with a management team for a new union contract. Many times the participants are asked to swap roles and play the scene again. In this way, employees are taught to see and understand the other fellow's point of view. In role playing, you know immediately whether or not you were successful by how you feel as well as the criticism that others give you. Involvement, interest, even excitement are high, and learning, as a result, is usually fast.

Other methods of classroom instruction, of course, are used by various instructors. Some teach by demonstrating how to do something. Simulation is another teaching technique where actual conditions are duplicated as nearly as possible with employees performing a task under these conditions. For example, your driving reflexes and skill can be tested by a machine simulating driving conditions. The machine is a realistic model of an actual automobile that you "drive" by watching a moving picture of traffic ahead. How you react to traffic is recorded, and your degree of driving skill is computed after you have finished the "drive."

The use of business games is another example of classroom simulation where actual market conditions are simulated on a computer with employees running a business and making decisions about such things as how much to buy, what the selling price should be, and how much to spend on advertising. As in role playing and cases, interest is typically high in simulation exercises because the actions tend to closely duplicate real-world conditions.

HOW CAN YOU MAKE A JOB EASIER TO LEARN?

A job that you do regularly may seem simple to you but difficult to someone just learning it. Therefore, you can do a better job of teaching and the other fellow can learn faster if you will remember just two things.

1. Break the job down into simple, easy-to-understand steps. The steps in frying an egg, for example, might be: (a) turn on stove and place pan on gas jet; (b) pour grease in pan; (c) put egg into pan; and so on until you have the egg on your plate. You've broken the job down into simple steps.
2. Give the learner some key points that will enable him to get the knack of doing the step correctly.

In the first step of frying the egg, for example, the key point might be, "Don't leave the pan on the stove without grease in it." In the second step, the key point might be, "Use about one tablespoon of oil or grease per egg to be fried, and never fry more than four eggs at one time." In the third step, the key point might be, "As soon as oil begins to sizzle, reduce heat by turning knob one-half way down; then break egg in a bowl and pour gently into pan, taking care not to let hot grease pop on you." These key points speed the learning process. Figure 11-1 illustrates the steps you would

learning aids

STEPS IN THE OPERATION	KEY POINTS
Step: A logical segment of the operation in which something is done to advance the work.	Key point: Any directions or bits of information that help to perform the step correctly, safely, and easily.
Place 8″ x 10½″ sheet of paper in front of you on flat surface.	1. Be sure surface is flat—free of interfering objects.
Fold lower left hand corner up.	2a. Line up the right hand edges. b. Make a sharp crease.
Turn paper over.	3a. Pick up lower right hand corner with right hand and place it at the top. b. Folded flap should not be underneath.
Fold excess lower edge up.	4a. Line up right hand edges. b. Fold should line up with bottom edge. c. Make sharp crease.
Fold lower left hand corner flush with edge "A."	5a. Keep edges "B" and "C" parallel. b. Hold bottom edge in the center with finger while making fold.
Fold upper corner to point "D."	6a. Hold cup firmly with left hand. b. Bring upper corner down with right hand.
Separate lower right hand corner and fold back.	7a. Hold cup with left hand. b. Fold back with right hand. c. Make sharp creases.
Turn cup over and fold remaining flap back.	8. Make sharp creases.
Check cup to be sure it will hold water.	9. Open cup and look inside.

FIGURE 11-1.
Operation breakdown for training. *(Courtesy of U.S. Air Force Department)* From James E. Morgan, Jr., *Principles of Administrative and Supervisory Management* (Englewood Cliffs, N.J.: Prentice-Hall, Inc., 1973), pp. 206–7. Reprinted by permission of Prentice-Hall, Inc.

follow to make a drinking cup, with key points shown opposite each step.
See if you can make a cup by following the steps.

HOW CAN YOU MAKE TRAINING MORE EFFECTIVE?

The secret to effective training is motivation. Make the employee want to learn. Show him how it will pay off in greater skill and more pay, in opportunities for advancement, or in job security. Tell him *why* something is done the way it is. An employee who only knows what to do and how to do it has just part of the picture. If he also knows why he should do it the prescribed way, he will be better motivated.

If you are training new employees, don't expect perfection in a short time. Most people have some kind of learning problem; some catch on to some things quickly, whereas others need more time and practice. Praise an employee for what he learns quickly, and give him encouragement on the steps he is having trouble with. Show him again how to do it. Tell him that others, too, have had trouble learning this part of the job, but they got the knack after a while, and he will too. If the job is a difficult one, go through the cycle with the employee, letting him do the easy steps and you can do the hard ones. Then gradually work the employee into doing the harder steps. Remember to tell him what to do, how to do it, and why he should do it that way. Heap on the praise and encouragement. See Figure 11-2.

In training employees, be on guard against several common mistakes:

- *Don't present the training as a bag of tricks and gimmicks.* Any training you might attempt based on this approach will serve to hurt the organization and to destroy or damage the employee's concept of the company and its programs.   *motivating employees to learn*
- *Don't stress the development by the employee of efficiency or productivity.* This will come later. Stressing it too early will make the learner apprehensive and will impede his learning ability.
- *Don't have one of the top bosses do the training.* This will serve to silence the trainee; it will make him nervous and will delay the training process.
- *Don't feed him too much at one time.* Give the learner just a "bite" at a time. Don't heap the facts on so fast that he can't assimilate them. Keep the pace slow and in line with the employee's ability to grasp and understand the steps.
- *Don't talk without showing.* An illustration or a demonstration is worth a thousand words. Have you ever tried to *tell* a person how to tie a four-in-hand tie? Try it! Then *show* him how. Which is better? Easier? Faster? Follow this same example in training employees. *Show* them how as you explain how and why.

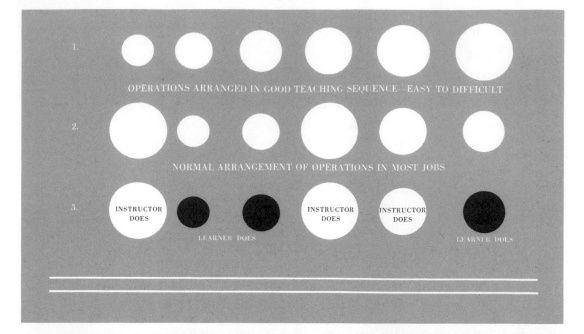

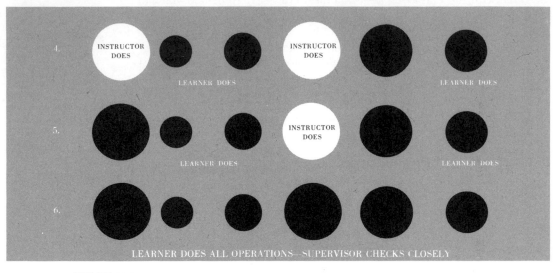

FIGURE 11-2.

Sequence for instructing the complex job. *(Courtesy of U.S. Air Force Department)* If a job can be taught by proceeding from the easy steps to the difficult, teaching becomes easier. Few jobs, however, have their working sequence arranged in an order of increasing difficulty as shown at the top of the chart. Instead, the difficult parts of the job are usually mixed in with the easy ones, like the second line on the chart. These steps have to be done on the job in the correct order and, therefore, they should be learned in that order. What can the supervisor-instructor do? He can keep the job in proper sequence and still teach the easier parts first by setting up his teaching plan as shown by the dark spots in each row of the chart. The instructor does the difficult or white spots while the worker does the easy or black spots; thus maintaining a learning sequence even in a difficult or long operation.

- *Don't be impatient.* Everyone can't learn as fast as you can. You must, therefore, give the beginner time to assimilate facts. Being an impatient instructor is one of the best ways to destroy a person's confidence and motivation—as well as to slow down the learning process. So be patient. Explain, explain, and explain again until everyone understands.

- *Don't make the employee tense.* This is the other side of the coin of patience. Tension breeds confusion, inhibits clear thinking, and virtually stops the learning process. Remember that the new employee has enough to be tense about without your adding even more to his tension. His mind is already confused by all he has been told in personnel, and he needs to be relaxed and clear-headed to assimilate the steps in the job. You should, therefore, put him at ease.

IS TRAINING WORTH THE EFFORT?

Yes—without question! In fact, business thinks that training is so worthwhile that it spent over $2 billion in 1977 to train employees. Numerous surveys have been made showing the impact that such training has had on various parts of a business enterprise. One survey, for example, showed that after a training program was completed, customer complaints dropped 24% and production rose 23%. Other areas, such as safety, employee absence, and turnover also showed improvements ranging from 6% to 45% after training programs had been conducted.

However, when top management approaches you as a supervisor and says, "Show me the value of your proposed training program and I'll give you the money for it," what do you say? What is your response?

It is hard to prove that a dollar spent on training returns more than a dollar in savings. Here are a few ways, however, that you can try to evaluate the effect of training programs.

One way is to get the opinions of employees who participate in the program. Get their opinions by interviews, or use questionnaires. Another approach is to measure the skill of employees before the program and then after the program. This can be done by giving them the same examination before and after. Of course if the program is to teach a skill such as using a typewriter, a before and after test would readily show the improvement. Many times, however, the purpose of training is to change an employee's attitude and behavior on the job, and this type of change can't really be measured. Tests might show that the employee has learned something, and the employee might say he liked the course, but he may not bring this new knowledge to the job.

*evaluating a
training program*

Another way to evaluate training is to compare an employee's work performance before and after training. For example, the amount and quality of work for salesmen, stenographers, production workers, and similar employees can be measured both before and after training to evaluate the effectiveness of the program. This is not a truly scientific way to evaluate a program, however, because we cannot be sure that an increase in output is due to the training program. It may instead be due to changes in economic conditions, better supervision, better production planning, and so on. If a salesman sells more after a program than before, is this because of the program or because economic conditions are better and customers have more money to spend? Or if he sells less after the program, is this because the training is no good?

The best way to make these comparisons is to compare the output of a group of employees who did not take the program, with the output of another group of employees who did take the training program. This might show, for example, that while an employee who took the course sold 10% less after the course, the sales of employees who did not take the course had declined 24%. This would show that the course had real value.

Other before-and-after information may be obtained from records of quality defects, employee turnover, grievances, cost, incentive earnings, absenteeism, and morale surveys. Most companies keep records of these factors, and comparisons before and after may give a strong indication of the value or the direction of a trend. The value of this measure, of course, depends on the adequacy of the records and the type of training provided.

A Case Study
THE SOUR WHISKEY

Bertie Lloyd answered the advertisement for a part-time waitress in the Sirloin Steak House. According to the advertisement, the job was a Tuesday-Thursday-Saturday job with hours from 4:00 P.M. to 10:00 P.M. This suited Bertie fine and allowed her to continue her schooling at the Monroe County Community College.

As she walked into the Steak House, she was impressed. "It was a first-class restaurant," she told her roommate, "and everything was so pretty and attractive." The manager asked her to fill out a brief application blank and then asked her if she had ever been a waitress before. When she replied that she hadn't, he told her not to worry. It was a simple job, he indicated, consisting of carrying food from the kitchen area to the customer. Tables were cleared and cleaned by bus boys, so the waitress's primary job was to wait on the customers.

Bertie asked about pay, and the manager told her it was $2.80 per hour plus the tips she earned. He hinted that some of the girls made an average of $6.00 per hour in tips, and that he believed Bertie could also. When he offered her the job, she took it and was told to report at 3:15 P.M. to be issued a uniform and be ready for work at 4:00 P.M.

Bertie was excited about her new job but wondered what kind of firm the Sirloin Steak House was. The manager had seemed friendly, but the interview was so brief. After reporting for work at 3:15 P.M. to get her uniform, one of the other girls took her to the employees' washroom and showed her where she could change clothes. When Bertie asked her for some advice on how to wait on tables, she replied, "There's nothing to it, Honey. Just smile, wink at the men, and wiggle when you walk."

Bertie wasn't sure where she was supposed to work, but one of the girls told her that she was responsible for tables eight through twelve. Bertie's first customer was a businessman who ordered a whiskey sour, a rare steak with french fries, a tossed salad, and coffee. When Bertie asked the cook for a "sour whiskey," he replied, "You're off your rocker? I don't cook sour whiskey!" When Bertie told the customer they didn't have any sour whiskey, he frowned at her and said in a loud voice, "What kind of a dame are you? I don't want sour whiskey! I want a whiskey sour!"

Hurt and confused, Bertie ran to the washroom in tears.

1. What changes would you suggest that the manager of the Steak House make in interviewing new employees for a job?
2. Do you think Bertie's orientation and training were adequate? What changes would you suggest?

A Case Study
MIDWEST OIL COMPANY

The Midwest Oil Company, with home offices in Dallas, operates in 32 of the 50 states. It is a progressive company and its management plans to have outlets in all states except Alaska within eight years.

Mr. B. C. Vawn is in charge of the company's retail outlets (service stations) in its midwest territory of Iowa, Missouri, Illinois, Indiana, and Ohio. In general, the company tries to locate a service station in every town of 15,000 or more population, but location also depends on competition, suitable site, potential for development, and the like.

Each of Midwest's service stations is leased or rented to a local manager. These units are somewhat autonomous and operate with minimum direct supervision. Indeed, each service station manager develops his business as he sees fit. Every station, of course, is required to sell Midwest's oil, gasoline, tires, batteries, and related products. However, additional products can be sold, and many stations carry a line of small home appliances such as toasters, mixers, electric ice cream freezers, etc. At company encouragement, most stations operate a service center where all types of minor automotive repairs are available. Most of these centers, for example, are prepared to give motor tune-ups, correct electrical troubles, reline brakes, balance and align wheels, grind valves, and install rings. Body repair and paint work, however, are not performed.

The manager of the company's station in Vancetown has notified Mr. Vawn that he will be leaving at the end of next month to accept a job as director of maintenance in a local manufacturing concern. The Vancetown station, located in an area with 88,000 population, is one of Midwest's most profitable and best stations. Situated at the intersection of two main highways, the station attracts a great deal of transient as well as local trade.

In terms of physical facilities, the station has eight islands (the raised concrete portion of a service station drive where gasoline pumps, oil, water facilities, etc. are situated) with four gasoline pumps on each island. In addition, the Vancetown station operates two wash pits, two grease racks, and one of the largest service centers, employing four full-time mechanics. With the exception of the service center, the station operates on a 24-hour basis. The Vancetown station is one of the company's largest and oldest retail outlets. Annual sales for the last ten years have climbed steadily and last year exceeded $780,000.

Finding the right man to replace the station manager has been difficult, but Mr. Vawn is encouraged by the background and record of one applicant, a Mr. Ralph Lewis. Lewis is a first-rate automotive mechanic who has been employed for the past twelve years with a local trucking firm. He has a good record with the company and at the present time is in charge of a fleet of twelve trucks, keeping them in tip-top running order. During his twelve years with the trucking firm, he has been the transmission mechanic, the tune-up specialist, and the front-end man.

1. If you were interviewing Ralph Lewis, what types of questions would you ask him? What facts would you need to know to make a decision about hiring him?
2. Do you think Mr. Vawn should employ Ralph Lewis as a manager? Why?
3. If he employed Lewis, what recommendations would you have for Mr. Vawn?

12
HOW TO HANDLE DISCIPLINE AND SETTLE GRIEVANCES

This chapter explains—

- The steps you should take to promote self-discipline
- The different types of disciplinary action
- How to handle complaints and grievances

If any one factor can make or break a supervisor, his actions in meting out discipline will be close to or at the top of the list. Thousands of workers go through life and are never a party to a grievance, but virtually everyone is subject to some form of discipline when they spoil some piece of work, break some rule, or have a run-in with another employee.

WHAT IS DISCIPLINE?

Most of us think of discipline as the use of authority to reprimand, to punish. This is one type of discipline. But discipline is far more than this. When we say that the Jones Company has good discipline, we mean that the workers understand and abide by the company's rules. In its broadest sense, discipline involves any action that attempts to generate compliance with rules and regulations. Thus, a training program to get employees to obey reasonable rules is one aspect of discipline. In this sense, then, discipline is the state of affairs that exists in a company. It is a condition that exists in a company where workers act according to recognized codes of behavior set forth by the organization. Discipline is good when employees willingly follow the company's rules and regulations. This is what the Navy calls a "taut ship."

"If any one factor can make or break a supervisor, the way he metes out discipline will be close to the top."

OH NO, MR. SILVERS, I LIKE WORKING FOR YOU FINE, BUT MY NEW JOB HAS A WINDOW WITH A VIEW.

HOW DOES DISCIPLINE RELATE TO MORALE?

Although closely related, discipline is not morale. As we have learned in Chapter 5, morale is a state of *mind*, an employee's attitude. Discipline, on the other hand, is a state of *affairs*, an employee's conduct. The two are closely linked, however, because the level of morale (the state of mind) affects the employee's conduct. When morale is high, we generally have fewer disciplinary problems than when morale is low. Of course, it is possible to have absolute compliance with rules and regulations—thus good discipline—but at the same time to have poor morale. When this condition exists, however, it is usually under strict conditions of fear and force such as could be found in a military unit or under dictatorial authority. So although morale and discipline are related, they are not the same thing.

a state of affairs

MUST SUPERVISORS DISCIPLINE EMPLOYEES?

Yes, but it's tough for most supervisors to apply the principle of sound discipline. In fact, most supervisors don't even think about discipline until they are faced by an infraction of a company rule. They know that discipline is one of their responsibilities, but they seem to ignore it until something happens that calls for corrective action. And then, in too many cases, they tend to jump in, show the employee who is boss, and clobber the guy.

Tough or not, it is the supervisor's responsibility to maintain control in his department. What every supervisor would like is for each employee to voluntarily follow company rules and regulations whether the supervisor is there or not. This can happen when the supervisor through sound leadership and expert teaching has developed a state of affairs where discipline is good—where there is self-discipline and self-control.

HOW DO YOU BUILD A CLIMATE FOR GOOD DISCIPLINE?

Good discipline grows out of a good work environment, a good state of morale, and a mutual feeling of respect, cooperation, and consideration. Virtually all the things we have discussed about human relations, communication, motivation, leadership, and supervision have an impact on the overall climate or work environment that influences employee behavior. If all these things have led to a positive work environment, then morale will be high, and self-discipline will be good. If the supervisor has generated a negative work environment, both morale and discipline will suffer.

need for disciplinary climate

It would be unrealistic, however, to say that just because the supervisor does everything right, all employees will be good and no one will ever break a rule. There is always something or someone that will require his

171

attention. Some rule will be bent or broken, and how he handles these infractions will determine how other employees will handle themselves.

WHAT IS SELF-DISCIPLINE?

Every supervisor would like to have his department run so that he would never have to reprimand anyone. He would like his employees to always do the right thing, to always do what needs to be done. In fact, he would like everything to run so smoothly that he would never have to use any discipline.

Almost everyone agrees that following instructions and generally accepted rules of conduct is a part of every employee's responsibility and a part of his job. Most employees, therefore, can be counted on to do their part, to *employee* get to work on time, to follow instructions, and to abide by company rules. *cooperation* This is self-discipline. When employees understand the rules and regulations and believe that they are not unreasonable, they will usually abide by them with little or no prompting. Rules are thus "self-enforced."

Supervisors, however, are the ones who have to generate the environment in which this state of self-discipline will exist. The employees must know that they will have the help and support of their supervisor as long as they abide by company rules and regulations in the performance of their assigned jobs. In addition to this, however, the supervisor must also set an example of self-discipline on his part for his employees to follow. A supervisor cannot expect his employees to impose self-discipline on themselves when he does not set the proper example. For example, the supervisor who comes to work with alcohol on his breath will have a hard time explaining to his employees why they shouldn't do likewise.

WHAT IS THE OBJECTIVE OF DISCIPLINE?

Although most employees are self-disciplined, it seems there are always one or two who try to get away with breaking company rules. These employees who refuse to be mature enough for self-discipline have to be handled by their supervisor.

Taking disciplinary action is an unpleasant task but one inherent in the supervisor's job. To avoid further infractions of company rules, the super-*the rule breaker* visor has to use his authority to take positive action to correct the rule breaker. If he doesn't, other employees who have a tendency to break rules may also move in that direction if they see that one person can "get away" with it.

The problem is what disciplinary action to take and how to take it. The objective of discipline is not to punish an employee or get even with him.

Instead, the purpose of disciplinary action is to improve the behavior of the offender so that the work environment in the department will be improved for all employees. The supervisor, therefore, should look upon a rule violation as an opportunity to help teach an employee to conduct himself in the proper way. The supervisor's problem is to choose a course of action that will teach the employee, as well as provide immediate corrective action.

WHAT STEPS SHOULD YOU TAKE TO PROMOTE A CLIMATE OF SELF-DISCIPLINE?

To promote a healthy climate of self-discipline, supervisors should follow several well-defined steps.

1. *Make sure that all employees are aware of and understand the rules.* This is such an obvious first step that many supervisors take for granted that "everyone knows this." But new employees, and sometimes even the older ones, have never heard of a particular rule until they break it. Some supervisors make it a practice to give all employees a copy of company rules and have them sign a statement that they have received, read, and understood the rules.

2. *Remain calm. Never lose your temper.* No matter how severe the violation, a supervisor should remain calm and in control. If he feels he is losing his "cool," then he should postpone action until he has regained his composure. How do you regain your composure? Hold your tongue and talk later. Do anything to stall for time. Tell the employee to meet you in your office in half an hour, or ask him to take a walk with you to your office or a rest area. Finally, remember that never, never in a fit of rage touch an employee. It may be misinterpreted as a punitive move.

3. *Investigate, get all the facts, before making any decision and taking any action.* A supervisor should not ignore a breach of company rules. If he does this, he is signaling to the other employees that he doesn't intend to enforce company rules and regulations. Neither should he go to the other extreme of moving in haste to take punitive or corrective action against a worker. Before he moves, before he does anything, the supervisor must get a clear picture of what happened and why the employee did it.

rules for taking disciplinary action

4. *Explain your actions.* Tell your employees why you decided the way you did.

5. *Take disciplinary action in private.* When corrective action is taken in public, the employee being censured will build up resentment over being chastised in public, and the situation may be blown all out of proportion to the infraction. The supervisor who reprimands in public also is asking for the other employees to serve as a "jury" to approve of his action. If they feel that the punishment doesn't fit the crime, that the supervisor was too severe, they will side with the employee. This

may lead to arguments with other employees and more disciplinary problems. Privacy, therefore, should be the rule for taking disciplinary action.

About the only exception to the privacy rule would be when an employee openly confronts a supervisor before the other employees. In this case, the supervisor would have to take quick and decisive action in front of the others or risk losing control of his department. If he fails to act decisively, he will lose his employees' respect, lose control, and do injury to the department's morale.

6. *Be consistent in enforcing the rules.* Rules were made for everyone to follow. Imagine the problem you would face if an employee approached you with the statement: "You didn't do anything to June when she was late last week. Why pick on me?" Of course, each violation doesn't call for the same punishment. Being consistent doesn't mean treating everyone in exactly the same way. It means that when an exception is made, it must be regarded as a valid exception by the employees. For example, the circumstances and conditions under which the incident took place and the employee's intent would influence and perhaps alter the type of reprimand. When June was late, it was because she had a flat tire. When Mildred was late, it was because she stayed in the ladies' lounge to grab another cigarette. Different reprimands would be called for here. One incident was an unintentional violation; the other willful. The consistency rule, therefore, means that under similar conditions and circumstances, the same type of reprimand should be used.

7. *Be firm but fair.* "Firm" doesn't mean getting tough or throwing your weight around. It means not being pushed around, holding to your position. "Fairness" applies to both the employee and the company. Being fair to an employee means being just. It includes explaining why the company has the rule, why the disciplinary action is being taken, and what the supervisor hopes the action will accomplish.

8. *Always express your confidence that the employee will not be involved again.* Remember that the objective of a reprimand is to teach, not to punish. A supervisor, therefore, should always show his employee that he is confident that the employee will correct his ways. Ending a disciplinary session on this positive note can help remove any bitterness or resentment that the employee feels.

9. *Tell the employee how to appeal your decision.* Don't hide company rules about appeal. Be sure to tell the employee that you won't hold it against him if he does appeal your decision—*and mean it!*

ARE THERE DIFFERENT STEPS IN DISCIPLINARY ACTION?

Yes. Many companies today are fostering the idea that discipline should be progressive in nature, moving in steps from a minor reprimand for the first offense to discharge as the final action. Step one in disciplinary action usually starts with an *informal talk* for the first offense or a relatively minor infraction of rules. It gives the supervisor the opportunity to discuss the employee's behavior in an informal, friendly way, emphasizing how well the employee performed in the past, how pleased he (the supervisor) has been with the employee's cooperation, but at the same time recognizing the employee's obligation to abide by the rules. If this friendly talk doesn't work, the next step is to recognize the violation and give the employee an oral reprimand.

The *oral reprimand*, step two, is firmer than the friendly informal talk. The supervisor is all business here, pointing out that the employee's behavior could lead to ultimate dismissal unless corrective action is taken. During the oral reprimand, the employee should be placed on notice by the supervisor that he will not tolerate continued violations, and that if they continue, the employee will be subject to more stringent disciplinary action.

A *written notice* is step three. This is a formal written warning that becomes a part of the employee's permanent record. It is a forthright statement of what the employee did and the consequences that he can expect from such an incident in the future. In unionized firms, this is an important step because it can serve as evidence in a grievance case.

progressive steps in discipline

If none of these steps have worked, the supervisor next tries step four, which is *disciplinary suspension*. In a disciplinary suspension the employee is laid off for several days or weeks, depending on the severity of his offense. Some employees don't respond to oral and written reprimands, but facing a Friday without a paycheck gives them a shock. They begin to recognize the seriousness of the situation and the need to comply with rules and regulations and will thus return to work with a better understanding of them. Suspension, however, doesn't always work like this. The employee may build up resentment while away from work and return in a more recalcitrant mood than when he left. For this reason, some companies refuse to use disciplinary suspension.

Finally, *discharge* is the last step in progressive disciplinary action. When an employee is discharged, the company loses a large investment in a skilled employee who knows the company. In addition to the loss of investment and of the employee, the company will have to replace the old employee with a new employee, which means an additional training expense as well as the expenses incurred in the disruption of production. Every reasonable step should be taken, therefore, to reconstruct and correct an employee's infractions before resorting to discharge.

Be sure, also, that you are on firm ground when you do fire an employee. In unionized companies, discipline and discharge are some of the most touchy actions you can take. Many times a "fired" employee has been returned to his job because his supervisor couldn't prove beyond a reasonable doubt that he (the employee) had broken a rule. Sometimes arbitrators will rule in favor of the employee because the supervisor did not give him fair warning that he would be fired if he continued his actions. The written notice is of value here. Finally, be sure that the crime warrants firing an employee. For example, would firing an employee be a just penalty for being one or two minutes late to work on several occasions? Firing could conceivably be justified in this case, but in all probability, some other type of punishment would be more appropriate.

HOW DO YOU TELL YOUR EMPLOYEES ABOUT COMPANY DISCIPLINARY POLICY?

Employees like to know in advance what the rules are and how they will be applied. The more they know, therefore, the better position they will be in to conduct themselves in accordance with the accepted rules of behavior in your company. This means you should post rules on bulletin boards, distribute them in printed form, and use any appropriate occasion to discuss them with your employees. Talking about rules is much more effective than posting them on bulletin boards or printing them in an employee handbook. As we saw in Chapter 3, oral face-to-face communication is the most effective method you can use. Thus, when rules are discussed, questions can be asked and employees can understand *why* the rules are needed. Knowing the rules in advance, the reason behind them, and the consequences of breaking them makes employees more receptive to abiding by them through self-discipline. Rules, therefore, should be fully discussed with employees as a part of their orientation.

talk about disciplinary policy

In addition, a supervisor should not hesitate to discuss a reprimand that he has given an employee. This is not to say that the supervisor should tell the whole department every time he reprimands an employee, but he should freely discuss the circumstances behind a severe reprimand such as laying off an employee for several weeks or actually firing him. Telling employees the facts will prevent erroneous speculation and grapevine talk about why the employee was fired and, at the same time, show that the supervisor was impartial and fair in the way he handled an infraction of the company's rules.

When an employee disagrees with a reprimand given him by his supervisor, he should have the right of recourse through a formal grievance procedure. In unionized companies, the steps in a grievance procedure are precise and well defined. These steps should also exist with the same degree of clarity in nonunionized organizations. The right of appeal is a real right and not just a formality, and supervisors should be mature and secure enough in their positions not to regard appeals as threats to their jobs. In like manner, supervisors should not tell an employee that he has the right to appeal to higher management and then hold it against the employee if he does. Employees are human and need the right to appeal what they consider to be an injustice. The supervisor who disciplines his employees properly will usually find his actions are upheld by his own superiors.

Handling grievances is just as much a part of your job as a supervisor as is the hiring of employees. Sometimes grievances can be so technical that you may feel more like a labor lawyer than a supervisor. Yet the skill with which you handle grievances is a direct measure of your ability to supervise.

At one time or another, each of us has complained or expressed dissatisfaction with some turn of events. These are not grievances; they are merely expressions of dissatisfaction. Grievances are complaints that have been *formally registered* with the employee's supervisor or some other management official in accordance with the recognized grievance procedures. Grievances usually arise when an employee thinks he has been done an injustice. Maybe nothing wrong has been done, but if an employee *thinks* he has been treated wrongly, he can file a grievance.

The beginning of a grievance is an employee's expression of some complaint or dissatisfaction. The complaint may be either real or imagined, but from the employee's point of view, it is real. Supervisors who brush aside such complaints as "routine gripes" are asking for them to be blown up eventually into full-size grievances. The sensitivity by a supervisor to this possibility means that he recognizes the key role that he plays at this point in preventing grievances. Frustration, anger, and hard feelings are at a minimum at this point, and now is the best time to reach a mutually satisfactory solution.

dissatisfaction vs grievance

If, however, the parties are unable to reach a satisfactory understanding at this beginning point, then the employee typically puts his grievance in writing to the supervisor. At this stage, the supervisor has to formally recognize and answer the grievance. The problem is still one between the employee and his supervisor. However, if the supervisor's answer is not satisfactory to the employee, he may then start formal grievance machinery, which takes the problem out of the hands of the employee and his supervisor. How the grievance is handled then depends on whether or not the company is unionized, and this will be discussed in the next two sections.

WHAT ARE THE GRIEVANCE PROCEDURES IN NONUNIONIZED COMPANIES?

Many companies have a published grievance procedure that guarantees an employee the right to file a grievance and to have it follow well-defined steps up to the top man. Company policy may further stipulate that employees who file grievances can do so without any fear of reprisal. Few if any employees, however, avail themselves of this procedure because they are keenly aware of the indirect means available to their supervisors to "get even" with employees who cross them—especially those employees who formally complain and thus question the wisdom and capacity of the supervisor.

steps in filing a grievance

Retaliation of this sort by supervisors may take the form of withholding a deserved merit increase, bypassing the employee for a promotion, consistently assigning the employee to undesirable jobs, or ultimately firing the employee on some other trumped-up charge. What can top management do to avoid this and make sure that an employee does get a fair shake?

First, be sure to have a written grievance procedure. Employees may not use it, but at least they know that management wants to be fair.

Second, set up some anonymous means for the employee to air his grievances. This may take such forms as a committee that airs grievances given to it anonymously, open meetings where "problems" can be discussed in a nonpersonal way, or a community board or committee made up of disinterested third parties with the authority to resolve grievances. In each instance, what management is trying to do is enable an employee to get his grievance aired without prejudice and possible retaliation. Unions have been able to secure this guarantee for their members by getting precise steps written into their labor contracts.

HOW ARE GRIEVANCES HANDLED IN UNIONIZED COMPANIES?

One of the first people to be contacted concerning grievances in unionized companies is the shop steward. His function is to represent the employee in any complaints or grievances that he might have against the company. The shop steward is a specialist, well trained to prepare and present a grievance. In dealing with these union stewards, supervisors would do well to remember not to lose their tempers with them, not to ridicule, bluff, or make threats to them, not to stall or try to slow down the process, and not to make statements they aren't prepared to back up with facts.

from supervisor to arbitrator

If the employee and his supervisor are unable to reach a satisfactory agreement, the next step is usually for the employee and his union representative to present the grievance in writing to the next higher authority. At this level, usually a superintendent or division manager reviews the case and either supports or reverses the decision of the supervisor. If the boss supports the supervisor's decision, the grievance may be carried to top management.

When grievances get this far, usually the best of the union's grievance handlers represents the employee. This might be the chief steward, the president of the union, the business agent, or a designated grievance committee. The case is typically heard by the plant manager, general manager, or president of the company. The case proceeds with the company's labor relations staff and the union's grievance specialists involved in hearing evidence, presenting arguments, and conducting discussions. The top manager who must make a decision at this point must weigh the effects on the entire organization of supporting or reversing the decision. It is now a total company problem and not just a departmental or divisional one. As was indicated previously, this level is the last "court of appeal" in a nonunionized company. However, in a unionized company, if the case is not resolved in favor of the union, then the union may take any grievance to arbitration if it wishes to.

Arbitration consists of referring the case to a disinterested third party for a hearing and a decision. Most union contracts specify arbitration as the final step in the settlement of a dispute. An arbitrator, approved by both union and management, is chosen, and both sides agree in advance to abide by his decision.

The arbitrator conducts a hearing, similar in many respects to a court of law. It is not unusual for both sides to be represented by legal counsel at the hearing. Charges are made, witnesses are called, statements are heard, and the arbitrator weighs the evidence and renders a decision. The supervisor at this point has no control over the process other than to watch it and hope that his initial decision will be affirmed.

Sometimes union agreements stipulate that conciliation may be used. A conciliator makes no judgments and renders no decisions. His only role is to help both parties find a common ground on which an agreement can be reached. If the conciliator fails, then the only recourse is through the courts or the National Labor Relations Board.

HOW SHOULD YOU HANDLE COMPLAINTS?

Every supervisor will get some gripes and complaints from his men, no matter how good a job he does. In fact, many management experts agree with the Army saying that "a happy soldier is a bitching soldier." When employees don't express complaints, many take this to be a sign of suppression, indicating that the employees are afraid to speak out. In the best-managed companies, therefore, you can expect a number of employee complaints. Try as hard as you like, you can't satisfy everybody. You'll have some complaints no matter what you do.

When you get a complaint, however, the way you handle it may prevent it from becoming a grievance, moving through the steps we have just covered. If you want to do a good job in handling the complaint, be sure to remember the following:

1. *Never ignore a gripe or complaint.* Don't think that if you ignore a trouble spot, it will go away. Don't think that if you soft-soap an employee, he will forget his complaint and live happily ever after. It doesn't work that way. An unsettled complaint continues to simmer in an employee until it reaches the boiling point. He'll gripe to his friends and fellow workers, and they'll probably agree with him. This is when you'll have trouble—when you ignore a small complaint and thus allow it to fester into a major problem.

2. *Be tactful.* Don't dismiss the employee by telling him he has no basis for complaining.

3. *If you are in error, admit it.* Correct the circumstances surrounding the complaint, admit your error, and offer an apology.

4. *Don't try to laugh off a complaint.* This could change a complaint into a grievance, and a mad employee into a furious one.

5. *Treat the employee and his complaint as being serious and important.* Never brush a complaint aside with a "so what" attitude. Even if you know there is no basis for the complaint, the employee thinks there is. Therefore, if it is important enough for the employee to bring it to your attention, it should be treated as an important complaint by you.

6. *Don't withhold any concessions.* Concede any point that you can.

7. *Listen carefully.* Listening carefully to an employee's complaint not only shows respect for him, it may also enable you to find out what is really bugging him. A typist may be complaining about her typewriter when her real complaint is that the file clerk upsets her and causes her to make typing errors. Listen carefully, therefore, to what is being said, and listen for hidden meanings.

8. *If an apology is called for, do so immediately.* Better to apologize for a complaint now than have it grow into a grievance later.

9. *Don't lose your temper.* When you're upset, you lose control. You don't think clearly. You may react hastily. Stay calm, therefore. If you feel yourself getting angry, delay the discussion until later in the day. But set a time to resume it.

10. *Don't decide until you have all the facts.* Although you may feel under pressure to render a quick decision, don't answer the complaint until you have investigated both sides. Get the facts—all the facts. And get them straight before you make a decision. Only then will you be in a position to make a sound decision. "Decide in haste, repent in leisure" holds true here. Remember that a small complaint and your hasty decision may become a major grievance.

11. *Speak to the problem.* When you answer a complaint, get to the heart of the matter. Answer the complaint head on. Don't try to avoid unpleasantness by talking all around the problem but never speaking to it. Be specific and definite in your answer. Make your statement so there can be no mistake in what you mean.

12. *Explain why.* Always tell an employee why you made the decision you did. Whether you agree or disagree with the employee, explain why you took the stand you did. If you can't explain the logic in your decision, you had better think it through again before you give it.

13. *Express confidence.* Every complaint isn't going to be settled in favor of the employee. "Yes" answers give you no trouble, but when you say "no," you'll need all of your administrative skills to make the employee understand and accept your decision in good spirit. After you've ex-

plained your decision to him, you should express confidence that he will accept the decision in the spirit it was made. Appeal to his reasoning, his sense of fair play, and his belief in equal treatment. Try to make him see the reason for your decision and agree to give it a try.

14. *Be fair, just, and honest.* Be sure that your decision takes into account both sides of the issue. Above all, don't play favorites. Get the facts, weigh them, then render an equitable decision that is fair and just to both parties. This can't be emphasized too much. Don't take sides. Get the employee's point of view clearly in mind before you make a decision. If you really understand his complaint, maybe you will make the decision in his favor. Don't hesitate to change your mind when the facts support it, but don't horse-trade. Be fair.

15. *Always be available to your employees.* Don't be afraid to listen to complaints. "A stitch in time, saves nine" was never truer than when it applies to nipping grievances in the bud. Keep an open door.

HOW CAN YOU AVOID COMPLAINTS AND GRIEVANCES?

Most complaints and grievances center around three areas:

1. Discipline.
2. Problems of promotion, seniority, layoff, etc.
3. Problems dealing with work assignments and job evaluation.

These are the areas you'll need to be extra careful with. Remember, too, that complaints and grievances are frequently symptoms of some other real problem. The symptom may be a backache; the problem may be a slipped disc. The symptom in a company may be that employee turnover is high. The problem may be that the employees don't think they are getting a fair shake in promotions and transfers.

Handle all matters pertaining to these three areas with particular care, with real caution, and with the utmost fairness. On all matters pertaining to these areas of sensitivity, be sure to keep your employees informed. Let them know in advance what changes are coming up and *why* they are being *keep employees* made. If you are going to have changes in raw materials, in methods, work- *informed* ing conditions, incentive pay, hours of work, and so on, tell the employees about these changes far in advance and tell them why. A thumping noise in the middle of the night may be frightening. But when you know the facts— that it is a limb being blown against the window—the noise is of no concern. A shift in hours of work may be frightening (Are we going on short time? Will I be fired?), but when you know the facts (The company is starting a new project on a second shift), the shift in hours is of little concern.

Finally, be alert and sensitive to any situation that might cause a grievance. Recognize the breeding ground, and then correct the situation.

Perhaps the best way to recognize these trouble spots is by looking at what has happened to your department in the past. Where have most complaints come from? What have most of the complaints been about? When you get a complaint that is out of the ordinary, poke around to see if a similar situation might exist elsewhere in your department. In other words, be on the lookout for trouble and trouble spots. The driver who watches out for trouble is less likely to have an accident than the driver who goes down the road looking neither to the left or the right.

A Case Study
HAZEL FRANCISCO'S PUNISHMENT

Hazel Francisco had worked for six weeks as a punch-press operator in a medium-size manufacturing firm. She liked her job but felt that the safety trip on the press slowed down her work so much that she couldn't earn more than 5 or 6% incentive pay. One of her fellow employees said that if she tied down the safety trip, the press would work faster and she could earn more pay. Hazel tried it and it worked.

A couple of days later, her supervisor happened to pass by when she had the safety trip tied down, and he really "let her have it" for tinkering with the machine. She was so overcome by his language and his ranting and raving that she didn't say anything.

When he left, she stopped her press and went to the restroom for a few minutes to "recover" from her bawling out. When she got back, her supervisor was standing by her press and "let her have it" again for being away from her job during work hours. This was too much for Hazel who was conscientious and tried to do a good job. She started to cry, and at that, the supervisor told her if she couldn't stay at her work place and work, he would find another person who could. With tears running down her face, Hazel started the press and began work. She ruined eight out of the next ten pieces she tried, at which her supervisor sent her home without pay for the remainder of the day.

When Hazel returned to work the following morning, she reported all this to her union steward who said that she had grounds for complaint and that she should immediately file a grievance. Hazel didn't want to make trouble. She liked her job and had about decided to drop the whole matter when her supervisor came by and said he hoped she had "learned her lesson" yesterday. That did it for Hazel. She decided right then to file a formal grievance with the company over the way she had been treated.

1. Do you think Hazel was justified in filing a grievance?
2. Do you think the supervisor was justified in taking the actions he did?
3. How should the supervisor have handled the situation? What did he do wrong?

A Case Study
DELWAY VACUUM CLEANER COMPANY

The Delway Vacuum Cleaner Company manufactured and distributed vacuum cleaners on a nationwide basis. Sales were made directly to consumers through field representatives. These representatives were not salesmen on a commission but were employees of the company who received a straight salary plus an annual bonus based on company profits and individual sales. The Delway Company was an old and reliable firm of 31 years, and its product was well established in the market. Because of its standing in the field and the fact that its representatives were not "salesmen" in the strictest sense, the company had a strict rule against an employee's selling any other product, even noncompetitive ones.

Norman Ellerbe came to work for the company in 1970 and was given the Dallas-Forth Worth territory. In 1975 the district manager, Mr. Purvis, called on Mr. Ellerbe and indicated that his sales volume had not been keeping up with the increases in the comparable territories of Houston and San Antonio. Mr. Ellerbe was somewhat surprised to hear this, but indicated that he would attempt to do better.

In March 1976, Mr. Purvis wrote Mr. Ellerbe indicating once again his dissatisfaction with Mr. Ellerbe's sales volume. He indicated that the dollar volume in comparable districts had increased an average of 97% since 1975 and that Mr. Ellerbe's volume had increased only 72%. His letter was rather strongly worded, and he implied that if improvements were not forthcoming, the company would have to take "appropriate action." Mr. Ellerbe replied that he did not understand why his sales were apparently lagging behind other districts because he was calling on housewives and demonstrating the cleaners in the manner prescribed by the company. In fact, he indicated that he was making 18% more calls per day than the company recommended.

In January 1977, Mr. Hoffman, the division superintendent for the Delway Company, wrote Mr. Ellerbe, with a copy to Mr. Purvis, indicating that his sales were unsatisfactory and that unless he increased his sales by 20% within the next six months, the company would be forced to take "appropriate steps" to rectify the situation.

At this point Mr. Ellerbe called on his union representative, told him the facts, and asked if the company could arbitrarily fire (as they had implied) an employee because his average was 25% below other supposedly comparable territories. The union representative was incensed over the threats made to Ellerbe and stated he would immediately contact Mr. Hoffman.

When the union representative called on Mr. Hoffman, he was shown that quarterly sales of employees in comparable areas had now increased by over 123% since 1975, whereas Mr. Ellerbe's still lagged with only a 90% increase. Furthermore, Mr. Hoffman had just discovered that Mr. Ellerbe had been working at night selling aluminum cooking utensils and electric food mixers. When asked about these facts, Ellerbe indicated that he had worked eight to ten hours per day selling vacuum cleaners, that he was unable to meet his family expenses from his income, and that out of necessity he had started selling the other items on his free time in the evenings as a "second job." The union representative then pointed out that Mr. Ellerbe had been with the company since 1970, that he had performed long and faithful service, and that the company's rules had not been infringed upon inasmuch as Mr. Ellerbe had sold the other items on his own time. The meeting adjourned at this point, and this is where the matter now rests.

1. What actions should have been taken by Mr. Purvis? Why?
2. Should Hoffman have been called into the act? Why?
3. What decision would you recommend to Hoffman? Why?

13
USING PERFORMANCE EVALUATION

This chapter explains—

- How and when performance evaluation should be used
- How to conduct evaluation interviews
- How evaluation can help you with promotions

$\mathbf{A}$ll of us continuously size up things in our daily lives. We are always forming opinions about people, products, advertisements, and so on. Many times we do this unconsciously. We know that we "like" a product or a person without having gone through any systematic evaluation procedure. However, if we are selecting someone to build a house or take out our appendix, we usually exercise a little more care in our judgment.

Like it or not, as a supervisor you will be called on constantly to evaluate your employees for various reasons. It may be for a possible transfer, for a promotion, for enrollment in a training school, or for a pay increase. How should you make the evaluation? By intuition? Hunch? Spur-of-the-moment reactions? Hopefully, you will do it by using some systematic, carefully thought-out process where the employee will be given a fair shake.

When a supervisor uses some formalized system of evaluation, he is showing an interest in an employee's potential for training and development. Using a formal approach, the supervisor observes the worker's behavior and skill, and records these observations as well as the employee's potential on a sheet of paper that is placed in the employee's personnel folder. This along with other evidence is used to determine an employee's potential for future promotions, for pay increases, and the like. So important is this careful evaluation of employees that about half of the major companies today have some formal system of employee performance evaluation.

WHAT IS PERFORMANCE EVALUATION?

Performance evaluation consists of a systematic appraisal of the employee's performance and of his potential for development and training. The evalua-

"Supervisors are called on constantly to evaluate employees."

tion is usually done by the employee's immediate supervisor and is then reviewed by the supervisor's superior. Such evaluations are used to determine an employee's level of performance on his job. Supervisors usually go over the evaluation with the employee, pointing out strengths and indicating areas that need improvement. In areas where the employee needs improvement, the supervisor can suggest training programs or formal courses in which the employee can enroll. Performance evaluations are usually made on an annual basis and are used to help make decisions about transfers, promotions, salary increases, and even layoffs.

rating an employee's performance

WHAT METHODS OF EVALUATION ARE COMMONLY USED?

Many performance evaluation methods have been developed and used over the years. The best known and most commonly used ones, however, are rating scales, employee comparison, and essay. Inasmuch as these methods are the ones typically found in business, let's take a closer look at each of them.

Rating-Scale Method. Using the rating-scale method, the supervisor is given a printed form for each person with the characteristics or traits to be rated listed on the form. Such things as quality and quantity of work, job knowledge, dependability, cooperativeness, industry, and initiative are listed on a scale on a form such as the one shown in Figure 13-1. The superior places a check on the scale at the spot he thinks best describes the employee's abilities. The rating-scale method is easy to understand and use, and with numerical values assigned to the scale, employees are easy to compare by their numerical scores.

evaluation techniques

Comparison Method. With the employee comparison method, the supervisor ranks all of his employees on the basis of their overall job performance and value. Starting at the top, he lists his best employee, then second best, and so on until the last man on the list is the worst employee. Using this method, someone must be chosen as the best and someone as the poorest employee. This method does have some disadvantages because it's difficult to compare every individual with every other individual. Therefore, in some ranking methods, employees are ranked as being in the top third, middle third, and lowest third instead of being ranked individually. Thus, the supervisor can say that Janie ranks in the top third of his employees (she is among the best employees), whereas Hank is in the middle third. Using this approach, no attempt is made to rank a person as "the best" or the "second best" and so on.

Essay Method. The essay method of evaluation uses no scales or ranking of employees. Instead, the supervisor simply writes down his impressions of each employee on a sheet of paper. His comments can be general in nature

EMPLOYEE EVALUATION

Name _____

Department _____ Section _____

Supervisor _____ Date _____

_____

    Please rate each employee in your section on the traits or qualities listed below. Following each trait is a line with points along it to serve as a rating scale. The phrases beneath the line indicate the number of points that will be awarded to the trait rated. Rate your employee by checking at any point on the line the position that best evaluates your employee.

_____

JOB KNOWLEDGE

0	5	10	15	20
Gaps in knowledge of a critical nature	Understands only routine aspects of job	Is well informed on all aspects of job	Has better than average knowledge of all aspects of job	Superior understanding of job; well informed

QUALITY OF WORK

0	5	10	15	20
Quality is unsatisfactory	Quality not quite up to standard	Quite satisfactory	Quality superior to typical employee	Quality exceptionally high

QUANTITY OF WORK

FIGURE 13-1.
A portion of an employee evaluation form—used in the rating-scale method.

or grouped under such headings as cooperativeness, job knowledge, performance, etc. This method requires a lot of thought and care on the part of the supervisor and is quite time-consuming. Some people can write better and more convincingly than others. Therefore, if the supervisor is not a good writer, his employees may suffer by comparison with those rated by a supervisor who is an excellent writer.

WHAT FLAWS SHOULD BE WATCHED FOR IN EVALUATING EMPLOYEES?

No matter how much care the supervisor gives to evaluating his employees, the results frequently reflect the supervisor's biases and weaknesses. The *halo effect*, for example, appears when a supervisor lets the rating he assigns one characteristic affect the rating he gives the employee's other characteristics. He may say the employee is average in his job skill, for example, and then have a tendency to rate everything else about the employee as average.

Also, watch for a tendency to be either too *lenient* or too *strict*. Some supervisors are easy raters. Others are tough. It's difficult to decide on which of two employees to promote when each of them has been rated by a different supervisor—one tough and one lenient in his appraisal.   *evaluation flaws*

Because some supervisors don't know their employees well enough, they don't want to go out on a limb and say anyone is either superior or poor. Therefore, they *rank everyone as average.* Supervisors who do this reason that they're not hurting anyone—but they're not helping the deserving ones either.

Watch for *personal bias.* A supervisor sometimes unconsciously rates an employee according to whether or not he personally likes him. This is particularly true for employees like color inspectors in textile mills where performance is difficult to measure and evaluate.

The *end use* of appraisals also materially affects the way supervisors rate average employees. If the supervisor knows the appraisals are to be used for wage increases, the ratings will tend to be higher than normal so that the employee will get a pay increase. If they are to be used to determine whether or not the employee needs training in an area, they are apt to be a little on the low side.

HOW CAN YOU MAKE AN EVALUATION OBJECTIVE?

Insofar as possible, every effort should be made by the supervisor to base every evaluation on the context of the employee's overall job and on the employee's total job performance. Basing a rating on only one aspect of an employee's performance or on the way he performed on a particular job would not be fair. Instead, the appraisal should be based on the total record of what the employee has done, how well he has performed, his total reliability, his overall skill, his resourcefulness, and so on. We all recognize that evaluations aren't perfect, but with some thought and work on the supervisor's part, they can be fairly objective and can serve useful ends in rewarding and motivating employees.

HOW SHOULD YOU CONDUCT THE EVALUATION INTERVIEW?

After the performance evaluation has been made, the second step is to review the rating with the employee. This is perhaps the toughest problem a supervisor faces in the appraisal process. When poorly handled, these interviews can be difficult and can lead to misunderstandings and hostility. It takes planning, skill, and practice to develop the sensitivity needed to tell an employee how he is doing on his job. The supervisor, therefore, should take every opportunity to prepare for this type of interview through classroom study and practice.

The interview itself should be held fairly soon after the evaluation takes place. The supervisor should assure the employee that the purpose of the appraisal is *not* to criticize the employee but to help him improve himself so that he will be in a position to be upgraded, thus helping himself and the organization. Prior to the interview, some supervisors even hand the employee a rating form and ask him to rate himself. This gives the employee a feeling for the difficulty one experiences in rating individuals and also gives the supervisor an insight as to how the employee feels about his own ability. Usually the employee will rate himself lower than the supervisor does, which makes the interview easier.

The thrust of the interview should be for the supervisor to review the progress the employee has made since he was last evaluated. Areas in which the employee has made real improvement should be pointed out, and the employee should be complimented. In areas where progress has not been shown, the supervisor should make constructive suggestions for improvement. These should be specific suggestions such as courses to enroll in, where they are taught, when and how to enroll, and so on.

One common mistake that some supervisors make is to take a salesmanship approach as though trying to sell an employee on his need for improvement. The employee is in a precarious position and can't very well argue with the supervisor's rating and his suggested improvement. He may outwardly agree to the "sale," but inwardly the employee may have no thought of changing his behavior.

reviewing the employee appraisal

An interview is almost always doomed to failure when the supervisor saves up a list of shortcomings and unloads them on the employee during the interview. A whole list of shortcomings at one time overwhelms an employee and puts him on the defensive. Instead of focusing on failures, the best approach is to focus on goals and a mutual agreement on the goals to be reached during the next period.

During the interview the supervisor should stress the fact that an evaluation was made of every employee, using the same standards of performance, and that no one was singled out for special study—no one was treated any differently from the others. If the employee shows any interest, the supervisor should show him how his rating was developed, what factors were considered, and how each one was related to the actual job demands. This is important for the employee who doesn't get a high rating and wants to know why. It is likewise important for the employee who gets a good rating, so that he can understand and appreciate the care with which his good work was appraised.

The evaluation interview should give the employee an opportunity to discuss his job problems and aspirations with his supervisor, as well as give the supervisor the opportunity to help the employee become a better worker. Questions should be answered truthfully, fully, and tactfully. Each employee's reactions and questions will be different, of course, and the supervisor will have to be a practiced and skillful interviewer to accomplish his mission with skill and sensitivity.

Finally, the supervisor should make sure that the employee clearly understands his rating and that there are no unanswered questions. The supervisor and the employee should both agree on some mutually established goals that will help the employee become a more useful individual. Given the proper encouragement, most employees will emerge from an evaluation interview with renewed vigor and determination to do a better job.

WHAT ARE THE BENEFITS OF AN EVALUATION PROGRAM?

Several advantages can be realized from using an employee evaluation program:

1. You have a permanent written record of the relative strengths and weaknesses of your employees, which can be used for salary changes, promotions, transfers, demotions, etc.

2. It forces you to evaluate an employee's performance and potential— forces you as a supervisor to analyze the strengths and weaknesses of each of your employees. Thus, you know them better, thereby putting you in a position to do a better job as a supervisor.

3. In case of contention over promotion, pay, and the like, you have a sound basis for your decision.

*need for
evaluation*

4. Once an employee comes to understand some of his weaknesses, he will be stimulated to set goals to improve himself.

5. Areas in which training is needed become more obvious, and training courses can be set up.

6. An individual employee's talents are more apt to be recognized and used where they are most needed in the organization.

7. The evaluation serves to help eliminate employees being poorly placed or misplaced.

WHAT ARE SOME TIPS ON EMPLOYEE EVALUATIONS?

1. Never let employees evaluate or rate each other. This is management's job and should be done only by a member of the supervisory staff.

2. Never discuss one employee's rating with another employee.

3. Evaluate the employee's performance at least once a year. Twice a year is better. If you wait too long, you forget. If you rate too often, you see day-to-day occurrences instead of the overall picture.

4. Measure an employee's skill against what the job requires, not what you think he can do. An employee may be an excellent typist but a very poor file clerk. If his job is to type only, measure his skills against the typing job only.

5. Take plenty of time for the evaluation interview. Tell the employee how well (or how poorly) you think he is doing; then give him plenty of time to ask questions about your opinions and tell you what he thinks.

6. Always include a discussion of goals and mutually agreed upon improvement programs for the next appraisal period.

7. Don't terminate an interview until you have cleared up all misunderstandings about the present rating, future goals, and what the employee can expect.

8. Be honest and candid in your appraisal. If an employee's work has been bad, say so. Then help him see where and how it can be improved.

9. Soften your criticism by saying something positive. You might, for example, say, "Mary, you are one of our best typists and I appreciate all of your efforts. However, you tend to neglect your filing and sometimes misfile items. Do you think you can do something to improve yourself there? If you get to the point where you can file as well as you can type, you'll be headed for a top secretarial job!"

10. Follow up interviews by subsequently checking with your employees on how they are performing, the progress they are making, and what their problems are. This show of interest on your part can serve as a stimulus for the employees to strive for improvement.

Yes. Every time a supervisor changes an employee from one job to another, he should be able to back up his action by a well-executed employee evaluation. Let's see why this is true.

Supervisors frequently make decisions that affect the pay of their employees as well as their placement, promotion, demotion, or discharge. Which is better—that all of these critical personnel actions be based on spur-of-the-moment decisions or that they be based on carefully thought-out judgments formulated in a systematic way? The answer is obvious. If the supervisor wishes to be fair, equitable, and just—and if the company wishes to protect its employees from arbitrary decisions—then such changes should be based on a well-executed performance evaluation.

Inasmuch as supervisors make such decisions, decisions that vitally affect their employees' jobs, the question is not *whether* the supervisors need to evaluate their employees' performances, but *how* they will do it. The overwhelming vote by most supervisors is for some formalized system incorporating either rating scales, employee comparisons, or essay evaluations. These systems, they have found, provide the most accurate estimate of an employee's capacity and value and, at the same time, provide the employee with the greatest protection against arbitrary decisions. Using performance evaluation, supervisors can move or promote employees from one job to another with greater assurance that the moves are fair and just for the employees as well as for the company.

for justice and fairness

WHY DOES AN EMPLOYEE NEED TO BE MOVED TO A NEW JOB?

You may need to move an employee to a new job either because you made an error in judgment in placing him in his original job or because you want to promote him.

Regardless of the care exercised in selecting and hiring employees, some mistakes will be made. Maybe the selection process was faulty. Perhaps a tight labor market made you accept an employee who would otherwise be rejected.

The job itself may not prove to be as challenging as the employee originally thought. There may be personality clashes. Or an opportunity for a promotion to a better job may open up. These are just a few of the reasons that employees are moved from one job to another within a company. Whatever the reasons, you should be certain that you select the right employee for the promotion or move.

SHOULD YOU PROMOTE FROM WITHIN?

Yes. Promotion from within the company is a great morale booster and provides a strong incentive for employees to perform better and upgrade themselves.

As you know, a promotion is the reassignment of an employee to a job of higher rank and higher pay. Most enlightened companies today follow the practice of promoting their own employees to better jobs rather than hiring outsiders to fill these vacancies. When companies don't promote from within, their employees suspect that better jobs will be reserved for outsiders, and as a consequence there is little motivation for them to work harder to develop themselves and to improve their job skills.

a morale booster For the company, promotion from within means having an old hand on the payroll who knows the company and its regulations and obviously wants to work for it, instead of some new employee who may not work out well. Promotion from within also means a better selection and placement process because management knows more about an old employee than it could ever learn about a new applicant. Promoting its own employees is important to the company because it means that in the new position, the employee can render a greater, more valuable service to the company. And finally, promoting from within lets the employee know that the company recognizes ability and rewards successful accomplishment. This spurs employee interest in training programs and in self-development in preparation for an eventual promotion.

WHO SHOULD GET A PROMOTION?

Some employees don't want to be promoted. They are happy where they are and don't want to disturb their routine by learning a new job. These employees place greater value on their leisure and freedom from pressure than they do on the status and added income of a bigger job. Other employees refuse to be promoted to a supervisory status because they find they cannot be responsible for what others do, because they are unwilling to give up the security of the union and being in a bargaining unit, or because they know their limitations and recognize that they would probably fail on a more demanding job.

performance vs seniority However, for those employees wanting promotions, we like to think that the person with the highest performance evaluation gets the job. But this is not always true. Sometimes a person who can adequately do the job and has the longest service with the company gets the job. He may not be the best qualified of all employees, but he can do the job, so the decision is made on the basis of seniority. Unions usually press for seniority as a basis for promotions because they feel that employees who have invested the greatest time should have the opportunity for the better jobs.

Promotion on the basis of seniority offers several advantages:

1. Seniority rights provide an employee with a greater sense of security. As he progresses in years, he is more comfortable with the knowledge that his job rights pertaining to promotion opportunities as well as to layoffs will be in accordance with seniority.

2. When a supervisor knows that promotions will be made on the basis of seniority, he will probably take more thought and care in initially selecting and hiring a new employee, thus getting a better man to begin with.

3. Knowing that the employee will probably stay with the company and be promoted, the supervisor will take greater efforts to provide training opportunities and suggest training programs that will better equip the employee so that when he is chosen for promotion on the basis of seniority, he *is* the best qualified for the job.

4. Promotions based on seniority serve to reward long and faithful service to the company, and therefore encourage good employees to stay rather than "job-hop."

5. Seniority promotions eliminate virtually all the grounds for dissension and resentment. Supervisors cannot be accused of favoritism or discrimination.

ARE THERE PROBLEMS WITH SENIORITY PROMOTIONS?

Problems can arise from promotions based on seniority:

1. Employees who are less competent, or even incompetent, may be pushed into a position because of seniority. Training under these conditions is undertaken in a perfunctory way, and the worker stays in the new job despite his poor performance.

2. Supervisors are reluctant to discharge or demote the senior man, arguing that his lack of capacity should have been noted long ago and that he should have been fired *then*, not *now*.

3. Most employees feel that they have a "right" to a new job based on seniority, and a discharge or demotion would be a blow to the morale and confidence of the other employees. Thus the marginal employee is kept in the job, and the company is not getting its money's worth.

morale and seniority

4. Well-qualified, aggressive employees with high-performance evaluations may leave the company or may have their morale seriously harmed by seeing the marginal employee get pushed ahead for no reason except seniority.

5. When qualified employees tend to leave the organization, it may find itself composed of largely marginal employees of questioned competence.

6. Seniority promotions may destroy incentives for study, self-improvement, and excellent performance. "Why bother to excel," employees say, "when all you have to do is stick around and eventually move up?"

SHOULD PROMOTIONS BE BASED ON ABILITY OR SENIORITY?

The supervisor has the responsibility to staff each position with the best man available if he expects to run his department in the most effective manner possible. Thus, when an employee extends his abilities through self-study and experience and thereby becomes the best qualified man for the job, many people think they should be rewarded by being moved to the higher ranking job. This is not to say that seniority should be entirely disregarded in the move. What is being said is that the supervisor should use seniority only to give the edge to the employee who has substantially the same qualifications for the job as another employee who has less service. Promoting the marginal employee strictly on seniority is an open invitation to possible stagnation, regression, even failure.

the best qualified

Sometimes the supervisor's hands are tied by a union contract that stipulates promotion should be on the basis of seniority. Most contracts, however, specify that it doesn't have to be *the* senior employee who gets promoted, but the senior employee who *has the capacity* to do the job. The problem is proving lack of capacity. Careful employee appraisals and adequate records that prove abilities and skills can be a big help here to the supervisor who wants to promote the more qualified junior man to a better job. If the differences between two employees are minimal or if the differences cannot be documented, the supervisor has little choice under most union contracts other than to give the nod to the senior man.

WHAT ARE OTHER CHANGES IN EMPLOYEE STATUS?

An employee's status may be changed for any one of several reasons. Depressed economic conditions, for example, may cause a shift in an employee's status. Building repairs, new machinery, and similar things may also make changes in an employee's status necessary. And, of course, when an employee is incompetent or undisciplined, a change in his status is likely. Whatever the reason for the change, a performance evaluation will be found of real value to the supervisor who must make such changes in an employee's work status and who wants to be as equitable and fair as possible. Most shifts in work status can be classified as either demotions, layoffs, or discharges. Let's take a look at each.

Demotions.   A *demotion* is a reassignment to a lower paying, less difficult job with lower status. In most instances, demotions are caused by factors beyond an employee's control. Recessions may cause some layoffs, with consolidations and demotions occurring among the remaining employees.

Supervisors should virtually never demote a person for disciplinary reasons. If an employee comes to work drunk, if he is absent a lot, or if he is insubordinate, demoting him will not change his ways. It may, in fact, make him more antagonistic and will emphasize his negative qualities. Discipline, as you know, should be used to train and correct. An employee demoted for disciplinary reasons would have to learn the new job, correct his negative habits, and make a psychological adjustment caused by his lower status and pay. It is highly improbable that an employee could or would accommodate himself to all three such adjustments.

shifts in status

Many companies today depend on government contracts for their business. When such sources of funds run out, the number of employees on the payroll may have to be drastically reduced, causing otherwise well-qualified employees to be lost. In order to salvage as many such employees as possible, some companies give an employee the option of either termination or accepting a demotion with the understanding that he will be promoted when a suitable position opens up. In other companies, the process of "bumping" is common, where an employee who is to be terminated is given the option of "bumping" the next lower-level employee and taking a demotion to his job. The "bumped" employee has the same option, with the end result being that the lower-level employees with least seniority are usually the ones to be terminated.

Where demotion may prove embarrassing to the company and inappropriate for the employee, the employee may be "kicked upstairs"—that is, he is demoted by being given a "promotion." This type of "promotion," however, is usually in title only with little or no change in pay, and typically occurs when an employee's job has outgrown his capacity to handle it. Because of his long and loyal service, however, the company may be unwilling to demote or discharge him, so he is eased out by being given a new title and stripped of his authority. Performance evaluations are of real assistance to supervisors in these situations.

Layoffs.   *Layoffs* are indefinite separations from the company due to reasons beyond the employee's control. At the time of the layoff, no one knows how long it will last. It may be a permanent layoff if business doesn't pick up, or it may be for only a few weeks until an increase in business warrants calling the employee back. In nonunionized companies, employees are usually selected for layoffs by considering their job performance, ability, and length of service. In some instances, financial hardship might also be considered.

*temporary vs.
permanent
separation*

In companies with unions, the union contracts are usually quite specific about the sequence in which employees will be laid off. Temporary and probationary employees are typically the first to go, with other employees laid off on the basis of seniority. Some contracts state that "seniority shall prevail provided the employee is capable of doing the work." Here again, adequate appraisal records are of a tremendous help to the supervisor.

Discharges. A *discharge* is a permanent separation from the company as a result of incapacity to do the job or some offense by the employee. Most discharges for lack of capacity occur during an employee's probationary period—the period of time during which the employee is on trial.

In unionized companies, it is virtually impossible to discharge an employee after his probationary period except for some clear infraction of company rules. However, whether the employees are unionized or not, most supervisors take pride in treating their employees fairly, in preserving their job security, and in demonstrating that they will not be arbitrarily fired. Thus, where employees have to be discharged, most supervisors take care to insure that they have "airtight" cases that can be documented. Employee evaluation records are virtually a necessity in these instances.

A Case Study
THE CASE OF THE PROBLEM EVALUATION

Don Reaton sat at his desk pondering what he should do. Yesterday he had completed the semiannual evaluation form on June Andrews, his secretary, and had "slept on" his comments overnight. As he reread the evaluation today, he was convinced that he had been fair and honest in his appraisal of her work, but he was worried about how she would take his comments during the thirty-minute review session scheduled later in the day.

He had rated June as follows:

Knowledge of job	good
Neatness in work	good
Ability	good
Dependability	excellent
Accuracy	excellent
Speed and productivity	fair
Ability to get along with others	good
Enthusiasm for work	good
Overall attitude toward job	good

As he recalled, June had protested vigorously during his last evaluation interview because she had not been rated "excellent" on her knowledge of what the job was, on her ability to do the work, and on her attitude toward her work. She had insisted that she knew the job inside and out, possessed all the necessary skills to do the job, and liked her work and looked forward to it each day. She implied, however, that "low ratings" like he had given her could certainly cause her to change her mind about her work.

During the six months since that interview, Don couldn't see that she had changed very much. In his mind, she was a solid, loyal, good employee but not an exceptional or excellent one. He didn't want to lose her, and yet he felt he had to be honest with her in his appraisal. She was not speedy, but then his work didn't require speed as much as reliability and accuracy. He knew what her reaction to his rating would be, and he didn't look forward to fighting or arguing with her about it. He felt he was fair and honest, and he refused to change the ratings to make her feel good.

1. How should Don conduct his interview with June?
2. What points should be stress? Why?
3. Should he change his ratings if she threatens to leave? Why?

A Case Study
TILLEY'S DEPARTMENT STORE

For some time now, Jane Tilley had been mentally debating the wisdom of trying to establish some formal system of rating the performances of the employees in her store. Jane's small department store employing 31 people was one of the leading stores in Florence. Her employees were friendly, seemingly loyal, and in general did good or average work for her. Jane's problem was how she could be certain that raises and promotions were given where deserved.

What Jane had tried to do in the past was to hire employees at the going rate in the community, then raise them annually based on (1) the quality of their work and (2) the increases that had occurred in the cost of living. Figures showing changes in the cost of living weren't difficult to obtain, and Jane systematically applied them to each employee's salary, thus compensating for inflation. Increases based on the quality of the employee's work, however, were more difficult to arrive at. In fact, the best she could do was to make estimates; and estimates, in her mind, were not very dependable.

At a regular employee meeting last week, several employees had suggested that she have conferences with each one and tell them how they were performing, indicating what was good and bad about their work, how they measured up with other employees, and what the employee needed to do to improve her performance.

When Jane thought about all this it made sense to her and sounded good. But she didn't know what should be done first, or how to start.

1. If you were called in as a consultant, what advice would you give Jane as to whether or not she needs an evaluation program?
2. What type of evaluation program would you suggest?
3. How should the evaluation program be started? How should it be introduced to the employees? How should it be conducted?

14
UNDERSTANDING EMPLOYEE UNIONS

This chapter explains—

- Why unions are attractive to some employees
- How unions operate in collective bargaining
- A supervisor's relationship with unions

The labor force in just about every industry is affected by unionism. Either the employees are union members, or they depend on other firms whose employees are unionized. In fact, the labor union today is just as much a part of our society as is the family and the morning paper. Unions have both legal status and social approval. They are an integral part of our management scheme and, as such, should be recognized, understood, and worked with effectively.

WHAT IS A UNION?

A union is an organization of employees that seeks to improve its members' social, economic, and political interests through the process of collective bargaining. Most unions emphasize improving wages and conditions of work. They seek through collective bargaining to get better pay, better fringe benefits, and better working conditions for their members. In addition, some unions seek to improve the workers' status by influencing political
types of unions   action in the local, state, and federal governments.

Some unions are craft unions and only accept members from a single occupation or trade. One craft union, for example, may represent only carpenters, whereas another craft union would represent only machinists.

Industrial unions, unlike craft unions, represent all workers in a particular company or industry regardless of what job the worker performs. The United Automobile Workers and the United Mine Workers are examples of industrial unions, where one union represents all workers in the automobile industry, and the other represents all the miners.

WHAT IS A UNION SHOP? CLOSED SHOP? CHECKOFF?

If a company has a union shop, an employee does not have to belong to the union before he is hired. However, after a given period of time—usually about 60 days—he must join the union or lose his job. With a closed shop (now outlawed by the Taft-Hartley Act), an applicant for a job had to join the union before he could be hired. The checkoff is where the company collects (or deducts from an employee's pay) union dues and fees and turns them over to the union.

HOW DID UNIONS DEVELOP?

The present strong position of unions didn't happen overnight. Their history goes back as far as 1792, when craft unions of carpenters and printers were founded to resist wage deductions. To give you an idea of how unions have grown, there were only 80 local unions in 1863 in twenty northern states. By the close of the Civil War, there were almost 300 unions in these same states.

The American Federation of Labor (AFL) started in 1881 as an informal organization of six crafts and some others calling themselves the Federation of Organized Trades and Labor Unions. It was a weak organization overshadowed by the Noble Order of the Knights of Labor. Then, irritated by a jurisdictional dispute, several craft unions formally organized themselves as the AFL in 1886 with about 138,000 members. By 1920, it had over 4,000,000 members representing about 70 or 80% of all union workers. *evolution of unions*

The economic recession of the early 1920s and the depression of the 1930s caused a setback in union growth. However, the passage of the Norris-LaGuardia Act of 1932, which limited the use of court injunctions in labor disputes, and the National Industrial Recovery Act (NIRA) of 1933, which gave legal sanctions to unions, set the stage for rapid union growth. The courts invalidated the NIRA in 1935, but it was quickly replaced by the National Labor Relations Act (the Wagner Act), which guaranteed the right to organize and bargain collectively and prohibited company-dominated or company-financed unions.

In 1938, a group of ten unions was suspended from the AFL, and they organized themselves as the Congress of Industrial Organizations (CIO). Growth continued for both groups through the war years. In 1947, the Labor-Management Relations Act (Taft-Hartley Act) was passed, which outlawed the closed shop and restricted or controlled such features as the union shop, welfare funds, grievance procedures, checkoff, and contract termination provisions. Secondary boycotts became unfair labor practices, and in strikes that endangered national health and safety, the president of the United States could prevent work stoppage for 80 days while a board investigated facts and tried to settle the dispute.

In 1955, the AFL and the CIO merged, and today, union membership fluctuates at around 18,000,000 members representing about 25% of our national labor force.

WHAT ARE LOCAL UNIONS LIKE?

Local unions are fairly simple in organization. They are headed by a president who presides at meetings, represents the union, and participates in bargaining with the company. The secretary-treasurer, because of his control over the money, can be a powerful man in the union. The business agent *local organization* (usually appointed) is typically the most powerful officer because of his intimate knowledge of unions and how they work. Usually a clever and experienced negotiator, he gives advice to the bargaining and contract committee. His main duty, however, is to represent the union in the administration of the union contract. The international representative in the local is a full-time employee of the international organization and represents the international in the local union's affairs. Shop stewards are elected by the employees to represent them in disagreements with the company.

Although the workers are theoretically in control of local unions, the president, business agent, secretary-treasurer, and international representative typically run the local union.

WHY DO WORKERS JOIN UNIONS?

One reason that workers join unions is that an individual doesn't have much of a chance trying to bargain over wages with a giant company. The firm can get along without the worker and can tell him to take the wages offered or leave. The worker's only bargaining strength is that he can quit. This obviously is not much strength for an individual, but when all workers join together and say they'll quit, they have some power over the company. Employees join unions, therefore, for *greater bargaining power*.

Another reason is the *need to make themselves heard*. Most employees want to be more than a cog in the wheel. They want the supervisor to listen to them and their ideas. They want a voice in the operations and procedures of the enterprise. The union gives them this voice.

bargaining power

Some workers are coerced to join a union as *a condition of employment*, in those businesses where unions have contracts specifying that employees must join the union within a certain period of time or be fired.

Man is a social, friendly creature whose actions are influenced by what others do. If all the other employees are joining a union, he will, too. Therefore, being "in," *being a member of the group*, or being identified with the organization that the employee feels is to his benefit is another reason employees join unions.

Employees also join unions because they want to eliminate or at least *minimize favoritism and discrimination*. In some companies, a few employees may be given the soft jobs, or they may be given the new machines, or they may be shown favoritism in other ways. Most workers resent this, and their unions, therefore, press for equal treatment, equal opportunity, and equal pay for equal work.

WHY DO SOME EMPLOYEES REJECT UNIONS?

Since 75% of the labor force does not belong to unions, everyone isn't in favor of unions. Why? A lot of Americans feel that *unions are socialistic or collectivistic in nature*. They distrust them and somehow feel they are "un-American" and contrary to the American concept of individual initiative, individual freedom, and free enterprise. They feel that a man ought to stand on his own two feet and get ahead by his own abilities and not have someone else fighting his battles for him.

Other employees reject union membership because they can see *no good reason to join.* They are happy with their jobs and their pay, and they see no reason why they should have to join a union and pay dues every month to fatten the union treasury.

Professional people typically reject unions because they feel that union affiliation would be *beneath their dignity.* Instead, they seek out and join their own organizations such as the American Medical Association, American Association of University Professors, and the American Bar Association, whose objectives are much the same as the unions'—to represent their members and better the members' positions.

Unions are typically composed of blue-collar workers because many white-collar employees feel that it is *below their social status to belong.*

*collectivistic
nature*

Finally, some employees reject unions because they *prefer to be associated with the managerial side.* This is particularly true of white-collar employees who work closely with the supervisors and managers and who tend to accept the management point of view. They feel their future lies in advancing upward in managerial circles and think that union membership might hamper this possibility.

HOW DOES THE UNION AFFECT THE SUPERVISOR?

The way a supervisor deals with his employees is considerably changed after the union comes in; he no longer can deal directly with an employee over such things as hours of work, adjustment in pay, and working conditions. The shop steward is the one who speaks for the employees and the one he deals with.

The supervisor is no longer the "cock of the walk" after the union comes in. He must now make sure he does nothing to violate the union contract. He is bound, so to speak, by the written word. He may not, for example, be able to shift a worker from one job to another with the freedom he did before. If he asks an employee to perform a task that requires better skills in some respects than the job the employee has been used to, both the union steward and the employee will demand a higher job classification. If a supervisor wishes to let two or three employees go because business is slack, he can't lay off the worst workers. Instead, he has to let those with the least seniority go. In other words, the freedom of action of supervisors is considerably restricted.

*restriction of
freedom*

Another effect on the supervisor is that he now *must* treat every employee alike. If one punch-press operator gets safety shoes at company expense, every other employee operating similar machines must also be furnished safety shoes at company expense. All employees assigned the same

"With a union present, a supervisor can no longer
deal directly with his employees about hours
of work, adjustments in pay, and working conditions."

SIR, THE SHOP STEWARD SAYS WE CAN'T PAINT THIS ROOM UNTIL MONDAY MORNING.

jobs get the same pay, except for seniority increases. Supervisors can make
no differentials.

Instead of dealing with dozens of employees, a supervisor now deals
mainly with the shop steward. If the supervisor wants to know his employees' preferences for vacation, he asks the steward. If he wants to know
their reaction to job rotation or job enlargement, he asks the steward. In one
sense, this simplifies his job because the shop steward usually knows the
employees and has a "feel" for their true opinions, thus giving a fair picture
to the supervisor. Because of this, the supervisor can easily check with the
steward about questions regarding such things as working conditions, safety
equipment, how to operate an employee suggestion system, and so on.

Decisions that supervisors used to make have a tendency to be centralized when the company has a union. For example, a small change in work
methods or the way a complaint is handled is no longer controlled by the
supervisor because such things might be in violation of the union contract or
cause a grievance. Management, therefore, tends to take the authority for
these and similar decisions away from supervisors and centralize them in the
industrial relations department. This is particularly true in the handling of
grievances. In many companies, the union contract specifies that the first
point of contact over grievances will be between the steward and the supervisor. In practice, the authority the supervisor has to handle the grievance

frequently resides in the industrial relations department, and before the supervisor can give a definite answer to a question, he has to check with industrial relations. In multiplant companies, this centralization of power is even more noticeable because management wants to make decisions with all plants in mind, not with just one department in mind. Afraid that the supervisor will do something to cause a work stoppage, top management in many instances has virtually taken away the power to discipline from the supervisor.

Thus, the supervisor really lacks authority and status in many instances. Although technically he is a member of the management team, he may feel as if he is the forgotten man because he is frequently left out of contract negotiations. In addition, the supervisor is often made to look ridiculous to his employees because his superior's concessions to union demands may contradict what he tells his employees.

And finally, among the many ways in which unions affect supervisors, you sometimes find the salary of the supervisor lower than some of his employees. This condition usually results from pay concessions made in union agreements pertaining to hours worked, overtime, and the like.

The above examples are illustrative of a few of the ways that unions affect the supervisor.

WHAT IS COLLECTIVE BARGAINING?

When authorized representatives of management and the union get together to bargain over and agree upon wages, hours of work, and working conditions, the process is called *collective bargaining*. By law, the process involves four steps:

1. Recognition of the appropriate bargaining unit.
2. Bargaining in good faith.
3. Meeting proposals with counterproposals.
4. Incorporation of the findings in a written contract.

legal aspects

The company must recognize the union chosen by a majority of its workers who voted in a government-certified election. The company must also bargain in good faith. It is not bargaining in good faith if it does any one or a combination of the following: meets with the union with no intention of reaching an agreement, refuses to bargain because its competitors haven't bargained, or claims the union is irresponsible and sets up unreasonable conditions before it will bargain. If the company fails to offer constructive counterproposals to the demands made by the union, it is not bargaining in good faith. Finally, it is unfair under the law if the company refuses to sign a written contract after reaching an agreement.

The actual bargaining is probably the least understood part of the process because it goes on in some hotel room or lawyer's office behind closed doors. The bargaining is given little publicity and is fraught with tension and emotions. Some people say it is like a high-powered poker game where the stakes are high. Actually, it is a bargaining process where the proposals and counterproposals are traded and bartered until the two sides finally reach an agreement. What the union usually strives for is to maximize the members' incomes, provide for job security, improve and maintain good working conditions, and make provisions for the continuance of the union.

WHAT ISSUES ARE BARGAINED OVER?

Obviously, wages, working conditions, and hours of work are bargained over. Other issues include administration of welfare, health, and pension plans; merit rating and job evaluation; and bonuses and incentive-pay schemes.

As time passes and contracts are renewed through the years, the issues bargained over expand tremendously. In many instances, these may be challenged as a management prerogative and not a bargainable issue. For example, in the B. F. Goodrich Co. 89 NLRB No. 139 case, the union wanted the company to tell it the salary of each employee before and after the last increase, the present salary of each employee, and the number of *unlimited variety* performance rating points received by each employee in the last performance rating. The company agreed to furnish the union with the information but refused to name the employees involved, whereupon it was held that this would impede the collective bargaining process, and the company was ordered to furnish the information. In another case, it was held a violation of the Taft-Hartley Act when an employer refused to bargain with the union over the increase in the price of meals given to the employees in the company cafeteria because meals were considered conditions of employment.

Instead of bargaining over such things as seniority, dues, checkoff, and so on, collective bargaining now includes such items as pension plans, insurance, hospitalization, etc. These fringe benefits cost a great deal, and both sides come to the bargaining table armed with amortization tables, vesting provisions, actuarial probability tables, legal provisions, and so on—a far cry from yesterday's pay increase and 40-hour week. Today, employees get more time off with pay and management gets nonstrike clauses as a result of bargaining agreements. There are lots of other issues, but this list serves to show the scope and variety of issues that can be bargained over. With such wide latitude given to the interpretation of the law, it is conceivable that virtually any activity that affects the social or economic life of employees in industry will someday be included in the area of collective bargaining.

When unions move in and try to organize the workers in a company, what can the supervisor do? What rights does he have? There are a lot of things he can do and a lot he can't do. We'll discuss a few of them.[1]

When union organizers appear on the scene, a manager can correct any untrue or misleading union propaganda but cannot ask an employee to talk in private about the union. A manager can, however, talk to employees openly, on company time, and in groups, just as long as the talk is not held during the twenty-four-hour silence period held before each election. During this period, however, management can mail material to employees' homes.

In talking with his employees, a supervisor can point out the disadvantages of a union, such as monthly dues, fines, wages lost from strikes, and so on. He cannot, however, threaten the loss of a job, reduction in pay, or discontinuance of any past benefit if an employee joins or favors a union. Neither can a supervisor use language that could be construed to be intimidating or language that would keep a worker from joining a union. He can, however, talk with his employees, telling them about any of his personal union experiences and can even show how the employees' present wages and fringe benefits compare with those in unionized shops, emphasizing that unions cannot do anything for workers that they cannot do for themselves. But in this talk, the manager must not do or say anything that might be interpreted as restraining or interfering with an employee's right to participate in union activities. In fact, he cannot do anything that would imply to employees that he is keeping an eye on them to see if they are participating in the organizing activities, nor can he ask them to tell him what they think about unions.

supervisory rights

Supervisors can, of course, insist that unions carry on their unionizing activities outside the plant work areas and during nonworking hours. Along this line, a supervisor may ask his employees to notify him if the employees are in any way threatened or coerced by a union member or organizer. A supervisor can also point out that a worker does not have to sign a union-authorization card or even talk to the union organizers unless it is his voluntary desire, and if a union-authorization card is signed, the employee is under no obligation to vote for the union.

When a supervisor sees one of his men taking part in unionizing activities, he cannot in any way discriminate against him or deny him his right to solicit other workers except during working hours and in work areas. In other words, if the solicitation is in outside areas and during nonworking hours, a supervisor cannot interfere. A supervisor cannot, however, stop a worker from soliciting other workers even on company property and during working hours unless management can clearly show that it is interfering with

[1]The following section is adapted from Claude S. George, Jr., *Management for Business and Industry* (Englewood Cliffs, N.J.: Prentice-Hall, Inc., 1970), pp. 362–64. Reprinted by permission of Prentice-Hall, Inc.

their jobs. In addition, supervisors cannot threaten in any way to discipline or fire a worker for favoring or joining a union, nor can a supervisor threaten to close, move, or in any way reduce operations in a plant if the employees join a union.

A supervisor can, of course, talk to his employees, but he must be careful about what he says. He can, for example, discuss the usual seniority provisions present in most union contracts, pointing out how they would serve to stifle the progress of ambitious and skilled employees, but he must not imply that if the worker does not join the union, he will be promoted, given a raise, or rewarded in some manner. He cannot imply or state that he will not deal with a union in order to discourage his employees from joining, nor can he ask a worker to report to him the names of other workers, including himself, who are either union members, favor unions, or are participating in union activities. A manager can legally *listen* to this type of information if it is told to him voluntarily, but he cannot ask any questions about it.

A supervisor has the right to point out in conversations with employees that the union will probably try for a union shop, which will force all employees to join the union whether or not they so desire. A supervisor, in addition, can suggest that if an employee joins a union, he will be paying for benefits he is already getting. He cannot, however, discriminate between union employees (and those thought to be union employees) and nonunion employees by giving the soft jobs to those who object to unions, saving the harder and more unpleasant tasks for the union members or those suspected of favoring the union.

Finally, a supervisor may advise his employees that they need not attend an organization meeting announced by a union organizer. In fact, under these conditions, a supervisor may call a meeting of his employees and advise them that the company has complied with all requests from the Labor Board and that the employees are not obligated to attend the announced union meeting. The supervisor should also point out that each worker must individually decide whether or not he will attend the meeting and that, whether he attends or not, it will not affect the employee's employment status. [*End of extract.*]

HOW IMPORTANT IS THE SUPERVISOR TO COLLECTIVE BARGAINING?

The supervisor is very important to collective bargaining. The first-line supervisor is usually the first contact between employees and management and between the union steward and management. What the supervisor does and says and the way he acts concerning labor matters are of vital interest to the company. His actions are not for his department alone but have company-wide implications. If the supervisor neglects or ignores an employee's grievance, assigns jobs in a thoughtless or unfair way, or encourages an employee to ignore safety practices, reports of his actions will probably find their way to the bargaining table as issues in future contract negotiations. The supervisor may, in fact, take actions that could precipitate a strike or get the company charged with breaking the union contract. He is, therefore, the key man in determining how testy the collective bargaining process will be.

Called upon to make decisions about and interpret the labor agreement, the supervisor is in a pivotal position. You can't expect him to be a "labor contract lawyer," yet he's got to know the proper responses to employee requests and union charges. If he doesn't, he may cost the company millions of dollars. Therefore, whenever a supervisor is in doubt about what attitude he should take, what the company's position is on a matter, the interpretation of a union contract clause, or how he should handle a request, he should get the answer from his boss or from the industrial relations department. He shouldn't guess. He should be sure of his grounds first and then move.

a key man

HOW CAN A SUPERVISOR HELP WITH COLLECTIVE BARGAINING?

A supervisor can help by making suggestions about union relationships. These suggestions should be specific and should be given well in advance of the start of the bargaining process. Many companies encourage their supervisors to give the management team suggestions throughout the year—any time the situation comes up and the supervisor has it clearly in mind. In this way, every suggestion can be evaluated with respect to how it would affect all other departments. Supervisors are especially encouraged to make suggestions about the three areas they are most heavily involved in: wages, seniority, and discipline.

WHAT RELATIONSHIP SHOULD EXIST BETWEEN A SUPERVISOR AND THE UNION STEWARD?

As a supervisor, you should by all means be friendly and cordial. Don't be anti-union. But don't forget that as the supervisor, you are in control of your department. The union steward's job is to protect his members' rights, and your job is to protect management's rights.

The steward has no authority to tell you what to do or boss any employees in your department. He may give you strong advice that you may later wish you had followed. But all he can do is advise. If possible, however, gain the steward's confidence and cooperation. This could be a mutually satisfactory agreement where each could help the other. You could keep him posted about what your plans are so that he can tell his members. And he can give you help by getting the workers to cooperate with, for example, a new work plan that you want to try out.

Try to work with the steward. Remember that the company has a contract with the union and that unions are a permanent part of our society. Don't waste time trying to annoy the steward or buck the union. Spend that same energy trying to find ways that the two of you can live in harmony.

A Case Study
JOE MANN VERSUS THE UNION

Joe Mann, supervisor of the testing department for Ace Electric Company, was upset because John Gordon, one of the lead testers, was absent again, the third time this year. And this time Gordon hadn't even bothered to call in sick as he had on the other two occasions. This meant a disruption in the testing program for the government job that had to be shipped tomorrow. He'd have to make some emergency changes to get the work done, which would mean a decrease in his department's efficiency record and a loss in pay for him.

In fact, as Joe Mann thought over the events, he got even madder. The Fourth of July had been on Monday of this week, which had made a long weekend for his men, and a short work week. So Mann had explained the need for an all-out effort on the testing of the government job, and Gordon, knowing all this, had taken an extra day—not even bothering to call in. Mann made up his mind that he'd "fix" Gordon when he did return to work.

At 10:30 A.M. on Wednesday, John Gordon finally punched in. Joe spotted him and immediately walked over to his position. "John, you've pulled this 'sickness' stunt once too often," he told Gordon. "You'll get no pay for Monday July 4th, for Tuesday July 5th, which you missed, and I'm suspending you without pay for today and tomorrow. I don't want to hear any of your excuses. Just punch out and report back for work on Friday."

John Gordon made no reply, but his look of disgust and contempt was evident. On his way out, he stopped by to see Ollie Jefferson, his union steward, to give him the story and ask him to see what he could do to help him.

When Ollie approached Joe Mann about the case, Joe lit into him with both barrels. "John Gordon was deliberately fouling up the testing procedure," he shouted. "He's been absent twice before this year, supposedly for sickness, and now he stretches a long weekend by taking an extra day and a half, not even bothering to call in. He's always one of the last men to return from a rest break, he 'jaws' with the other men too much, and in general he's an agitator. The union contract allows suspension for poor attendance, and that's exactly what I'm doing. Maybe it will teach him a lesson."

Ollie opened his mouth to protest but decided to hold his tongue. Instead, he simply replied, "Mr. Mann, you are dead wrong about John. This suspension is illegal. John Gordon is right and you are wrong."

The union filed a written grievance, and when it came to the hearing, Ollie Jefferson stated that Joe Mann had blown his stack without the facts, that Mann had just *assumed* that John Gordon had stretched his long weekend arbitrarily. Actually, what had happened, he explained, was that John took his wife to the hospital at 6:00 A.M. on July 5th, stayed by her side during an emergency operation, and remained at the hospital until she came from the recovery room at 9:30 A.M. on July 6th. Knowing that she was all right, he immediately reported back to work. Although it was true that the union contract called for forfeiting the holiday pay if an employee was absent on the day prior to or following the holiday, Ollie stated that the facts in this case called for an exception to the rule. Furthermore, the other absences, he stated, were because of actual sickness as shown by a doctor's written statement. Finally, Ollie indicated that Joe Mann apparently "had it in" for John Gordon, by accusing him of being the last to return (but not late) from rest break, of talking with other employees "too much," and of being an agitator.

"I submit, therefore," Ollie stated, "that John Gordon was misjudged, that his supervisor was more interested in getting even with him for petty things, and that he used this absence as an excuse to suspend him without pay."

1. How well do you think Joe Mann handled his problem? What do you think he should have done?
2. How should "returning late from rest breaks," excessive talking, and "agitating" be handled by Joe Mann?
3. How would you decide this case? Why?

A Case Study
ABE SALEM AND THE UNION

Abe Salem walked into his office to find the union steward and two of his employees waiting for him. "What's the problem, men?" he asked.

John Hickory, the union steward, started the discussion with a blast at management. "Damn it all, Abe, what are you trying to do to us?" John demanded. "Just when we thought we understood each other, you tell Ed Johnson, here, that he'll be fired if he joins the union. You know this isn't so. You know it's illegal to do this, and I'm going to have your hide for this. I've overlooked too many slips on your part already, and I'm waking up to the fact that they were all planned.

"Take the time last week," he continued, "when you made my men leave the loading platform during their lunch hour to talk about unions and to carry on unionizing activities. You know this isn't right as well as I do. Then on Monday you tried to get Saddie Jones to stop talking about unions on the sewing line while working. You know that those women carry on a constant stream of conversation all day long. You name it and they talk about it. If Saddie wants to talk about unions and try to get others interested in it, I say, 'More power to her.'

"But the straw that broke the camel's back was when you indicated to Ed here that if he was in favor of unions, he could look for a job elsewhere. Oh, you didn't come right out and say it in so many words, but Ed said that you really gave him a hard look when you overheard him say that the union would see to it that all of its members got their just desserts in pay from you, and that union membership would assure equality of opportunity and equal pay for equal work."

"Now wait a minute, John," Abe countered. "You've got it all wrong. I don't know who has been feeding you this pack of lies, but let me set the record straight. Yeah, I did talk to Ed and Jim here about what your union was and what changes it would make. I told them in no uncertain terms that your union was for seniority and that in most of your contracts, seniority means that ambitious employees like Jim and Ed here might well be stifled in their progress in the company. You know as well as I do that seniority provisions give opportunity for promotion and pay increases to the senior man—not to the junior man in the group. So, if your men want to get ahead based on ability and not seniority and pull, then joining the union isn't the way. And I'll also say to you and any other employees, that joining the union is a waste of money—you'll be doing nothing but paying for a benefit you are already getting.

"And one more thing I want you to get straight," Abe stated, "is that I can say what I damn well please to my employees. And for your information, I am going to have a meeting on Friday with all my employees in the cafeteria and give them the straight dope on you and your union. I'm not going to pull any punches. If the truth hurts, then you'd better prepare to get hurt." With that Abe turned and left the three men sitting in his office.

1. Criticize Abe Salem's actions. What did he do wrong? What did he do right?
2. How do you think Abe Salem should have handled the meeting?
3. Do you think that John Hickory had any grounds for complaints? On what basis?
4. What advice would you give John Hickory as to how he should conduct himself at future meetings like this?

PART THREE
SUPERVISING YOUR DEPARTMENT

15
HOW PLANNING HELPS YOU MANAGE

This chapter explains—

- What planning is
- Why you need to plan
- How you plan

Like it or not, every manager has to plan. It may be a plan for tomorrow's work, or next month's vacation, or next year's production. It may involve one department or it may involve the entire business. Whatever its scope, planning is a function performed by every manager.

When a supervisor makes plans for the future of his department, he projects a course of action for some future period of time. It may be a complex plan for the efficient utilization of his equipment next month or a simple plan for staggering work hours. Whatever it is, his aim is to achieve coordinated action so that a desired goal can be reached with minimum disruption.

Just because you plan, of course, doesn't mean something will come true. However, without planning, the probability is remote that you will achieve a goal other than by accident. Plans are our rudders that guide us toward given objectives. For example, if we want each employee to sell $500 worth of merchandise each day, some plan has to be developed to help make this come true. Just wishing for it doesn't make it happen. And although planning won't make it happen either, it will increase your probability of success by as much as 80%.

WHAT IS PLANNING?

Planning is a managerial function that every supervisor uses every day. It's not something he puts aside for a rainy day and pulls out when he has nothing else to do. When a supervisor plans, he typically:

planning actions

1. Takes a realistic look at the future.
2. Tries to accurately anticipate problems that will be involved.
3. Determines alternative ways to handle and solve these problems.
4. Weighs the advantages and disadvantages of each alternative to see which one is best.
5. Decides on which course of action he will follow.

Planning then, consists of looking ahead, thinking about the future, anticipating what will probably happen, and determining what should be done in order to be ready for it.

IS PLANNING EASY?

planning and the supervisor's job

Yes and no. For a lot of supervisors planning is difficult to get around to but not hard to do once they get started. Whereas a lot of a supervisor's work is physical in nature, planning is mental work. Physical work is easier for most of us than mental work, and planning, therefore, falls in the category of being harder than most managerial tasks.

DO YOU NEED A PLAN FOR SIMPLE JOBS?

Yes. When you really think about it, you'll see that you have to plan for everything you do. When you get ready to do something, say, wash your car, you have to plan for it and act on the basis of *facts*—not on guesses. For example, you may not be able to wash the car whenever you choose because others may need to use the car. You will, therefore, have to find out when the car will not be needed for an hour. You also have to plan how you will wash it—whether you will use a hose or a bucket of water. By getting the facts, you find that your family will not need the car between 2:00 and 4:00 P.M., so you plan to hose it down then. Before you act, however, you have to get the facts about the availability of the hose, bucket, and water. The water is OK, you find out, and so is a bucket; the hose has a split in it. This means you will have to change your plan about hosing the car down and instead wash it with a sponge and a bucket of water.

For the complex job of running an entire department, a supervisor has to have his goals clearly established, and he has to have plans made whereby he can achieve his goals. If he doesn't have plans, the probability of his reaching his goals is fairly remote.

WHO IS RESPONSIBLE FOR PLANNING?

Every manager is responsible for planning: the chairman of the board, the president, the division manager, and the first-line supervisor. Not everyone is involved in the same sort of planning, however. The president and other top-level managers are involved in planning about where the company will be next year or five years hence. They plan long-range company strategy, whereas the first-line supervisor plans about the daily, weekly, or monthly operations of his department, about how he can supervise his employees best, and about what will have to be done to ship the Smith order next week.

HOW FAR IN THE FUTURE SHOULD YOU PLAN?

How far into the future you should plan will depend on what level you are in the organization. If you are a member of top management, your planning will be for at least five years into the future. This type of planning will be broader in scope and have a far greater impact on the total firm than other short-range planning. Middle management will probably be involved in planning that is more operational in nature than that by top management. Also, it will not look as far into the future—maybe eighteen to twenty-six months.

First-line supervisors make plans for work to be done by their own departments. Most of these plans are on a weekly or monthly basis and seldom project further than six months into the future. What this means is that the supervisor must find some free time, usually early in the morning or late in the day, when he can look over what his department is responsible for in the future so that he can plan or size up what has to be done in order to reach these objectives. Occasionally, a supervisor will be asked to project or plan his activities for a year or so in advance so that overall plans can be made to assure an adequate supply of, say, labor or materials.

IN A NUTSHELL, WHAT ARE THE ESSENTIALS OF GOOD PLANNING FOR A SUPERVISOR?

We all know that the future is uncertain, and as a consequence, we have to make plans. Before you plan, however, you have to predict or project what the future will be like. Most of us are fairly good at predicting what will happen a short time in the future—like this afternoon, or tomorrow, or next week. But the further we try to predict in the future—like next year or three years from now—the poorer our predictions become. For this reason, the further we plan in the future, the less precise our plans can be. Two essentials for a supervisor's plans, therefore, are (1) you should not project your plans too far into the future and (2) you should make them clear, easily understood, and concise.

Another essential for supervisory planning is that you should include allowances in your plans for any changes that might come up. You might, for example, plan to have a picnic in the park this afternoon and then have to change your plans because of rain. In other words, you need to make contingency plans in case something changes. A contingency plan for the picnic, for example, might be to hold the picnic in your recreation room in case of rain.

essentials of
planning

Finally, supervisory planning calls for you to be precise about *what* is to be done, *when* it is to be done (today, tomorrow, next week), *where* it will be done (at the work place, in the stockroom), *how* it will be done (steps, processes involved, tools to use, etc.), and *who* will do it (list the employee by name).

As the supervisor, of course, you have to remain flexible because these plans may have to be changed as conditions change. An employee may be absent, a machine may break down, or raw material may not be available— all of which would mean a change in plans. But the important thing for you as the supervisor is that you have a plan—that you know what needs to be done and how you will do it. You have thought through the problems and have decided on how to handle them. A supervisor who plans his job carefully is seldom caught by surprise. And the supervisor who plans his job is the successful supervisor.

WHAT ADVANTAGES CAN A SUPERVISOR REASONABLY EXPECT FROM GOOD PLANNING?

When you as a supervisor give some thought to the future and make specific and concise plans about it, you will find that your employee's jobs are coordinated so that disruptions are minimized and schedules are more easily met. When plans are set forth on paper, you can spot areas where no one is responsible for the work or where two or more people are supposed to be doing the same thing. Thus, duplication or omission is avoided by having a plan. Inasmuch as employees know what to do, they have a better mental *rewards* outlook and feel that things are "under control," and consequently morale is better. By planning ahead, the best employee can be placed on the most difficult job—that is, the 16-cylinder man can be assigned to the 16-cylinder job and not to the 2-cylinder job.

Planning the work and then following the plan gives you better control over employees and costs. You know what your employees are or should be doing, and by utilizing their efforts most effectively, your operating costs will be kept at a minimum. Since you know what will be done in the future, you can take adequate steps to insure that needed tools and materials are available to meet your requirements. And, finally, good planning should enable you to operate your department at a high level of quality and efficiency and at minimum cost.

MUST YOU PLAN?

Some supervisors say they don't plan, when they actually do. They may not recognize it as planning, but they are always staying "one jump ahead." They are good enough to do this mentally; therefore they say they are not planning when actually they are planning.

Most of us aren't smart enough to keep it all in our heads. We have to put our plans down on paper so that we can study the plan, spot flaws, and make changes. If you want to be a good supervisor, therefore, you will need to plan.

CAN YOU SPOT A SUPERVISOR WHO DOESN'T PLAN?

There are lots of "signals" that tell you a supervisor is not planning his work. When delivery dates and schedules are missed, for example, or when some work gets overlooked, poor planning is usually the case. When you look around and find some employees not working and their equipment idle, poor planning is probably the cause. When employees are working at a slow pace, it is probably because they don't have anything else to do, and they are stretching out their work—again, the result of poor planning. Any time you see a supervisor in a "crash program" going around like the proverbial chicken with its head cut off, it's probably because he has done little or no planning.

DO PLANS EVER FAIL?

Yes, plans often fail. Just because you plan doesn't mean that you will meet your goal. Lots of things can make plans go astray. Strikes at a supplier's plant might mean a delay in the receipt of materials. "Acts of God," such as floods, fire, and lightning, may cause delays. Having employees out sick or having key employees quit could throw a monkey wrench into your plans.

Or maybe the plan itself is poor and wouldn't work under any conditions. Some supervisors don't understand the fundamentals of planning, and although they've tried, their plans are inadequate.

Just because plans can fail, however, is no reason not to plan. Even with major catastrophes, the probability of reaching your goal is better under planned conditions because you know what has to be done and you know what should be done, who should do it, how it should be done, etc. And you know all this because you had a plan you were following. Now all you have to do is modify the plan in light of the inflicted change. You don't have to start from the beginning with no plan at all.

SHOULD A SUPERVISOR PLAN HIS OWN JOB?

spotting look of planning

The supervisor who doesn't plan his own job can easily be spotted. He has to be in ten places at the same time (he says), or he claims he needs 36 hours per day to do his work. What he's really saying is that either he doesn't know how to plan, or he doesn't understand what his job as a supervisor is.

A manager who fails to plan his own job—how he will use his time—is continually chasing about putting out fires unnecessarily. People who complain often about not having enough time are the ones who kill their days doing wasteful and unnecessary things. How do you spend your day? If you don't have a precise picture of what you are doing, maybe you need to make a chart to record how you spend your day. How many hours do you spend in meetings? How much time are you losing by extending coffee breaks for a "few minutes"? How much routine clerical work are you doing that someone else could do? Answers to these and similar questions will show up on a time-analysis chart.

A time-analysis chart is nothing but a sheet of paper on which you've listed vertically the hours in your workday in 15-minute intervals, like 8:00, 8:15, 8:30, 8:45, and so on. Make a separate chart for each day. Then as you go through the day, keep an accurate account of what you do, and record it by the appropriate time interval. Be conscientious and accurate. Don't fudge and try to make it look good. Remember, you are trying to find out how you *actually* spend your day—not how you *think* you spend your day. At the end of a week, summarize the number of minutes each day you spend doing different things. You might find, for example, that you are spending eight hours each week reviewing and discussing your employees' work with them. This means you spent 20% of your week doing this. Maybe you'll see you spend ½ hour each morning and ½ hour each afternoon at coffee breaks— 12½% on this. And so on. As you review the sheets, ask yourself whether or not you are wasting an excessive amount of time on coffee breaks and other activities. Search for places where you think you are not spending enough *how the supervisor* time. Search for activities where you could save time and thus have it avail- *spends his day* able for more critical activities. Ask yourself if the things you are doing have to be done by you—or can one of your employees do them. How much of the routine work are you doing that you can assign to one of your employees? Look at the regular work that you need to do. Are you spending enough time on that?

By analyzing your time-analysis chart, you will find out what you *are* doing. Next you should ask yourself what you *should be* doing. Are you doing everything you should? Can some of your work be discontinued for more important things? It's your job and you know it best, but remember that you should be giving more than 60% of your time to supervising the work of your department. Do you find that you are doing too many special jobs "that only you know how to do"? Special jobs that crop up can kill you as a supervisor. If you don't watch them, you'll find you are spending 50% of your time on them, when 10 to 15% is a better time allocation.

Finally, do you have time to think, to be creative, to plan ahead? If not, rework the way you spend your day. Eliminate the unnecessary. Reassign other jobs. Leave yourself time for the important job of supervising!

WHAT HAPPENS TO A SUPERVISOR WHO DOESN'T PLAN?

If the situation is bad enough, the supervisor may lose his job. Certainly he will surely lessen his chances for promotion. If he can't plan and operate his own department, the chances that he could do well with a larger job are pretty poor. This is how his boss will see it, and promotions will probably not *poor operations* come his way.

His department is probably one of the poor departments in the company, and consequently his employees do not take pride in their work. No

poor operations

one wants to be on a losing team, and good employees, therefore, might transfer. This means the department's record gets poorer, its costs go up, and the supervisor gets pressured by top management to "get on the ball"— to increase production and lower costs. Harried and pressured, the supervisor starts on the "fire-fighting" routine. The confusion that results along with employee dissatisfaction might cause an increase in accidents. And thus the snowball grows larger and larger—all because the supervisor would not or did not take a little time to think through his work and make some plans.

WHAT KINDS OF PLANS SHOULD A SUPERVISOR BE INVOLVED WITH?

A supervisor should be involved with every kind of plan that affects his department. Top management should ask the supervisor to participate in setting goals for his department, and he should make certain that they are realistic since he is in the best position to know the department's capabilities and potential.

plans that affect the department

A supervisor should also have a part in developing plans affecting various operations in his department, such as a plan to reduce scrap by 3%, a plan to reduce employee absences by 10%, a plan to reduce employee turnover by 2%, a plan to reduce expenses by 15%, and so on. For each of these, the supervisor will need to determine how the goal will be reached and what his overall plan of attack will be.

In like manner, he should be involved with plans concerning the scheduling of production, the development and maintenance of a trained work force, the organization or reorganization of the people and work in the department, a plan for the systematic replacement of old equipment with new machines, and so on. In other words, the supervisor should be a part of any plans that have anything to do with the work of his department. This is true whether the responsibility is his or that of a specialized staff. In any case, he should be a party to the development of the plan and should have the opportunity to review, change, and finalize a plan involving the work and processes in his department.

IF PLANNING IS SO IMPORTANT, WHY DON'T MORE SUPERVISORS PLAN THEIR WORK?

Most supervisors are in a tough spot, serving as a buffer between top management and the employees. They are constantly called on to justify the actions of employees to management and top management's actions to their employees. Many supervisors, therefore, simply state they don't plan because they don't have time to do it. And the supervisor who "doesn't have time to plan" is usually the one who needs it the most.

lack of understanding

When a supervisor cites time as the reason he is not involved in planning, he's usually too busy putting out "brush fires" to develop an overall plan of "fire prevention." Or he may say there are so many physical demands on his time that he doesn't have time for the mental work involved in planning. Both of these excuses point to the need for planning. Time spent in planning pays off in preventing the "brush fire" emergencies, thus cutting down on physical work and leaving time for the equally important but less pressing mental work.

Some supervisors don't plan because they have never had any instruction in it, have never thought about it, and don't have the foggiest notion about how they should go about it. This may be an excuse for today but not for tomorrow. Every supervisor can avail himself of help either from experts in the company, from evening courses, from individual study, or from talking and working with supervisors in other companies who are involved in planning.

HOW SHOULD YOU PLAN AND USE YOUR TIME?

After you've made a time-analysis chart of your day, try *budgeting* how you would like to spend your time. Use your desk calendar or a sheet of paper, and plan what you will do with your time for each day in the week. Break it down into half-hour intervals. Your budget for one day might read something like this:

- 8:00 – 8:30   inspect presses; check oiler
- 8:30 – 9:00   inspect drills
- 9:00 – 9:30   interview new employee
- 9:30 – 10:00   attend monthly staff meeting
- 10:00 – 10:30 attend monthly staff meeting

and so on.

Making a budget is a plan for work. It might not work out exactly as you hoped at first. If not, make the adjustments necessary until you have a plan that allows you flexibility but still provides you with a way to spend your day effectively. The idea is to plan your work, then work your plan.

Other tips for planning and using your time are:

Don't Procrastinate.   Make up your mind with due speed, but don't make snap judgments; then tell your employees what you want done. If you haven't made up your mind, if you are "still thinking about it," you obviously don't know what you want done, your employees don't know, and nothing gets done about it.

plan your work

Be Specific.   When personnel calls, for example, and wants to know when you can interview a prospective employee, don't say, "Any time this week." Look at your calendar and set a time that will provide you with ample time to devote to the interview; otherwise the prospect might show up in the middle of a grievance session. Or ask your assistant to "get this done on Tuesday," not "when you get around to it," and make a note of it on your calendar for Tuesday to remind you to ask your assistant about it.

Watch the Open Door.   Too many supervisors kill their day by shooting the bull with first one person, then another. They have a policy that says: "You can always see me. My door is always open." This sounds good but is a sure way to ruin your plan and waste your time. See people if they need to see you and be polite; but when they just drop in to tell you about their latest vacation plans, ease them out with, "I'm sure enjoying your visit, Gerry, but unfortunately I've got to get a report ready for the boss. Let's continue this later."

Don't Trust Your Memory.   Jot down reminders of things you need to do. If necessary, make yourself some "things-to-do" folders—one for each day, one for each week, and one for each month. Then, as you think of something that needs to be done on Wednesday, scribble yourself a note and drop it in the appropriate folder. When that day arrives, pull out the folder to see what you need to do. When you're away from your desk, always carry a pocket pad and pencil to jot down reminders. Then put the reminders in the appropriate folder when you return to your desk.

work your plan

Use the Exception Principle.   The *exception* principle will make your work easier by calling to your attention only those things that need your action. It works this way. Suppose you want to be sure that the #4 shear is working at a high rate of efficiency. Its normal output is about 1600 pounds a day. You tell the operator to let you know whenever a day's production falls below 1500 pounds. In this way your attention is needed only when production drops. And as long as you're not called, everything is OK. The exception (in this case, less than normal production) is called to your attention.

The exception principle is easy to use on many parts of your job. First pick out the job you are concerned about, such as the number of units shipped, the number of letters filed, or the number of accounts posted, etc. Next, decide what is an acceptable level of daily performance for your department, such as shipping 112 units, filing 75 letters, or posting 250 accounts. Then set up a system so that you will be notified when the performance drops below the acceptable level. In this way, you won't waste your time on things that do not need your personal attention and action.

Delegate.   Examine everything you do, and ask yourself questions like: "Is it necessary for this to be done? Can it be eliminated? If not, can one of my employees do it, thereby freeing me for more important matters?" If you don't have an employee who can do it, can you train one to do it? By systematically going through your job in this way, you'll probably find that you're doing some things that can be eliminated and that you can assign much of what's left to your employees.

You may think this is passing the buck. But remember, you can't do it all. That's why you have people helping you. People won't think you are lazy; neither will you lose control of your job by delegating. As a supervisor, your job is to get things done through other people. So start getting things done by assigning other people the routine jobs that you have been doing yourself.

If you find yourself using the following excuses for not delegating, take another look. They're probably *excuses* only and not valid reasons:

1. My subordinates are too inexperienced to do this. I have to do it myself.
2. It takes more time to explain the job and farm it out than it does to do it myself, so why go through the routine?
3. I can't afford to have my subordinates make a mistake for which I will be responsible.
4. This job is different. It demands my personal attention.
5. My men are all busy, too, and don't have time for additional work.
6. I don't have anyone who will take the responsibility for work like this.
7. I got where I am today doing this type of work, and I don't plan to stop now.
8. If I pass it on to a subordinate, I'll lose control of the job. I won't know what's going on.
9. People will think I'm lazy—that I'm just passing the buck.
10. No one knows exactly how I want this job done.
11. If you want a job well done, you've got to do it yourself.
12. This job is too important to trust to a subordinate.
13. Doing this sort of thing is my occupational hobby, and I don't plan to turn it over to someone else.
14. I've got to OK the final product anyway, so why not do it to begin with?

Use Three Baskets for Paperwork.   When you use the three-basket system, label one basket "Do today." Label another "Do next week." And label the third "Do when there's time." Now when anything comes to you, the first thing to do is decide its urgency—"today," "next week," or "sometime later." Put it in the appropriate basket (or drawer). Don't leave work until you have done all "today's" things today. On Monday of each week, take the material from basket number two, and decide what part you will get done on each day of the week. Then stick to the plan. When you have free time, check basket number three.

Think Before You Act.   I once knew a supervisor who always managed to jump into the middle of every problem and thrash about furiously, not really knowing what he was doing or what should be done. The moral here is don't rush into action without doing a little thinking and planning. Be willing to take time out to think and plan what needs to be done, rather than diving in

"Use the three-basket approach."

...AND THERE'S NO PROBLEM WITH TIME SINCE I ADOPTED THE THREE BASKET APPROACH.

headfirst in an attempt to be *doing something.* At times like this, doing nothing is better. If you'll only take time to reflect on your work, you'll probably see shortcuts and timesavers that you would not otherwise discover.

rules to use

Even in emergencies when someone yells, "Fire!" don't rush head-on into the problem without thinking: "Where is the fire? Where are the closest extinguishers? How should the alarm be turned on?" Deciding the answers to these and similar questions would probably take no more than 45 seconds, and they would be 45 seconds well spent in thinking before you act.

Stay Off the Phone. You'll be surprised how much of your time is spent on the phone, just talking and waiting for the other fellow. Spending as much as 25 or 30% of the day on the phone is not uncommon for many supervisors who have made no attempt to plan their work. Try to limit your calls to three minutes. Some conversations will take longer, but shoot for three minutes. You should use the phone to save your legs, but conduct your business first; then if the other fellow is a talking machine, ease him off by having "someone waiting for instructions."

Tackle the Tough Jobs First. Most supervisors who tackle the tough jobs first get the most work done. Those who postpone the tough jobs soon find work piling up, and they really get behind. Studies have shown that many supervisors spend their time doing things they like to do or are good at, rather than working on the tough jobs first. Check your priority scale. Do you put off the tough or unpleasant jobs as long as possible? This type of job may be physically easy to do—like a monthly efficiency report—but it's a job you don't relish. Tackle the tough or unpleasant jobs first—when you are at your peak of energy, when you feel your best.

Start the Job.   Even if you can't finish the job, start it today. An unfinished job is much more of a motivator than an unstarted job. When was the last time you were able to wash only half of your car?

Plan Tomorrow Today.   Never leave your place of work until you have looked over what you will have to do tomorrow and have made plans about how it will be done, when it will be done, who will do it, and so on. You will find that when you come to work in the morning, nothing motivates you better than having a plan of action for the day. Lacking a plan, you'll waste time trying to get something going.

Analyze Your Work Every Month.   Review every job that you do at least once a month to see if it is necessary, if it can now be eliminated, or if it can be combined with another job. See what you can do to rearrange or cut down on a job. Study after study has shown that supervisors who don't take time to analyze their work in order to eliminate some of their activities and improve the work sequence of others are the ones who virtually always are ineffective in utilizing their time.

Each Day, Set Aside Some Time to Think.   Allow some time to think each day. It may be only 15 minutes at the beginning of each day, but set this time aside *without* interruption. Use it to think through your job—to look ahead at what needs to be done. Try to think in broad terms of planning your work, improving your operations, and in general, trying to work "smarter" not harder.

At the End of Each Day, Review What You Have Done.   Review your activities at the end of each day. Ask yourself why *you* had to do the job. Could all or part of it have been done by someone else? If so, make plans as to how you will handle the job next time. Then stick to your plan.

ARE YOU MAKING THE BEST USE OF YOUR TIME?

Perhaps you are thinking that you are already doing your job well, that there are no frivolous parts that could be eliminated, shortened, or combined. Maybe you've already analyzed your job and eliminated the soft spots. If this is where you are, then ask yourself the following questions:

1. *Am I a detail hugger?* Do I check up on small details that are important to some jobs but have little meaning for mine? Things like: "How long does it take to change ribbons on your typewriter, Sally?" "How much string do we use per year in tying up packages?" "How many of our employees drive a full-size car?"

2. *Am I constantly on the go?* Do I find that the only way to get things done is by doing the work myself? Am I spinning my wheels rather than getting help from others?

3. *Am I a conference caller?* Do I have to get everyone's opinions before I can make a decision? Is every decision I make so important that I have to have a meeting of my key people to discuss it?

4. *Am I always thinking about what we could do, not what we are doing?* Using your imagination and some daydreaming are important ways to discover new approaches to your job; but when you spend all of your time thinking about what you are going to do tomorrow, and thus accomplish little today, you aren't making the best use of your time.

best use of time

5. *Do I need more time?* If you reduce the time it takes to do the individual parts of your work, you can save time on the whole job.

6. *Do I have a hang-up?* Do I love figures or statistics or solving personnel problems so much that I neglect all the other parts of my job?

7. *Is my desk always overflowing with work?* Do I spend my time routinely working through stacks of paper, reading, approving, disapproving, signing, and routing papers put in front of me? Couldn't someone else do this for me?

If you answered "yes" to many of the questions above, take another look at yourself. Chances are you are killing the day doing everything except supervising people. Make a conscious effort to correct these personal deficiencies by planning your own work better.

A Case Study
MATT HINSHAW'S PROBLEM

Matt Hinshaw didn't like it when his boss told him he needed to pay more attention to the work in his department, that he needed to concentrate on the important things and leave the rest to other people. "I don't know what he expects," Matt thought. "I never loaf, and I always work overtime—have more to do than one man can do. He must want a superman to run this department. It's more than one man can do." With that, he turned his attention to the work of the day.

As the whistle blew, he checked his work stations and saw two empty spots. "Wonder what happened to Slim and Mavis," he mused. Then he noticed that four stations weren't operating. "Wonder why? Before I wade into this, I'd better take an ulcer pill." After a walk to the fountain for water, Matt remembered the weekly report that he always made out. Of course his secretary could do it, but he felt that these production figures should be kept from her, and besides if everyone knew what was going on, he might lose control.

After the weekly report, Matt turned his attention to what he thought of as his "fun job," computing each employee's efficiency on the basis of the number of rejected products. He knew his secretary could do this as well as he could, but he enjoyed doing it, and it didn't take too much time. In the middle of his computations, he remembered about Slim and Mavis, and went to check on them. Mavis had come in late, but Slim wasn't at work. Matt decided he would have to double up on Slim's work by putting one of the stock men there.

Forty-five minutes later, he was back at his desk waiting for his secretary to finish typing his weekly special report to top management. He always personally took this to the front office and delivered it to the "top boys." In this way he could have a cup of coffee and butter up the bosses some.

During his lunch break, he talked with other supervisors about their work, asking for tips on how to get things done. One suggested that he stop going to the routine supervisors' meeting each week. It just took time. Matt knew that Joe Dawson would like to have the assignment, and it would be good training for him since he had been picked to be acting supervisor during Matt's absences. But Matt had always kept this job for himself because he was afraid something would happen that he should know about.

When he got back to his desk, he reviewed the weekly stock report prepared by his storekeeper, which he telephoned into central records—at the home office in Chicago. It usually took about 15 or 20 minutes. Joe Dawson could do it, but Matt always believed it should be an accurate report, and he didn't want the big boss to jump on him because of inaccuracies.

Later, his secretary put a stack of routine forms in front of him and as he systematically signed them, he wondered what his boss would say if he saw all the things that he (Matt) had to do during the day. Maybe he would not say he needed to pay more attention to the work in his department.

1. What is Matt's major problem?
2. If you were Matt's boss, how would you handle him?
3. What do you think Matt should do?

A Case Study
NEW LONDON FURNITURE COMPANY

The New London Furniture Company was a medium-size manufacturer of bedroom and dining-room suites, and in addition fabricated a small line of occasional living-room pieces such as coffee tables, end tables, and odd chairs.

In the fall of 1978 the purchasing agent, Mr. Henry Parden, resigned his job to accept the position of purchasing agent and vice-president with a similar company specializing in the manufacture of upholstered furniture. Because of the nature of the offer, Mr. Parden had to leave the employ of the New London Furniture Company with only a week's notice.

To fill his position, the company hired Mr. Burch Kelford, a long-time buyer for a chain of furniture stores. The officials of the New London Company felt that because of Mr. Kelford's familiarity with furniture in general, and their lines in particular, he would be able to assume Mr. Parden's duties without too much difficulty. On Mr. Parden's last day, Mr. Kelford reported for work, was shown around the plant, and was introduced to Miss Virginia Bellamy who served as the secretary for the purchasing agent, the designer, and the accountant. Insofar as possible, Mr. Parden gave Mr. Kelford an outline of his duties and indicated his plans for reorganizing the purchasing department. Because of the time situation, however, his instructions to Mr. Kelford were necessarily brief.

During the following week, Mr. Kelford began analyzing the work of the purchasing section and found several disturbing facts. For example, a supply of core stock (lumber used as a base for veneers) sufficient to last for sixteen months was on hand. In addition, two boxcar loads had been received and waybills showed that six more were on the way. All available space was at that time being used to store this material, and he had real doubts as to where the additional material could be stored. Although he and Miss Bellamy searched the files, they were unable to find a purchase contract authorizing the shipments. On Wednesday, five rush calls from the assembly plant informed him that the plant was out of drawer pulls, hinges, and braces for a particular dining-room suite and that unless a new supply could be obtained immediately, production of this item would necessarily stop. Later in the day, the accountant requested him to OK a bill from a paint and varnish supplier. Upon checking, Mr. Kelford found that although the material had been received, no purchase order had been issued for it. Instead, he found that Mr. Parden's practice had been to allow the paint salesman to inspect the company's stock and ship whatever supplies he (the salesman) thought appropriate. As a result, Mr. Kelford estimated that the New London Company had an eighteen to twenty month's supply of various types of fillers, paints, and varnishes.

At various times during the week, several plant foremen brought him bills for brushes, sandpaper, etc., indicating that they had practically exhausted their supplies and so had replenished them locally.

1. If you were Mr. Kelford, what immediate action would you take? Why?
2. What would be your long-range plans?

16
HOW YOUR COMPANY IS ORGANIZED

This chapter explains—

- The organization structure of a typical company
- Where the first-line supervisor fits in the organization
- How organization charts are made and used

The place where you work is important to you. You earn your living there, and you spend at least 50% of your waking hours at work. In view of this, you should understand how your job fits into the total company organization structure, how the company is organized, what it consists of, and how the parts work together to make it a coordinated, "well-oiled" operation instead of a disjointed, poorly working firm.

WHAT ARE THE ORGANIC FUNCTIONS OF A BUSINESS?

Most firms are operated to make a profit, and they attempt to do this by supplying a product or a service at the right time, at the right place, and at the right price that will induce the customer to purchase the product or service. To do this, every firm must make provisions for performing three absolutely necessary activities:

1. It must make arrangements to have the necessary money to *finance* and run the company.
2. It must *produce*, *assemble*, or in some fashion *acquire* the product or the service it hopes to sell.
3. It must make provisions to *distribute* the product or service to the customer.

needed activities These three activities or functions are found in *every* firm and are frequently referred to as *finance, production*, and *distribution*. Because you find them in every firm and because they are necessary for the firm to exist or "live," they are called the *organic functions* of an enterprise.

The *finance function* is performed by the company treasurer and his team. These individuals are usually known by such names as treasurer, controller, chief accountant, etc.

The *production* or *manufacturing function* includes all the activities directly concerned with making a product, such as the "shop" where products are made.

The third function is concerned with getting the product to the consumer and is known as the *distribution function*. In typical companies, you will find marketing, advertising, and sales included in this function.

WHY HAVE A BOARD OF DIRECTORS?

The board of directors of a corporation is required by law. It represents the stockholders of the firm and speaks for them. As such, the board is the "supreme commander" in a modern corporation.

"What are the organic functions
of an enterprise?"

What Does the Board Do?   A board of directors appoints various corporate
officers and fixes their wages. For example, the board usually appoints the
president, vice-president, secretary, and treasurer. The board also establishes company policies. The board for a shirt manufacturing firm, for example, might decide that the company should make a shirt that is the finest in
the world—even though it would cost the buyer $45.00. Or it might make a
policy that the company would make the best shirt it could that would retail
for less than $5.00.

board structure

    The board sets general objectives for the firm, like aiming for a 10%
return on investment or expanding operations to every one of the 50 states.
After these policies and objectives are set by the board, it is up to management to carry them out. The board also reviews and approves or rejects plans
and actions of the corporate officers. The president, for example, might
propose building a new plant in Arizona. The board would either approve or
disapprove of the president's proposal.

Who Makes Up the Board?   The board members may come from within the
company, in which case it is known as an *inside board.* If the board members
are not working for the company but are executives of other corporations, it
is known as an *outside board.*

An inside board has the advantage of having members on it who know the workings of the firm and the technical aspects of its operations, and who are familiar with its problems. Its major drawback is that the members are all insiders, and they don't bring outside, fresh points of view to bear on problems and policies of the firm.

Outside boards are considered to be more effective than inside boards because they bring a wide range of experience and ability to a company. However, a mixed board, consisting of both insiders and outsiders, is probably the best type of board because you get the best features of both. Most of the nation's leading companies have mixed boards with from 20 to 60% of the members coming from outside the company.

WHAT DOES THE PRESIDENT OF THE COMPANY DO?

Appointed by the board, the president is the top boss, the overall manager of the company. He is supposed to operate the firm profitably (if it is a profit-making firm), within the guidelines and policies set by the board. Because of the comprehensive aspects of his job, he is given broad powers and authority by the board.

Some firms have a vice-president or executive vice-president who is second in command. He does whatever the president directs him to do, but his duties are usually similar to those of the president. A lot of times the responsibilities are divided between these two by having the president responsible for the long-range aspects of operating the firm, whereas the vice-president's job is concerned with the short-range aspects.

WHY HAVE A CORPORATE SECRETARY?

Sometimes companies don't have an individual secretary, but rather a secretary-treasurer. In large firms, there is an individual secretary whose duty is to transmit the policies and recommendations of the board to the company's corporate officers. To do this, the secretary must attend all meetings of the board, keep minutes of the meetings, maintain the corporate books, and handle all the board's correspondence. The secretary also has the job of issuing and transferring all stocks, bonds, and securities for the company.

DOES THE TREASURER KEEP THE MONEY?

No, not personally. However, every firm has to have money to operate, and it is the treasurer's responsibility to look after *all aspects* of the firm's finances.

"Does the treasurer keep
the company's money?"

The treasurer is appointed by the board and is responsible to the president for all financial activities of the corporation. He has the job of getting credit or borrowing money and then using it appropriately to finance the operation of the company. Because of his responsible position with money, the treasurer must be a person of proven financial and business ability. In large companies, he hires credit managers, cashiers, controllers, and security managers to help him in his work.

IS THE CONTROLLER THE CHIEF ACCOUNTANT?

The controller is the chief accountant, in a sense. He reports to the treasurer and is responsible for such activities as accounting, cost control, payroll, and financial analysis. To help him with his job, he usually hires accountants, auditors, and budgetary directors.

ARE ACCOUNTANTS REALLY NECESSARY?

Accurate records are essential for any business to succeed. You've got to keep records of what you buy, your sales, your cash discounts, the money you take in, and so on. These records are kept by bookkeepers who periodically summarize them and prepare statements that analyze and interpret the figures for management.

Management needs financial facts on which to make decisions, and accountants typically keep the records and supply management with the necessary facts. To get this information, the accounting organization works closely with production supervisors to gather labor cost figures, with the purchasing agents to get material cost figures, and with the sales organization to gather figures on sales revenues and costs.

In addition to these figures for management, accounting is also responsible for preparing figures for people outside the firm—figures such as reports to stockholders, reports for bankers and other creditors, and reports to the government for tax purposes.

WHAT DOES THE PERSONNEL DIRECTOR DO?

As we saw in Chapter 10, the personnel department is charged with securing, training, and maintaining an adequate work force for the whole company—not just for one department. In single-plant firms, the personnel director usually reports to the plant manager. In large multiplant companies, the personnel department is usually located in the home office, and the personnel director reports to a vice-president.

The duties of the personnel officer (or department) vary from company to company. In large companies the personnel officer may be responsible for promotions, transfers, union relations, discharges, employee recreation, wage payment plans, health, safety, fringe benefits, financial aid to employees, and community relations. For all these, he provides the appropriate help or service to the supervisor, giving him advice to help him operate his department in a more effective way.

When a personnel director has all the many responsibilities indicated above, he usually has the following people to assist him: an employment manager, a training supervisor, a safety director, a medical director, and a director of industrial relations.

WHAT IS THE PURCHASING AGENT'S JOB?

The purchasing agent's job is to procure the necessary parts, tools, materials, and supplies from outside vendors. Like the personnel director, the purchasing agent (or director of purchasing) reports to the plant manager.

In small firms, you may well find the president or vice-president also performing the purchasing job because he wants to have more control over the spending of money. You may also find the purchasing agent responsible for the receipt and storage of the purchased material. The purchasing agent works mainly with production to find out what is needed, and with accounting to get the materials paid for.

You might find as many as four types of engineers in a company:

1. The *plant engineer* is responsible for selecting, installing, and maintaining the machines and other physical facilities of the enterprise.

2. The *process engineer's* job, on the other hand, is to effectively and economically maintain the manufacturing conditions in the plant. The process engineer, for example, is responsible for determining the best lighting conditions, temperature, humidity, etc., for the good of the employees.

3. The *product engineer* makes sure that the product being manufactured meets the customer's needs. In some companies, he designs the product and also has control of how it will be manufactured. A part that is typically made from a casting can be changed by the product engineer to a part of equal quality that can be fabricated more cheaply. He has final control over which part to use and how it will be made.

   varieties of engineers

4. An *industrial engineer* develops economical ways to do work. His job is not to get people to work faster but to devise better ways to perform work using the same or less effort. He looks for better, easier ways to work and, in doing this, studies the motions an employee uses, the tools employed, the layout of the work area, the materials used, and the work process. The industrial engineer may also be called the *methods engineer, motion and time study engineer, methods analyst,* or *methods and standards analyst.*

   He does methods work all over a firm: in the office, the assembly department, the manufacturing department, and the testing department. In addition, he also determines how much work an employee should do in a normal day; that is, he determines what a fair day's work is. In doing this, he may make time studies or use some system of predetermined time standards.

WHERE DOES PRODUCTION CONTROL FIT IN?

The production control manager usually reports to the plant manager and serves to coordinate all the factors of production so that a smooth flow of products will be produced with efficiency and dispatch.

Production control acts as the brain and nervous system of a firm and, as such, coordinates the work of engineering, purchasing, production, and sales. To do this, production control plans the work that needs to be done, determines when and where it should be done, and issues manufacturing orders to get the work accomplished. Production control also follows up on these plans, and where manufacturing is not proceeding according to plans, production control will make the adjustment necessary to get production back on the beam. Because of its broad coordinating responsibilities, production control is in close contact with practically every department and activity in a plant.

WHO IS IN CHARGE OF THE INSPECTION DEPARTMENT?

The inspection department practically never reports to the manufacturing superintendent because inspection would most likely suffer if the person responsible for making a product were also responsible for inspecting it. Instead, the plant manager or his assistant is usually the person to whom the manager of the inspection department reports.

As its name implies, the inspection department is charged with determining whether or not purchased materials as well as manufactured products meet the prescribed specifications. The inspection department's major contacts, therefore, are the receiving department, for the inspection of incoming materials, and the production department, for the inspection of the products manufactured.

DOES EVERY FIRM HAVE ALL OF THE ABOVE DEPARTMENTS?

No. The major activities described in the preceding sections are not found in every organization. Some companies combine the activities of one or more functions and put them in charge of one person. Other firms, because of the nature of their manufacturing operations, may not have need for some of the activities discussed. A brewery, for example, with a great many of its processes enclosed in kettles and pipes, might have little if any need for industrial engineering. The functions discussed, however, are quite common activities that are typically found in a great many industrial enterprises today.

WHERE DOES THE SUPERVISOR FIT INTO THE ORGANIZATION?

The supervisor is the man who is frequently caught between the proverbial "rock and a hard place." He is the middle man who works with both labor and management. To the employees, he is "management." To the top managers, he is the low man on the managerial totem pole. He is, however, the key man in the organization structure.

On his shoulders rests the responsibility for correctly and tactfully interpreting management's wishes to the workers. Because he works so closely with the employees, he is almost one of them and, in some cases, was one of them before his promotion. This may at times give him real problems with his loyalty. But because of this closeness, he is in the best position to correctly interpret the workers' feelings to top management. Being in this strategic position, the first-line supervisor is the key man in knitting both management and workers into a coordinated organization that works effectively and harmoniously to achieve its objectives.

first-level management

DO YOU NEED AN ORGANIZATION CHART TO "SEE" AN ORGANIZATION?

An organization chart is the best way to clearly depict the structure of a company. It is an attempt to "photograph" or picture how people are grouped, to tell who reports to whom, and to show the lines of authority and responsibility. It shows how the dynamic activities of enterprise are held together and are coordinated into a properly working unit.

Drawn correctly, an organization chart shows each man's assignment and its relation to other jobs. As a result, it helps avoid confusion and conflict that might arise because of an overlapping or haphazard arrangement of duties. When you try to depict a company's organization structure on paper, you might see inconsistencies or problems and thus be able to solve them. It might, for example, point out an illogical grouping of personnel and marketing activities, which when recognized can be corrected. Sometimes a chart points up the omission of an activity or function, thus allowing management to put it in the organization before serious problems result.

advantages of charts

Although a chart doesn't make a firm have a good organization, companies that keep up-to-date charts generally have the best organizations. The reason for this, of course, is that the charts serve to keep the managers aware of the company's structure and thus afford them the opportunity of making changes and divisions where they appear needed.

An organization chart is a good way to help get a new employee oriented with the formal organization structure of the company.

ARE THERE RULES FOR MAKING AN ORGANIZATION CHART?

Constructing an organization chart is not hard once management has determined what the general structure of the firm should be. Figure 16-1 illustrates the way most line and staff organizations are shown by a chart. Some good rules to follow in drawing an organization chart are:[1]

[1]These rules are from Claude S. George, Jr., *Management for Business and Industry* (Englewood Cliffs, N.J.: Prentice-Hall, Inc., 1970), p. 36. Reprinted by permission of Prentice-Hall, Inc.

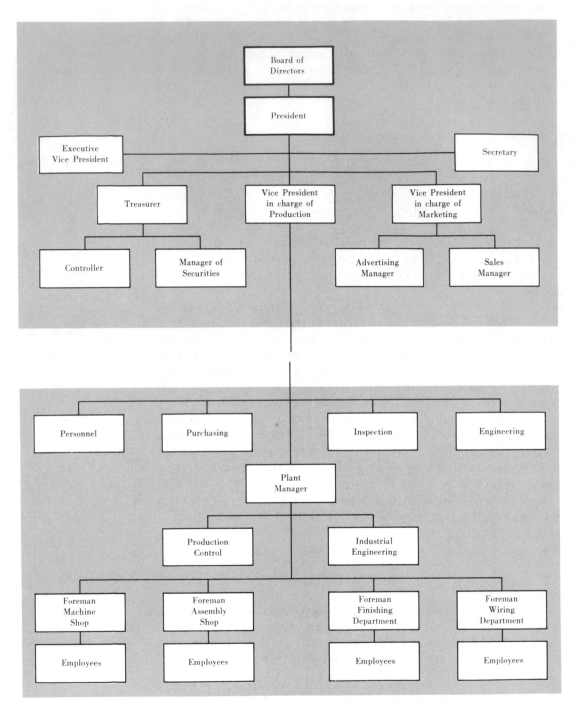

FIGURE 16-1.
Organization chart illustrating typical line and staff organization.

1. The vertical arrangement of functions, departments, or persons should be according to the grade or position in the company.
2. A rectangle should be used to indicate a unit or a person on a chart. Use straight vertical and horizontal lines to show the flow of authority.
3. Heavy black lines may be used to show the flow of line authority between any two positions.
4. Light lines may be used to show functional supervision.
5. Broken lines may be used to show the sources of advice and service.
6. Make the rectangles on the same level of equal size.
7. Place all rectangles for positions on the same authority level on the same horizontal line.
8. Normally, lines of authority enter each rectangle at the top center and leave at the bottom center. Lines of authority do not run through a rectangle.
9. Rectangles for personnel are normally placed under the individual or unit that they serve but above the line units in such a manner that they do not interrupt the lines of authority to line units.
10. If the chart centers around a person or unit, make the rectangle representing this person or unit the largest one on the chart. The rectangles above and below the key figure should be a smaller size. Rectangles on each lower level may be one size smaller.
11. On any individual chart, show at least one level above and two levels below the primary organization or person being charted.

CAN A SUPERVISOR PROFIT BY USING AN ORGANIZATION CHART?

A supervisor can use a company organization chart to show the relationship of his department and each individual in the department to the rest of the firm. Each box on the chart represents one job, and the way these boxes are grouped and connected by lines shows which activities fall within a division, department, or section. Having an organization chart of a department shows who reports to whom and can prevent misunderstandings and conflicts over authority.

Having a departmental organization chart may point out problems of duplication of effort or possible areas where the source of authority may be confused. It would readily show where an employee reports to two or more bosses or where confusion might result because of overlapping positions. It might point out situations where one person is supervising too many employees and another person is supervising too few.

Finally, if you'll keep an up-to-date organization chart of your department posted for your employees, they will understand you and your department better, how it is made up, and its relation to the rest of the company. They will also see where they fit in and possible lines for promotion.

A Case Study
ORGANIZATION STRUCTURE

Describe to the class how a firm or group of which you are a member is organized. This can be a company, a store, a civic organization, or a social group. Draw an organization chart of the structure showing how all the members fit into the overall organization. Have members of the class criticize your chart and the general organization and operation of the firm or group.

1. What changes would you suggest in the organization structure?
2. If you were president of the firm you have presented, what would you tell the other members about the organization chart and its uses?

A Case Study
EASTSIDE FLOUR MILL

In 1911 Sam Harris established the Harris Hickory Plant to manufacture and sell hickory handles for all types of hand tools and implements. Because of the quality of his work and the care with which he selected lumber, the company grew and prospered. By 1977 the organization of the company had developed into the seventeen-man structure illustrated in Figure 16-2.

Sam Harris was a strong-willed individual who had ruled and run his company with an iron hand. In a sense, he distrusted everyone and personally wanted to direct and supervise the efforts of all his employees. Insofar as possible, he did so, giving orders directly to his salesmen as well as to the plant workers. His "second in command" was Tom Jenkins, his mill foreman, who had been with the company for 52 years. Tom was well liked by the employees, was a capable worker, and was to a great degree responsible for the success of the firm. "T.J.," as everyone called him, had a "way" with people that made them like

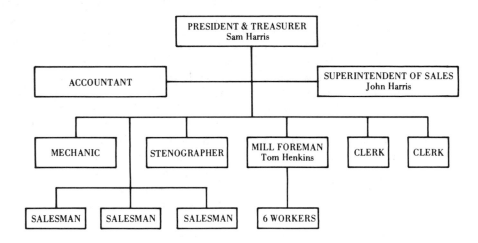

FIGURE 16-2.
Organization chart of the Harris Hickory Plant.

and respect him; he was the one who most often coordinated the overall efforts of the plant personnel after Mr. Harris had made a disturbing comment or observation.

Sales were under the direct supervision of Mr. Harris's youngest son, John, now 38 years of age. After receiving a college degree in chemistry, John Harris had been quite successful with one of the larger chemical companies. Five years ago his father had insisted that he return home to work in the family concern, and somewhat reluctantly he returned. Although John did a respectable job, it was apparent to most of the employees that he did not have the drive of his father nor the personality of Tom Jenkins. The accountant and the mechanic for the plant were both satisfactory in their respective areas, although neither was thought to possess the characteristics necessary for further advancement.

On January 18, 1977, Mr. Sam Harris died, and the business was sold to the Eastside Flour Mill. At the request of the new owners, the operation and name of the Harris Hickory Plant was to remain the same until some form of reorganization could be made.

The Eastside Flour Mill was located three miles from the Harris Hickory Plant and was a bustling concern. Originally, the company was founded to mill wheat and distribute flour and flour products. In 1936, however, lumber and mill work were added to the flour operations, and by 1950 the lumber operation (including the lumber milling work) had virtually taken over the Eastside Flour Mill with only 4% of gross sales coming from flour operations. As a result, flour milling and flour products were dropped from the company's line in 1965, and attention was devoted exclusively to lumber and wood products. Figure 16-3 illustrates the current organization structure of the company.

The Eastside Flour Mill was a locally owned corporation, managed by Mr. Tim Sykes, president and largest stockholder. Mr. Sykes had an outgoing personality and was generally regarded as a "natural-born" salesman. Although 63 years old, he often traveled the territory with his salesmen, and invariably when he made the rounds with them, sales increased by 15 to 60%. The controller, J. R. King, was highly regarded by Mr. Sykes as a man of rare abilities. He was a good coordinator, well liked, levelheaded, and possessed

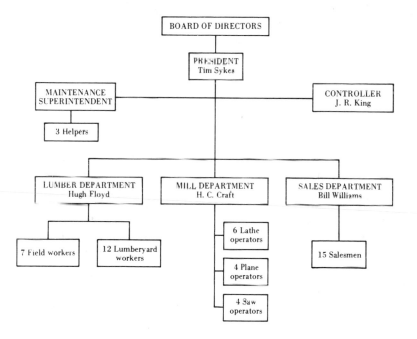

FIGURE 16-3.
Organization chart of the Eastside Flour Mill.

a keen insight into sound financial management. Hugh Floyd, in charge of the lumber department, was a lumberjack type of employee who did a good job in keeping the company supplied with the needed lumber of the right kind and quality. In fact, he devoted his major attention to the field and cutting operations, often to the detriment of the lumberyard at the plant. H. C. Craft, head of the mill department, was recognized by all employees for his ability in mill and lumber work. Not only did he run his department efficiently, but he often found time to help Hugh Floyd in his lumberyard operations.

Sales were under the direction of Bill Williams, 42 years of age, who was quite competent as a salesman, but he had experienced some trouble in keeping his salesmen satisfied and enthusiastic about their work.

After acquiring the Harris Hickory Plant, the Board of Directors of the Eastside Flour Mill was faced with the problem of how to consolidate and effectively organize the operations of the two plants.

1. If you were called in to give advice to the Board, what organization structure would you suggest for the consolidated firm?

17
WHAT YOU SHOULD KNOW ABOUT ORGANIZATION

This chapter explains—

- The difference between line and staff
- What authority is and where it comes from
- What an effective span of management is

If you stop to think about it, most of our lives are spent working with and in organizations such as families, clubs, churches, schools, governments, and business firms where we earn our living. We work with all these organizations for only two reasons: (1) we can accomplish objectives through them that we could not accomplish as easily or as effectively by ourselves, and (2) we can do things together that we could never do alone.

Some people complain about organizational relationships by saying that business would be a good place to work if it weren't for the organization. But think for a moment about the trouble you would have trying to provide food, clothing, and shelter for yourself and your family if you could not work in an organized way with other people. Of course, you might be able to survive, but what you could provide for yourself would not nearly equal what we have today, and you would have to work at it every minute of the day—not just 40 hours a week!

When we organize ourselves, we can do things working together that we couldn't do alone. For example, we put a man on the moon through organized endeavor. We built a Golden Gate Bridge through organized endeavor. And we can accomplish smaller tasks even more easily when we organize. For these reasons, we organize ourselves in business—to make the work easier and more effective and to do things that we could not do alone.

WHAT IS ORGANIZING?

Organizing is the process of coordinating the efforts of men to achieve objectives in the most efficient manner possible. For our businesses, this means that organizing consists of combining and coordinating what employees do in such a way that they get the most output for the least effort. Thus, in our businesses when we organize ourselves, we are working most effectively toward a goal we want to reach.

WHAT IS A LINE ORGANIZATION?

definitions

A line organization is the oldest and simplest type of organization. It's the kind of organization you would find in a small manufacturing plant, such as that shown in Figure 17-1. This organization is easy to understand, there is no problem about who is the boss, and decisions can be made quickly. Its drawbacks are: if the leader leaves or dies, usually no one is prepared to move in, and the business suffers; and, because the leader has no assistants, he is frequently overworked and places undue reliance on his subordinates. In many cases, this results in jobs being poorly done.

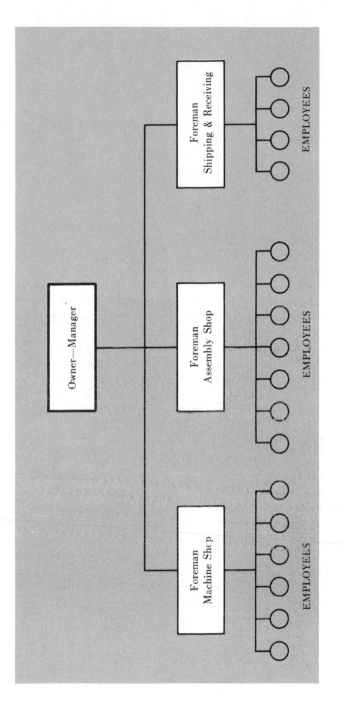

FIGURE 17-1.
Organization chart of a small manufacturing plant.

WHAT IS A LINE AND STAFF ORGANIZATION?

A line and staff organization is essentially a line organization to which staff assistants have been added. If our small manufacturing plant grew in size, the owner might need to add accountants to keep his books, a personnel supervisor to look after his employees, a production control man, and an industrial engineer. When he adds the new *staff* people, his organization would now look like that in Figure 17-2.

The line organization is indicated by heavy lines and is much the same as it was except that more men have been added. The staff organization, however, is new. The owner has hired the staff people to give expert advice and help to himself as well as to his supervisors.

WHAT'S THE DIFFERENCE BETWEEN LINE AND STAFF?

line vs staff

The line organization *directly* aids in accomplishing the goals of the firm. The staff aids *indirectly*. Staff is usually advisory in nature, helping other people know what should be done and how to do it. Staff has no command authority over the line; it only recommends. The staff's purpose is to be on tap for advice but not on top authoritatively.

Production and sales departments are most commonly thought of as line organizations, whereas such activities as engineering, accounting, personnel, and maintenance are usually thought of as staff activities.

DOES STAFF HAVE MORE AUTHORITY THAN LINE?

the line commands

It might look as if staff members have more authority than line members, but they actually don't. When staff men are present, however, the problem usually arises as to how much authority these staff men should have over the shop foreman. For example, does the foreman control the work of his employee, or does production control tell the employee what to do? Remember the staff's job is to advise and help but not to command—and production control is staff. The line supervisor is the one who has the authority to act and to command. The line supervisor, therefore, runs his department. The staff man has no authority over him or his employees.

HOW DOES STAFF GET AWAY WITH TELLING LINE WHAT TO DO?

Staff can tell line what to do in two ways:

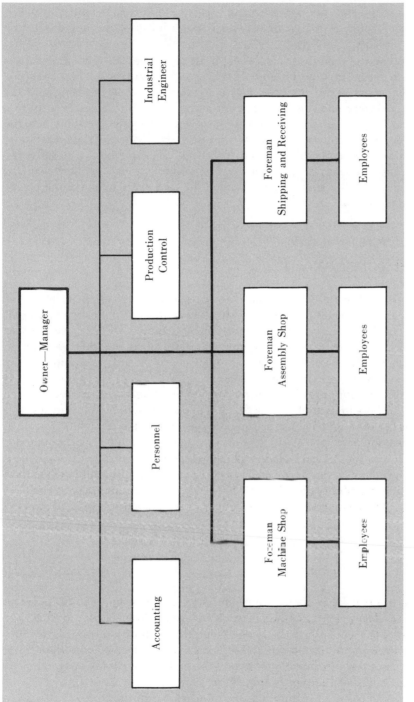

FIGURE 17-2.
Organization chart of a small manufacturing plant that has grown.

1. If you listen carefully, the staff isn't giving commands to the line. Instead, the staff man is saying, "This is what I think you should do," or, "You'd better do this if you want to improve the quality of your work."

2. When the staff gives this advice, most supervisors take it and make the changes. The supervisor could refuse to do what the staff man suggests, but most of the time the staff man is an expert in his field, and the supervisor knowing this, doesn't argue with him. When you go to a doctor and he says you need to have your appendix out, do you argue with him? You could if you wanted to. In fact, you could even refuse to have your appendix removed. You would, of course, have to suffer the consequences. In like manner, the supervisor can fail to follow the advice of the staff, but in doing so he may have to suffer the consequences.

ARE AUTHORITY AND RESPONSIBILITY ALIKE?

Authority is the right to command or act and is the power you have over others. If you have authority, you can cause a person to do something that you want done. Every supervisor is vested with the authority necessary to secure the cooperation of his employees. He might get this cooperation through his dynamic leadership, through coercion and persuasion, or by promise of some economic gain or loss.

Responsibility, on the other hand, is the obligation that an employee has to his boss to do a job or task that has been assigned to him. The key idea here is one of *obligation.* You are hired to do a certain job; therefore, you have an obligation or responsibility to your boss to do the job he hired you to do.

It wouldn't be fair to hold a person responsible for doing a job without first giving him the authority necessary to get it done. Thus, although authority and responsibility are different, they should go together. Where you have authority delegated, it should be coupled with responsibility.

WHERE DOES AUTHORITY COME FROM?

There are two ideas about where authority comes from. The first idea or *classical theory* says that authority is delegated from above. If you have authority to hire and fire, you were given this authority by your boss. Suppose you were delegated the authority by him to hire no more than thirty men. You could hire any number up to thirty, but you couldn't exceed thirty without additional authority from him. Thus, you get your authority from your boss. He gets his from his boss. And so on up the line.

The other theory of authority is called the *acceptance theory.* The idea here is that the authority you have over your employees is only the authority that your employees give you. In other words, they give you the authority to tell them what to do. In similar fashion, the only authority your boss has over you is what you give him, and the only authority that teachers have over students is the authority that the students give the teachers. Suppose you tell your employees that starting tomorrow, everyone must wear red uniforms and yellow shoes to work. Will they do it? If you have authority over them, they should do it. But they probably won't come to work with red uniforms and yellow shoes—which means you don't have authority over them. Suppose a teacher assigns 115 math problems as homework. Does he have the authority to make you do it? Not unless you give him the authority. Of course your boss or teacher can withhold pay or grades if you don't do what they say, but neither of them can make you do it unless you give them the authority to command you to do so.

sources of authority

There's some truth in both of these theories. The authority to hire thirty employees comes from your boss—not from your employees. But the authority to force an employee to do a job a certain way comes from the employee and not from your boss. Thus, part of every supervisor's authority, the right to command, comes from his boss, and part comes from his employees.

WHY IS DELEGATION OF AUTHORITY IMPORTANT?

Delegation of authority is the key to organization. If you don't delegate, you won't have any organization—only one-man operations. No one expects a supervisor to personally tell every employee what to do, or to inspect every product, or to prepare shipping papers on everything that goes out. But he may well be responsible for seeing that all this is done, and the only way he can get it done is to delegate authority to his employees. Since the job of a supervisor is to see that his department operates smoothly through the efforts of his employees, he must, therefore, delegate authority to the appropriate employees in order to get the work done.

need in organization

Another reason for delegating is that it gives your employees a sense of participating—of being somewhat in control. Being in control, or having authority to make decisions, is a great source of job enrichment for your employees and enhances their job potential. In addition, letting your employees make decisions is a great motivating influence. It makes them feel that they belong, that they are not just cogs in a wheel.

TO WHOM SHOULD YOU DELEGATE?

Delegate authority only to a person who has both the knowledge and the competence to make a decision. If the person has information about the job but is not competent to make a decision, he should not be given authority to

information and
competence
make the decision. Likewise, if he has competence to make the decision but does not have sufficient information, he should not be delegated authority nor be required to make the decision. If you delegate authority to a person who lacks both competence and knowledge (information), you will probably get bad decisions.

WHAT HAPPENS IF YOU DON'T DELEGATE?

You won't keep your job long if you don't delegate. You'll be the supervisor who is always pushing carts around the floor, cleaning a machine, relieving an operator, and doing a thousand other jobs—rather than doing your own thing of supervising. You'll be constantly interrupted by your employees to give them help. You'll be called on by your secretary to tell her how to spell a word. In short, you'll be so busy doing odd jobs—work that isn't yours—that your own work will suffer. Your desk will be overflowing, and your employees will be in a state of confusion because you haven't organized things properly.

poor
organization
If the above sounds like you, then your basic problem is that you don't understand what delegation is, how it makes for good supervision, and how it can be a sanity saver for you. Perhaps you don't trust your employees to do their jobs. Whatever your reason is for not delegating—remember that if you don't delegate, you aren't supervising. Your job is to get things done through others. You can't do it all. You have to let someone else do something. You must, therefore, give the authority to your employees to make decisions and to do things where they have the competence and information necessary to get the work done. Only through wise delegation can you get on with your job of supervising the work and workers in your department.

Don't forget that *the job of a supervisor is to get things done through others.*

HOW SHOULD YOU DELEGATE AUTHORITY?

rules that help
1. Call in the employee to whom you are delegating the authority, and tell him what authority you are delegating to him. Give him the whole picture and scope of the job. Tell him clearly what he has to do, how far he can go, and how much you will check on him. Tell him the relative importance of the job and how it fits into the scheme of work. Remember that you understand the total situation, that you can see the whole picture, but that an employee does not have your vantage point. When he comes to a crossroads and has to make a decision, you want him to choose the right road, but unless he can see the whole picture, he will not be in a position to do so. Be sure, therefore, that you give

him the whole story, all the facts. When an employee says, "But you didn't tell me that," you've done a poor job of delegating.

2. It is a good idea to take the employee around and introduce him to all the people who will be concerned with his new authority, and explain his job to them.

3. When you tell your employee about his additional job, be sure to tell him why you picked him. In other words, prepare him psychologically. Explain your confidence in him and in his ability to do the job. Don't let him leave wondering, "Why did the boss pick on me to do another job when I already have more than I can do?" If he thinks you are pushing things off on him, he may embarrass you by doing a poor job.

4. Be sure you only delegate those things that you should delegate. Don't push off a "hot potato" on an employee. Don't ask him to do an unpleasant job or one that you wouldn't do. And don't give him the job of discipline. That is a supervisor's job and should never be given to someone else.

WHAT'S THE PRIME RULE OF ORGANIZATION?

The purpose of organizing is to help us achieve goals. The first rule of organization, therefore, is to always remember what you are trying to do before you develop an organization to do it. Your goal, what you are trying to accomplish, should determine to a large degree what your organization looks like. A lot of people forget this and develop an organization that works, but doesn't work well, because it was not developed with the particular job or goal in mind.

If you were called on to organize some men to build a reviewing stand for a parade, you wouldn't try to appoint a board of directors, a president, a sales manager, and so on, because that is not the kind of organization you need to get the stand built. Instead, you would probably hire yourself a couple of carpenters and tell them the size of stand you want and where to get the materials. This is a temporary organization that will end as soon as *know your* the stand is built, and it does not have to be elaborate. *objective*

Contrast this hastily developed organization with one that would be needed to operate a bank. In a bank, you would want permanence, safety for depositors, compliance with state and federal banking laws, etc. In this instance, your objectives are different, and the organization structure will be different. You will need a board, a president, a controller, a loan officer—lots of people you didn't need for the organization to build the reviewing stand.

Even though you can easily see the different needs of these two organizations, a lot of people overlook this rule when they begin to organize men. They often get carried away with the development of an organization and forget *why* the organization is being formed. Then they wind up with an eight-cylinder organization to do a two-cylinder job.

The rules, then, are:

1. First get clearly in mind what you want to accomplish.
2. Then build an organization to achieve what you want done.

IS UNITY OF COMMAND IMPORTANT?

Unity of command means that every person in an organization has only one immediate superior who is his boss. In other words, only one person should give orders to an employee. Some companies are organized in such a way that sometimes two or more supervisors boss one man. This is poor organization for several reasons. If the employee has two or more bosses and he is conscientiously trying to do the work for all of them, he will probably reach the point where he gives up because of excess work (no boss knows how much work he has to do), frustration (he gets conflicting orders from different bosses), and maybe ulcers from worry.

have only one boss

Having two or more bosses for one employee is poor from a supervisor's point of view because it provides an employee a good place to goldbrick or goof off. Neither boss knows exactly what the other one has given the employee to do. As a consequence, the employee can loaf pretty much as he pleases. Or it might end up as a situation where the "squeaking wheel gets the grease," that is, the boss who yells the loudest at the employee and beats the desk the hardest is the one whose work gets done. The other bosses take whatever time the employee has left.

"Having two or more bosses is poor organization."

For all these reasons, having two or more bosses should be avoided. It
helps nothing and presents all sorts of possibilities for conflicts.

257

*What You Should
Know About
Organization*

WHAT IS AN INFORMAL ORGANIZATION?

Every organization has two systems in operation: the *formal* and the *informal*. The *formal* system is composed of the recognized and formalized lines of authority, communication, and control. This is the system we see "pictured" in the typical organization chart of a company.

The second or *informal* system is much more difficult to see and to understand. In any group of employees, some informal leader always emerges. He sets the pace, and the others give him the authority to lead them. He is not the leader designated by management, but he has authority just as surely as the supervisor does. For example, in a sewing operation where a team of women work to produce certain parts of garments, one lady might emerge as the leader and spokesman for the group. Whatever she says should be done, the group does. If she tells the group to sew slower, they do it. If she says she thinks the group should complain to their supervisor about the quality of the material they are sewing, they will complain. Thus, she is the informal leader of a group who have organized themselves informally. This is not a formal organization structure set up by management. A supervisor can rescind or change a formal organization, but he cannot rescind or change an informal organization. The employees are the ones who set up the informal organization, and they are the ones who have the power to change it.

*organization
developed by
employees*

Some informal organizations are made up of employees who get together to get work done without the benefit of formal direction or authority. In a great many companies, these are the ones who actually make things go, who work with the sticky problems, and who give aid to the formal organization. However, they can also be just the opposite by being the ones who cause all the problems. It depends on their leadership and the direction their efforts take.

WHAT SHOULD SUPERVISORS DO ABOUT INFORMAL ORGANIZATIONS?

Every supervisor should recognize that informal organizations exist and that they are susceptible to human manipulation and opportunism because of their undefined structure. An informal organization might make trouble as well as give help. The alert supervisor, therefore, should try to develop a sensitivity to the presence of these informal organizations and should be alert to possible problems they may cause before the problems fester and erupt as full-blown complaints or grievances.

Inasmuch as informal organizations are going to exist whether the supervisor likes them or not, a wise course of action might be to view them as a positive force, and use them to make the work of the department easier. This can be done by thinking of the informal leader not as a "ringleader," but as a person "in on things," whose talents can be used. By building good relations with him, the supervisor might get him to use his influence to settle a knotty problem between two employees or to give the supervisor help in getting some concept accepted by the workers.

IS IT POOR PRACTICE TO COMMUNICATE OUT OF CHANNELS?

A channel is the official path through which orders and communications flow from management to workers and vice versa. On an organization chart, the lines that join various jobs show the path through which orders and communications flow from the top to the bottom man in the organization.

use of channels

Most companies set up these channels carefully and for good reasons. They are the highways for orders and communications to follow, and as such, they keep everyone aware of what is going on. They serve to coordinate and unify the organization into a whole unit instead of a series of parts. When you leave these channels and take a shortcut, you are apt to run into problems. If an employee takes his grievance straight to the president of his company instead of to his supervisor, he would be going out of channels. Most companies frown on going out of channels, so it is best to conform to the company's practices and wishes.

Sometimes, of course, the normal channels of communication can delay work, and you might choose to take a shortcut and go around some individuals. If you do, be sure to tell those you bypassed, including your boss, what you have done and why. In this way, you will preserve the wholeness of the organization and keep your boss and others from thinking that you are doing things behind their backs.

WHAT IS SPAN OF MANAGEMENT?

Span of management is the number of people who report to a supervisor. If a supervisor has too many employees to look after, he will not be able to do a good job of supervising them. If he has too few, the company is not getting full value from him, and he may oversupervise and thereby destroy some of his employees' initiative. The problem is, how many employees can one supervisor effectively supervise? There is no magic answer, because the number that can be effectively supervised depends on a lot of factors. Let's look at some of them.

Factors Affecting Span of Management. If all the people you supervise are in one room or area, you can supervise more employees than if they are scattered all over the plant. If all of them are doing the same thing, you can supervise more than if they are doing different things. With everybody doing the same job, you can tell them what to do in groups (like classes), thus saving time. Also, your work of planning, control, etc., will be easier because everyone is doing the same job. If their work is interdependent; that is, if what one person can do depends on what another employee does and so on, then you cannot supervise as many employees because you will have to plan and watch the work closely to be sure that there is no bottleneck. If the people you supervise are very intelligent, you can supervise more than if the level of intelligence is very low. Also most of the time, employees with a good education catch on quicker than those with a poor education. They don't, therefore, need as much supervision.

Another factor, of course, is the supervisor himself. Some people seem to have the ability to keep eight or ten irons in the fire, whereas others have difficulty looking after two or three. The supervisor who has the capacity to look after seven or eight things at once can supervise more employees than the supervisor who gets confused if he has over three or four items going.

Finally, factors like how exacting the quality standards are and how much time you have to get the work done have to be considered in trying to figure out the right number of employees for a supervisor to look after. As was stated earlier, there is no magic number. For one set of circumstances, the "right" number of employees for a supervisor might be twelve. In another case, it might be eighteen or twenty-two employees.

What you have to do is consider the types of things that affect your span of management, look at the situation you have, and come up with a reasonable number. Experience will show if your judgment is wrong, and you can make adjustments.

SHOULD A SUPERVISOR HAVE AN UNDERSTUDY?

Absolutely! Every supervisor needs someone he can call on to take over while he is out of the department. Even in the smallest departments, someone should be designated as an understudy or backup man. You never know when an emergency will call the supervisor away or when the opportunity will present itself for the supervisor to attend a conference or educational session. Also, there are always vacation periods to be considered. And, of course, the supervisor may miss a promotion opportunity for himself if no one has been groomed to take over. For these and other reasons that you can think of, every supervisor at one time or another will need a backstop. The problem is selecting the right man.

Selecting an Understudy. When you select an understudy, look for a person to whom other employees seem to turn naturally for help and advice about their work, a person who has the respect of the other employees, and a

effective span of management

selecting and training an understudy

person who is regarded by them as a leader. He should be a levelheaded individual who is able to handle problems without getting excited. He should be the type who wants to learn, has an open mind, and is motivated to accept larger responsibilities. And finally, he should have demonstrated his loyalty and dependability. You may not see all of these in a worker right away, but when given the opportunity to prove himself, you may find that he possesses many latent or hidden qualities that weren't readily apparent.

Training an Understudy.   Once you've decided on your understudy, it is not necessary to have a press conference to announce it. Instead, you can start giving him small assignments to test his capacity and indicate your confidence in him. These will be signals to the other employees that it looks like Sam Jones is learning your job. When you leave, of course, you should tell your department that Sam will be in charge until you get back.

There is no definite procedure that can be outlined for training every understudy. What will work in one case may not in another. You should, however, develop a plan to gradually bring Sam into focus on the details of how your department works, the reports issued, problem areas, and so on. If company policy allows it, you may also take Sam to supervisors' meetings, so he can meet other supervisors and get a larger picture of the company's problems. Finally, you can give Sam the responsibility for certain areas or activities in your department to let him try his wings. Using steps similar to these, you should be able to gradually get Sam into a position to take over your department. And then, just when you think you've got him trained, you have to start the process all over because he is transferred out of your department to be the supervisor in another! But you've done an important job for the company: you have identified and developed a person with managerial capacities. And you have given a fellow man an opportunity to try to improve himself.

WHAT IS THE PERFECT ORGANIZATION?

ideal organization

Every supervisor should have in mind a plan for the perfect or ideal way he would like to have his department organized. This would be the organization structure that in his mind would be most desirable and would best enable the department to achieve its objectives. The ideal organization might mean that old John, the strawboss, would not be in the picture. It might combine two or more jobs in a new operation. These things can't be achieved now, however, because John has four more years before retirement, and you don't want to change his job now. But having an ideal organization in mind is important to you because when the time comes that a change can be made, you will know what changes you want to make. When an employee suddenly leaves, for example, it might present an opportunity for you to make a change *provided you know what you want to do*. Your idea of what a perfect organization would be like also gives you a standard by which you can compare and evaluate your present organization, in addition to giving you a guide for making future changes when the opportunity presents itself.

WHAT ARE THE REWARDS OF GOOD ORGANIZATION?

An organization conceived and developed along the lines we have discussed will more than reward you for your efforts. Not only will you achieve your objectives more easily, you will also find that the physical operation of your department will be greatly enhanced. Everything will go more smoothly. This situation is achieved because a good organization typically:[1]

- Establishes responsibility and prevents "buck passing."
- Provides for easier communication.
- Eliminates jurisdictional disputes between individuals.
- Helps develop supervisory ability.
- Aids in measuring a person's performance against his charges and responsibilities.
- Aids in equitable distribution of work functions and/or personnel supervision.
- Permits expansion and contraction without seriously disrupting the structure.
- In times of change, affords movement in the direction of the "ideal" organization.
- Makes for closer cooperation and higher morale.
- Points out "dead-end" jobs.
- Delineates avenues of promotion.
- Prevents duplication of work.
- Makes growth possible with adequate control and without literally killing top executives through overwork.
- Aids in wage and salary administration through forced job analysis and description.

A Case Study
THE CASE OF THE OVERWORKED SUPERVISOR

The Amos Construction Company was one of the largest and most successful building contracting firms in the state. By and large, its business consisted of erecting public buildings such as schools, city halls, auditoriums, dormitories, etc., and private buildings for factories, offices, and the like.

[1]The following points are from Claude S. George, Jr., *Management for Business and Industry* (Englewood Cliffs, N.J.: Prentice-Hall, Inc., 1970), p. 109. Reprinted by permission of Prentice-Hall, Inc.

Joe Thompson was one of its best project foremen. The project foreman's work consisted of completely supervising all work performed on the site from the ground breaking to the final ribbon cutting. On a normal project, this involved the supervision of over 80 men, and on the larger projects, this number frequently exceeded 200. The project foreman was responsible for hiring his men, keeping records of their work, making up payrolls, paying the men, maintaining various social security records, etc. In addition to these activities, he was completely responsible for planning what should be done, how it should be done, and giving instructions to the men to do the work. By interview and questions, he determined each man's best qualifications and used him accordingly.

As the building progressed, the project foreman had to contact the suppliers and have them deliver certain quantities of material as needed. For example, the home office would place an order for all bricks necessary for a building and would tell the project foreman with whom they had placed the order. The project foreman would then contact the brickyard and make arrangements for them to deliver certain quantities and types of bricks on specified dates as demanded by the progress of the building. The same sort of thing held true for steel-fabricated parts, ready-mixed concrete, and the like.

As the building developed, the project foreman also had to make arrangements to have bricklayers, carpenters, and other workmen available when needed, as well as tell them what he wanted done and supervise their work. In addition, he usually worked closely with the architect, and frequent conferences were often necessary to "iron out" certain points of disagreement.

Accurate time records had to be kept for cost and payroll purposes, and receipts for all material delivered to the job had to be verified and sent to the home office for payment. As material was delivered to the job, the project foreman had to decide where it should be placed to be most convenient for use without blocking access to other material that would be required.

In other words, the project foreman was the "plant manager" of a construction job. Everything that happened on the job was his responsibility, and it was his job to see that the work was completed according to specifications in minimum time.

Despite the fact that Joe Thompson was one of their best foremen, he did not apparently have the capacity to handle a big job. His work was superior on small jobs where he could personally supervise every operation and attend to each detail. On the major projects, however, the very quantity of things to be done weighed him down. The company, however, needed Joe for the big jobs—they wanted the advantage of his superior knowledge and construction know-how—but they couldn't decide how to break Joe into a big job. They first tried giving him a medium-size job and sending him an assistant. In six weeks, however, the assistant reported that he was wasting the company's money because he had nothing to do. At the completion of this job, however, Joe Thompson had to take a two-month sick leave to regain his health. The extra work of the larger project had caused him to overwork, and his physician recommended complete rest.

1. Construct an organization chart of how you think Joe Thompson ran the project.
2. If you were the owner of Amos Construction Company, what steps would you take to get Joe on the road to handling the larger, more complex jobs? Construct an organization chart showing your recommendations.

A Case Study
STAFF VERSUS LINE

The discussion was calm at first, but then it grew heated between John Lancing, head of Organization Planning, and Pete Bogs, the supervisor of the Purchasing Department. Pete claimed that John was trying to reorganize his department (Purchasing) out of existence, whereas John claimed that he was only trying to place the Purchasing Department in proper perspective within the company.

Basically, John's plan was this: The Purchasing Department was a staff activity in his mind, and as such should be organized along those lines. Inasmuch as it was a staff department, he thought that it should report to the VP of Staff Services, Harry Council. This would mean that Harry would have Transportation, Purchasing, Personnel, Legal Relations, and Accounting reporting to him.

Pete claimed that this was not the logical place for Purchasing to be located. Purchasing, he argued, was not a staff activity. It was, instead, a line operation and should continue to be a part of Bill Marston's Manufacturing Department. Purchasing, he continued, was a necessary and vital part of Manufacturing. Without purchasing activities, Manufacturing would have no raw material to work with, no parts to assemble, and nothing for its employees to do (according to Pete). In addition, Pete claimed that Purchasing was vital to producing products at a minimum cost through control of inventory and the inflow of materials. Without question, in his mind, Purchasing aided directly in accomplishing the objective of the company, and as such should continue to remain as an important part of the basic line function of Manufacturing.

John Lancing couldn't see Pete's side of the question at all. To him, Purchasing was a pure and simple staff function. It served not only production, but all components of the company as well. Like the Personnel Department, it served all components of the firm by going into the marketplace and buying requisitioned materials at the best price and delivery available. In John's mind, it didn't matter whether a requisitioned part was to be used on a typewriter, a milling machine, or on the cafeteria stove—the Purchasing Department served all equally. As a result, John reasoned, it was a service function that should not be placed under the control of Manufacturing. In Marston's organization, he reasoned, it would be subject to pressure to get Manufacturing's parts first, to serve Manufacturing first, and to give whatever time was left to the procurement of materials for other parts of the company.

In addition to these arguments, John indicated that he thought that leaving Purchasing under Manufacturing would stretch the unity of command principle. He explained this by saying that instead of having one boss, Pete would, in effect, be responsible to the supervisors of Manufacturing, Transportation, Personnel, Finance, Accounting, and so on—all the departments that had him buy material for their use. If the Purchasing Department were located under the VP of Staff Services, however, he reasoned that it would have only one boss, Harry Council, to report to.

1. Do you think that John Lancing's arguments were sound? Why?
2. Where do you think that the Purchasing Department should be located? Why?
3. Is Purchasing a line or a staff activity? As such, where would you normally expect it to be located in a typical manufacturing organization?

18

HOW TO MAKE WORK EASIER AND INCREASE PRODUCTION

This chapter explains—

- How to go about making a motion study
- Which jobs are best to study
- How to make and use process charts, flow diagrams, and operations charts

Management is always interested in finding easier, simpler, and more effective ways to perform work. If you can find a way to make a product cheaper and thus reduce production costs, then your company can be more competitive in the marketplace and can make more sales. More sales mean more business, and more business means more jobs and more profits. All of this is desirable from management's point of view.

When it comes right down to your own personal job, you can improve the way you work in lots of ways. Sometimes you get a sudden idea that really makes the job easier, and you wonder why it hadn't occurred to you before. Or maybe a neighbor makes a suggestion. Or something you see or read triggers your mind. Although all of these ways may occasionally work, they are unsystematic, and if you do improve your job, it is inspirational or accidental and not because you have made a systematic study of what you are doing and how to improve it. The best and surest way to improve your job is through systematic study of what you are doing, using a process called *methods improvement*. Whether it is called work study, motion stud methods improvement, or work simplification, it all means the same thing: a systematic attempt to eliminate unnecessary work and to make what remains easier to do.

There is nothing new in this, of course. Man has always searched for ways to make his work easier. When he substituted the sail for oars and added wheels to his sled, he was working "smarter," not harder. We are

"The idea in work simplification is to work smarter, not harder."

doing the same thing today when we try to find an easier, better way to
perform a task. As a supervisor, you want your employees to do their jobs in
the simplest, easiest, most effective way. This makes your department more
efficient and lowers your operating costs. The best way to approach this is
through methods improvement.

WHAT IS METHODS IMROVEMENT?

Methods improvement is the name given to the process of trying to improve
the way you do a job. You would be making a methods study, for instance, if
you tried to figure out a better and easier way to set a table or to wash a car.
To do this, you would study each part of the job to see if you could eliminate
it, improve it, or in some way make the work easier.   *working easier*

The steps you use in making a methods improvement study are:

1. Select a job to be improved.
2. Break the job down into steps and record these on a piece of paper.
3. Analyze the steps, questioning the necessity for each one. If the step
   can't be eliminated, see what you can do to make it easier to do.
4. Develop a new method of doing the job using the improved steps you
   have designed.

Process charts and flow diagrams are frequently used in methods improvement. Let's look at what these are and how they are used.

WHAT IS A PROCESS CHART?

A process chart is nothing but a piece of paper on which you record the parts
or steps in a process. When you write down the steps in a process, you place
them in the right sequence. Then you can study the whole process without
forgetting a step or getting it in the wrong place.

Once the whole job is recorded, you then sit down and look at each
step, asking such questions as the following. "Is this step actually necessary
in order to get the job done?" "Can it be eliminated?" "Can it be simplified
or made easier?" By asking questions like these about each step, you will
frequently find that the job can be simplified or reorganized so that it can be
done more easily and in less time than before.

How Can a Process Be Described?   Every process or job can be described
by using some combination of the five following steps.

1. An *operation* consists of doing something like painting a table, washing a plate, putting the top on a jar, or typing a letter.

2. A *transportation* occurs when something is moved from one place to another. Moving a letter from the file cabinet to your desk, moving raw materials from the stockroom to the assembly area, or moving a dish from the cabinet to the table are examples of transportation.

3. A *delay* occurs when something stops or delays what is taking place. If you are moving raw materials from storage to the shop floor and had to wait for the elevator, this would be a delay in the transportation of the material.

understanding the
job

4. A *storage* describes storing a part or product to prevent unauthorized use. Dishes in a cabinet are in storage, as are materials in a stockroom. A storage is not a delay but is a regular part of the process.

5. An *inspection* is what the word says. A clerk checking the weight of a bag of potatoes or an inspector checking the hardness of a piece of steel are examples of inspections.

By using these five steps, any process can be broken down quickly and easily into its basic parts. To save time in writing, the following symbols for these five steps are frequently used in constructing process charts:

○ = Operation
⇨ = **Transportation**
D = Delay
▽ = Storage
□ = Inspection

A further explanation of these symbols is shown in Figure 18-1.

Where can a Process Chart Be Used?   You can use a process chart anywhere in order to study and improve what is being done. You could make a process chart of getting out of bed and dressing in the morning. Everything that you do would be classified under one of the five steps. Or you could make a pro-

making and using
a process chart

cess chart of what happens to a soft drink in a bottling plant. Everything that happens to the bottle would be classified under one of the five steps and would be recorded on the chart.

How Do You Construct a Process Chart?   A process chart can be made on a sheet of paper or on a form similar to the one shown in Figure 18-2. To construct the chart, you first follow the person about his work, noting and classifying on the chart everything that he does. For example, if a typist carried a letter to her supervisor, you would draw an arrow because this is a transportation, note how far she walked (say 35 feet), and describe what she did as, "Carried letter to supervisor." If she waited for the supervisor to read and sign the letter, you would draw a "D" (for delay) and note by it, "Waited

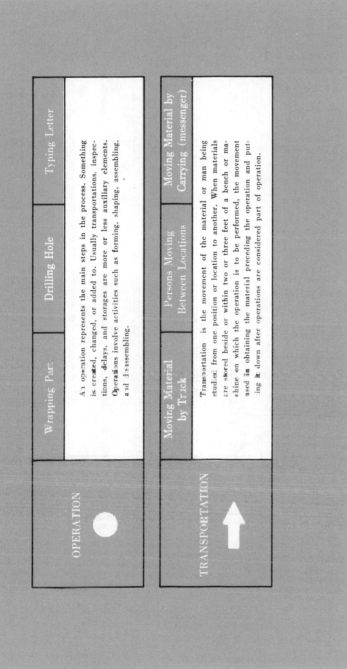

FIGURE 18-1.
Flow process chart symbols. (From James E. Morgan, Jr., *Principles of Administrative and Supervisory Management* (Englewood Cliffs, N.J.: Prentice-Hall, Inc., 1973), p. 336. Reprinted by permission of Prentice-Hall, Inc.

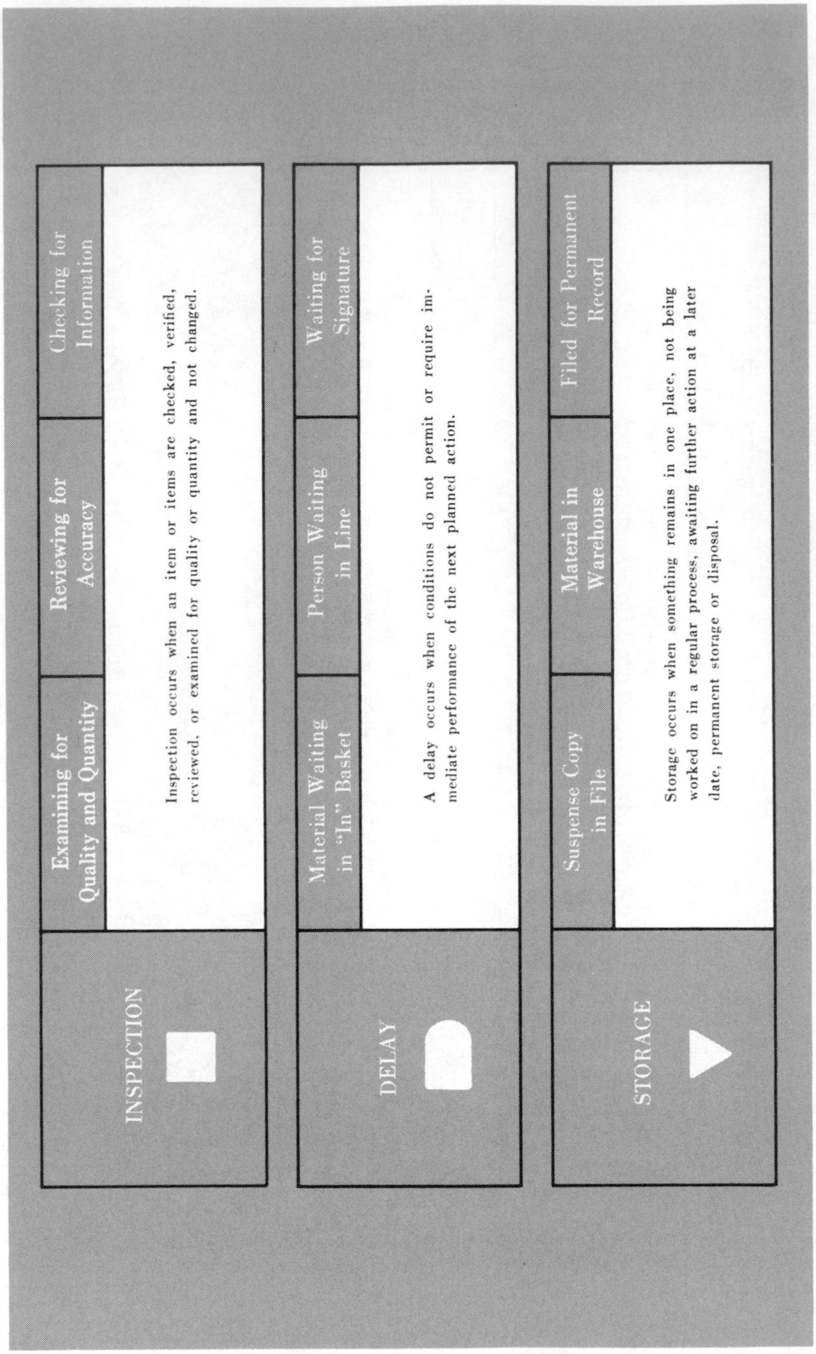

INSPECTION

Examining for Quality and Quantity	Reviewing for Accuracy	Checking for Information

Inspection occurs when an item or items are checked, verified, reviewed, or examined for quality or quantity and not changed.

DELAY

Material Waiting in "In" Basket	Person Waiting in Line	Waiting for Signature

A delay occurs when conditions do not permit or require immediate performance of the next planned action.

STORAGE

Suspense Copy in File	Material in Warehouse	Filed for Permanent Record

Storage occurs when something remains in one place, not being worked on in a regular process, awaiting further action at a later date, permanent storage or disposal.

FIGURE 18.1 (continued)

SUBJECT CHARTED _Carton of forms_
LOCATION _Warehouse_

		SUMMARY					
		PRESENT		PROPOSED		SAVING	
		NO.	TIME	NO.	TIME	NO.	TIME
PRESENT [X]	○ OPERATION						
PROPOSED [ ]	⇨ TRANSPORTATION						
CHARTED BY	DIST. IN FEET						
_R.K.M._	☐ INSPECTION						
SHEET _1_ OF	D DELAY						
_1_ SHEETS	▽ STORAGE						

DIST IN FEET	SYMBOL	DESCRIPTION	TIME	REMARKS
	▽	Carton on floor		
5	2 ⇨	To Glue stand		
	③	Carton glued		
9	4 ⇨	to center storage		
	▽5	In storage		
6	6 ⇨	To scales		
	⑦	Weight written on Carton		
6	8 ⇨	To storage		
	▽9	In storage		
6	10 ⇨	To stamps		
	⑪	Stamps affixed		
6	12 ⇨	To storage		
	▽13	In storage		
14	14 ⇨	To shipping platform		

FIGURE 18-2.
Process chart of old method of shipping cartons of printed forms.

for supervisor to read and sign letter." In this way, every step in a process is recorded so that it can be studied later. Figure 18-2 is a process chart of the old way of shipping cartons of printed forms.

How Do You Analyze a Process Chart?   Once you have made the process chart, your next job is to question and study each step in the procedure, using such questions as:[1]

[1]From Claude S. George, Jr., *Management for Business and Industry* (Englewood Cliffs, N.J.: Prentice Hall, Inc., 1970), pp. 398–99. Reprinted by permission of Prentice-Hall, Inc.

Questions about each step

1. What is being done? Is it necessary? Why?
2. Who is doing it? Can someone else do it better, easier? Why?
3. Why is it being done? Can it be eliminated or perhaps shortened in duration or reduced in scope?
4. When is it done? Can it be performed at a better time in the sequence? Why not?
5. Where is it done? Can it be done easier at another location? Why?
6. How is it being done? Can it be done more easily? Can it be combined with another step?

In addition to the above general questions, specific questions similar to the following are asked about each component.

Operations

1. Have conditions changed, making this operation unnecessary? Can it be eliminated?
2. Can it be performed more easily at another place in the process—perhaps during the idle time of another operator?
3. Can it be performed more easily at a different work place—perhaps on a table, conveyor, or rack?
4. Can it be performed more easily and quickly by another operator or person?
5. Can material be purchased that would eliminate or reduce the effort involved in this operation?

Transportations

1. Can the previous operation and the succeeding operation be combined or eliminated, thereby making this transportation unnecessary?
2. Can work areas be rearranged to eliminate or shorten this transportation?
3. Can some material handling device (conveyor, cart, etc.) make it easier to move materials and shorten the time required to make the move?
4. Can gravity conveyors, chutes, etc., be employed to shorten distance or time?
5. Can special equipment be relocated to eliminate or to shorten the transportation?
6. Can a new layout be developed for the area that would eliminate or materially reduce the transportations involved?

Inspections

1. Is inspection necessary? Can it be eliminated completely?

2. Is the inspection necessary at this point for completion of the productive process? Can it be performed more easily at a later time?

3. Can any of the inspection requirements be eliminated or reduced to shorten the inspection time or to eliminate it?

4. Can inspection be performed in combination with another step? During an operator's idle time?

5. Can a mechanical or electronic inspection device be employed, thus eliminating the operator's time and effort?

Storages

1. Does the storage aid in the overall productive process (such as aging tobacco or wine)? If not, can it be eliminated?

2. Do subsequent operations bottleneck the material, thus making storage necessary? If so, can the bottleneck be eliminated?

3. Can the storage time be reduced or eliminated by better planning and a better balance of the subsequent operations?

4. Can the steps immediately preceding and following the storage be eliminated, thus obviating the necessity for the storage?

Delays

1. Does the delay occur with any degree of regularity? If so, can the cause be controlled to prevent recurrence?

2. Can mechanical controls, electric signals, or other apparatus be effectively used to eliminate the delay?

By asking questions like these, you can usually simplify jobs, making them easier and quicker to perform.

WHAT ARE FLOW DIAGRAMS?

A flow diagram is a picture of the *movement* or *flow* of products (or people) that you described on the process chart. It is a map of the work area on which you show where the various operations, delays, transportations, etc., take place.

Figure 18-3 is a flow diagram of the work described in the process chart on p. 277. Note that the symbol for a step in the process is placed on the flow diagram at the place where it occurred. For example, the third step in the process chart (the operation of gluing the carton) is shown on the flow diagram by a circle (the symbol for an operation) at the exact spot where the gluing operation took place. Numbers corresponding to the step number on the process chart are placed inside these symbols for easy reference and identification.

map showing
movement

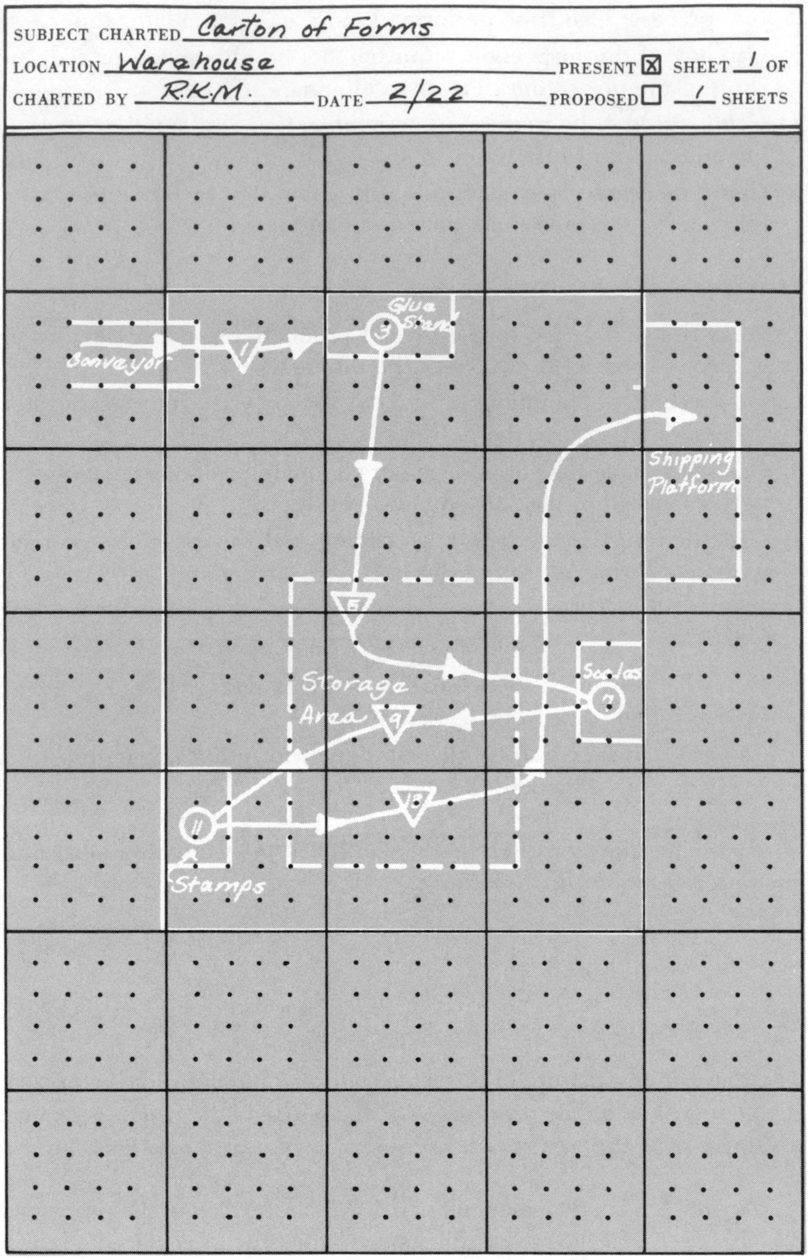
SUBJECT CHARTED Carton of Forms
LOCATION Warehouse
PRESENT ☒ SHEET 1 OF
CHARTED BY R.K.M.
DATE 2/22
PROPOSED ☐ 1 SHEETS
Conveyor
1
Glue Stand
3
Shipping Platform
5
Storage Area
9
Scales
7
11
13
Stamps

FIGURE 18-3.
Flow diagram of old method of shipping cartons of printed forms. (From George, *Management for Business,* p. 400.)

HOW DO PROCESS CHARTS AND FLOW DIAGRAMS HELP MAKE WORK EASIER?

Process charts and flow diagrams make work easier because they help you understand and study the whole job. For example, by analyzing the process chart and flow diagram shown in Figures 18-2 and 18-3 and questioning each step as indicated by the preceding checklist of questions, a new method for shipping material was developed. A process chart and flow diagram of the new method are shown in Figures 18-4 and 18-5. Note the savings in the summary shown in Figure 18-4 that you would realize if you used the new method. By analyzing this shipping room function using a process chart and flow diagram, this company was able to reduce the work force in the shipping room, thereby saving $8,765 annually.

use in studying work

Process charts and flow diagrams are very simple yet effective tools of analysis. Both are of value in establishing the overall sequence of operations and in determining the best layout for an economical and effective flow of materials. They present a clear picture of a process and are very effective

SUBJECT CHARTED *Carton of forms*
LOCATION *Warehouse*

PRESENT ☐
PROPOSED ☒
CHARTED BY *R.K.M.*
SHEET *1* OF *1* SHEETS

SUMMARY	PRESENT		PROPOSED		SAVING	
	NO.	TIME	NO.	TIME	NO.	TIME
○ OPERATION	3		3		0	
⇨ TRANSPORTATION	7		3		4	
DIST. IN FEET	52		12		40	
☐ INSPECTION	0		0		0	
D DELAY	0		0		0	
▽ STORAGE	4		0		4	

DIST IN FEET	SYMBOL	DESCRIPTION	TIME	REMARKS
3	⇨ 1	To Glue stand		
	○ 2	Carton glued		
3	⇨ 3	To scales		
	○ 4	Weighed		
	○ 5	Stamps Affixed		
6	⇨ 6	To Shipping Platform		

FIGURE 18-4.
Process chart of proposed method of shipping cartons of printed forms. (From George, *Management for Business*, pp. 401–2.)

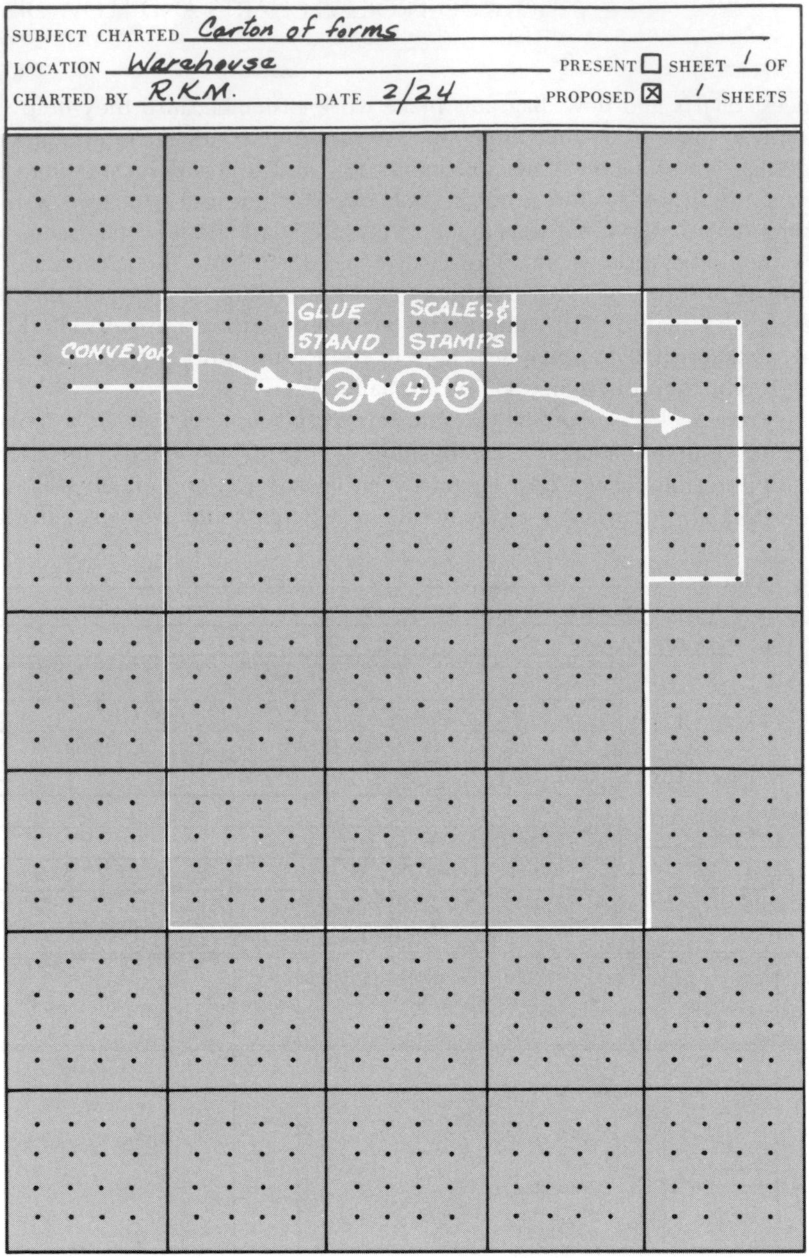

FIGURE 18-5.
Flow diagram of proposed methods of shipping cartons of printed forms. (From George, *Management for Business,* pp. 401–2.)

tools for studying and improving a complex job. Both process charts and flow diagrams are particularly useful in the following ways:[2]

1. Effectively locating work areas.
2. Establishing the best sequence of operations.
3. Eliminating unnecessary work.
4. Pointing out idle times and delays.
5. Establishing a better layout for an effective flow of material.
6. Suggesting means of eliminating ill-directed effort.
7. Reducing the number of steps in a process.
8. Making the remaining steps as economical as possible.
9. Reducing materials handling.
10. Decreasing the distance material is moved.

WHAT IS THE BEST WAY TO STUDY A PROCESS?

The easiest way for you to study a process is as follows:[3]

1. Choose a definite starting and stopping point for the process studied.
2. Make a process chart of the work as it is currently being performed. Be sure that no steps are omitted.
3. Construct a flow diagram of the process showing the steps and path of movement of materials or persons, and indicating relationships.
4. Analyze the process chart and flow diagram. Question each step. Determine the validity of each step in the process. Devise a better method of performing the work.
5. Construct a process chart and flow diagram of the proposed way of performing the work, establishing proper relationships between departments and steps. Take particular care to find the shortest, easiest route.
6. Test the new method to assure its effectiveness.
7. Instruct the operators and others concerned, and put the new method into effect.

WHAT IS MOTION ANALYSIS?

Up to this point, we've been talking about improving a process by looking at each step. In motion analysis, we try to improve whatever a *person* is doing.

[2]From George, *Management for Business*, pp. 401–3.
[3]Adapted with permission from George, *Management for Business*, p. 403.

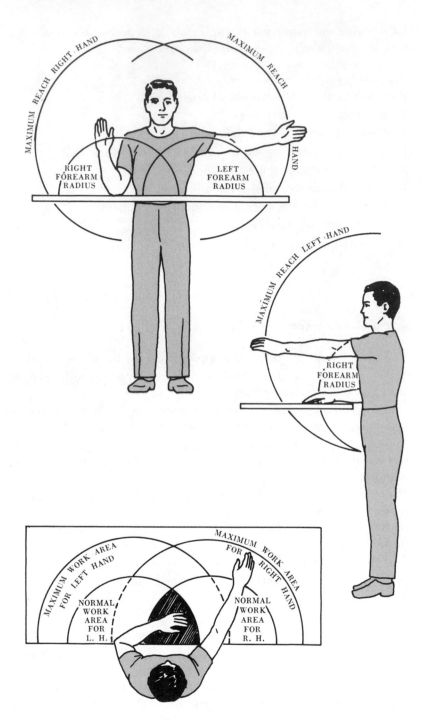

FIGURE 18-6.
Normal and maximum work areas in horizontal and vertical planes. (From George, *Management in Business*, p. 409.)

Most work is performed with the hands. If you watch what a worker's hands are doing instead of the product he is working on, you can usually spot many wasted or nonproductive movements. This study of body motions is called *motion analysis*. To help improve work motions, you should apply the rules of motion economy as noted in the next section.

WHAT ARE SOME OF THE RULES OF MOTION ECONOMY?

Most untrained workers use first one hand and then the other performing work. For example, if your job called for you to pick up four different items and put them in a box to be shipped as spare parts for a product, you would probably use one hand exclusively to pick up the parts, or you would use first one hand and then the other. According to the rules of motion economy, neither of these methods would be a good way to do the job.

The first rule of motion economy is that *the work should be distributed between the hands so that both are working simultaneously*. To better balance the work of the two hands, the second rule adds that *the two hands should follow opposite and symmetrical motion patterns*. You can "feel" the logic of this rule when you move your hands through opposite and symmetrical motion patterns. For example, place your left hand on your left shoulder and your right hand on your right shoulder. Now move both hands straight up above your head, now back to your shoulders. Now extend them straight out on each side, now back to your shoulders. Now extend them straight out in front of you, then back to your shoulders, and so on. This is a routine exercise. Now try moving one hand up and the other out. Notice how "unbalanced" and "unnatural" this feels.

making work easier

Another rule of motion economy is that *tools and materials should be located for easy accessibility and in a way that will employ the best possible sequence of motions*. Figure 18-6 illustrates the areas where materials and tools are most easily accessible.

Apply these rules to your job of picking up four different items and putting them in a box. The best layout and sequence would probably be to arrange the four parts in a semicircle in front of you as shown in the diagram on page 286. Now reach for part #1 with your left hand and at the same time reach for part #4 with your right hand. Pick up the parts *at the same time*, bring both parts back to the box *at the same time*, and drop them in the box *at the same time*. Now repeat the process picking up parts #2 and #3, and put them in the box.

To prove how these principles of motion economy have helped, actually go through the motions of picking up four items one at a time, placing them in a box one at a time. Time yourself using the second hand on a watch. Now do the job the improved way using both hands. You'll probably cut your time in half!

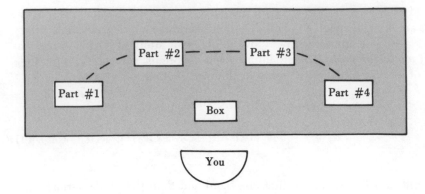

Some other rules of motion economy are:

1. Study any hesitation to see if its cause can be eliminated.
2. Make hand motions as simple as possible, so they are easier and faster. Hand motions classified from fastest to slowest are:
   a. Finger motions only
   b. Finger and wrist motions
   c. Motions involving the fingers, wrist, and forearm.
   d. Motions involving the fingers, wrist, forearm, and upper arm.
   e. Motions involving the fingers, wrist, forearm, upper arm, and body.
3. Locate tools and materials within the normal work areas and as close to the operator as possible.
4. It is usually quicker to slide, roll, or shove a small part rather than pick it up and carry it.
5. Motions that require sudden changes in directions are slower and more tiring than smooth, continuous, curving motions.
6. Arrange the parts of a job so they are as simple, automatic, and rhythmical as possible.
7. Have a place for all tools and materials and have all tools and materials in their place. This will eliminate the necessity of having to fumble and look for parts and tools.

SHOULD YOU STUDY A JOB MORE THAN ONCE?

Yes, you should study a job a number of times. You'll never reach perfection, and you'll never find the one best way of doing a job. The loom, for example, is much the same today as it was 100 years ago. Yet at this very moment, men are studying looms and their operators in textile plants across the nation, trying to find a still better way to get the job done.

This doesn't mean that you should study a job, then turn around and study it again. You should first study jobs that haven't been studied or jobs where the possibility of striking "pay dirt" is greater.

WHICH JOBS SHOULD YOU STUDY FIRST?

Your common sense will probably be a good guide. Study jobs first that are causing you trouble. Improving these will probably do the most good. After that, maybe the following will give you some hints on where the payoff will be.

1. Look for jobs that involve a large expenditure of man-hours, machine hours, and dollars. These usually afford good hunting.
2. Study the main process that the company is involved in. If the company bottles soft drinks, study this operation before you do the clerical operations.
3. Study jobs whose probable life will be long. If a job is only going to last a couple of weeks, it may not be worth studying it.
4. Study bottlenecks, jobs where performance requirements are not being met, or jobs where a lot of overtime is worked.
5. Look for jobs involving a lot of people doing the same thing.
6. Study jobs that are short in duration and repetitive. Short-cycled, highly repetitive jobs involving a lot of people usually offer good opportunities to make a little improvement amount to a great deal.
7. Try to improve work that requires a great deal of physical activity along with frequent rest periods.
8. Look for jobs where excess material is wasted.
9. Try to improve jobs that are dangerous, where the accident rate is high, or where it is undesirable to work because of such things as noise, temperature, fumes, and so on.
10. See if you can simplify the job being performed by highly skilled employees so that less skilled workers can do the job.
11. Look for jobs where quality or quantity standards are not being maintained.

sequence of jobs
to analyze

WHAT PARTS OF A JOB SHOULD YOU STUDY FIRST?

Some parts of a job offer a better opportunity to make improvements than other parts. Think of every task as being divided into three parts:

Part 1, you *get ready* to do the job. This means getting tools, supplies, parts—everything you'll need. Before you ice a cake, for example, you have to get out the cake, icing mix, milk, etc. Before you mow your lawn, you have to get your mower, shears, etc., in preparation.

Part 2, you *do the work*. This is the part that counts. This is the part that adds value to the product. You push or ride a mower around. You trim the edges. Your home looks better and is more valuable with a well-trimmed lawn versus an overgrown mass of weeds two feet high. Or you ice a cake in a bakery, and it adds value to the dry layers.

three parts of a job

Part 3, you *put away* the tools. This involves everything that has to be undone, unloaded, washed, put away, and cleaned up. Cleaning the pots and pans and returning the icing to the refrigerator are part of "put away." Cleaning your lawn mower and storing it and your shears in the tool shed are parts of this step.

The part to study and try to improve is part 2, the "do" part. The reason is simple. If you can eliminate or simplify the "do" altogether, you will also eliminate or change the "make ready" and "put away" parts. After you have done everything you can to improve the "do" part, then move to the "make ready" and "put away" steps to study and improve them.

WHAT IS AN OPERATIONS CHART?

An operations chart is simply a "picture" of the simultaneous work that the right and left hands are doing. Sometimes we call it a left-hand/right-hand chart. The operations chart shown in Figure 18-7 shows what an employee is doing to assemble a pipe clamp. Note that we use the same symbols that we used in the process charts.

making and using operations charts

By studying Figure 18-7, you can see that the work of the two hands is not balanced. One is working and the other is either idle or merely holding a part. Applying the rules of motion economy and using a jig instead of the left hand to hold the parts, an improved procedure was developed, as illustrated in Figure 18-8. Note that two hands are now productively employed in a balanced manner and that output has been doubled with no increase in the number of steps in the job.

WHO CAN DO METHODS IMPROVEMENT STUDIES?

You can do methods improvement studies with a little practice. However, there are specialists in motion study who are called *industrial engineers*. They use the same techniques we have discussed so far. In addition, they also use micromotion analysis. To do the most refined work in this field, you need to have some formal training in order to know how to do film analyses, multiple-activity analyses, and so on. However, anyone can do the type of motion study we have been talking about. Supervisors are good at it. And the

anyone can improve jobs

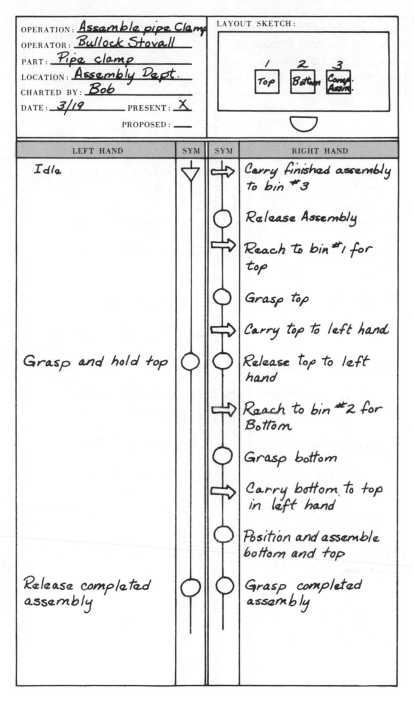

FIGURE 18-7.
Operations chart of original method of assembling pipe clamps. (From George, *Management in
Business,* p. 422.)

OPERATION: *Assemble Pipe Clamp.*
OPERATOR: *Bullock Stovall*
PART: *Pipe Clamp*
LOCATION: *Assembly Dept.*
CHARTED BY: *Bob*
DATE: *3/19* PRESENT: ___
PROPOSED: *X*

LAYOUT SKETCH:

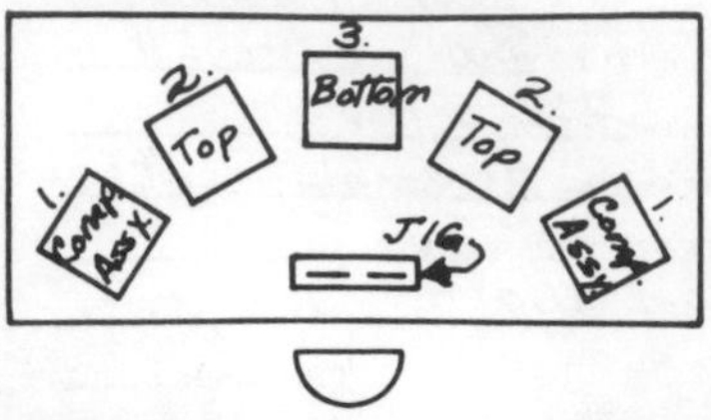

LEFT HAND	SYM	SYM	RIGHT HAND
Carry finished assembly to bin #1	⇨	⇨	Carry finished assembly to bin #1
Release assembly	◯	◯	Release assembly
Reach to bin 2 for top	⇨	⇨	Reach to bin 2 for top
Grasp top	◯	◯	Grasp top
Carry top to jig	⇨	⇨	Carry top to jig
Position top in jig	◯	◯	Position top in jig
Reach to bin 3 for bottom	⇨	⇨	Reach to bin 3 for bottom
Grasp bottom	◯	◯	Grasp bottom
Carry bottom to jig	⇨	⇨	Carry bottom to jig
Position and assemble bottom to top	◯	◯	Position and assemble bottom to top
Grasp completed assembly	◯	◯	Grasp completed assembly

FIGURE 18-8.
Operations chart of proposed method of assembling pipe clamps. (From George, *Management and Business,* p. 423.)

employees themselves who are doing the jobs frequently can figure out better ways to do the work than anyone else.

285

How to Make Work
Easier and Increase
Production

DO EMPLOYEES FEAR METHODS IMPROVEMENT?

Employees sometimes distrust and suspect methods improvement because it involves changing their jobs so that work can be done more easily and in less time. This in turn makes them think that fewer employees will be needed and that they might lose their jobs. You have to assure them that this will not be true. You have to explain what methods improvement is and assure your employees that their jobs will not be eliminated—that they will not be fired, that their pay will not be decreased, and that they will not have to work harder. And be sure you mean what you are saying and abide by it. If you don't, you're in trouble before you start.

explain the
need for
job study

Explain to your employees what methods improvement is. Try to get their cooperation in improving their own jobs. Consider offering rewards for the most improvement made. If you have a union, get the steward to explain what the company is trying to do, and assure the employees that they will not be penalized. We all fear the unknown, but if we know what is being done and if we ourselves are applying the principles of methods improvement, then one of the greatest obstacles has been overcome.

HOW CAN METHODS IMPROVEMENT HELP THE SUPERVISOR?

Your job as a supervisor is to produce more and better products at less cost. One of the best and easiest ways you can do this is to apply methods improvement to the work done in your department. When work is thus improved, it means that your department is typically out front in terms of efficiency, costs, and job performance. As a result, you will have fewer problems getting what you ask for in terms of equipment, overtime, and working conditions. Inasmuch as you are running a good department, you will usually get what you want from management.

Methods improvement also makes supervision easier because the supervisor's employees are working "smarter," not harder—they are doing their jobs in a more efficient manner. When employees know what their jobs are and how to do them in the simplest and easiest way, they are typically happier with their work. And the satisfied and happy employee is usually the productive employee.

advantages
of study

Finally, methods improvement helps you personally, because it puts your supervisory abilities in a favorable light when raises and promotions are up for consideration. Good work methods, productive employees, and a smoothly running department—all resulting from methods improvement— call attention to your good supervision.

The girls in the office of Greystone Manufacturing were preparing for the annual sales convention to be held in Miami. Some were cutting stencils, some were checking addresses and accommodations, and others were assembling packages of material. Over 700 salesmen were expected to be present, and preparing for them was no small task.

Mary Littleton and Nancy Hester probably had the two most monotonous jobs. Mary's job consisted of picking up and placing in a folder four sheets of paper, which outlined the tentative program for the convention. The program sheets, standard 8½″ × 11″, were picked up and placed in a standard manila file folder. Mary's work place is illustrated in Figure 18-9. She assembled the sheets as follows: Picked up sheet #1 with her right hand and placed the sheet in her left hand. Her left hand then held the sheet while the right hand picked up sheet #2 and placed it in her left hand along with sheet #1. In similar fashion, she picked up sheets #3 and #4. Using her right hand, she got a manila folder from the stack on her left, opened the folder, placed the four sheets in the folder with her left hand, and placed the folder on the completed pile on her right hand.

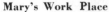

Mary's Work Place

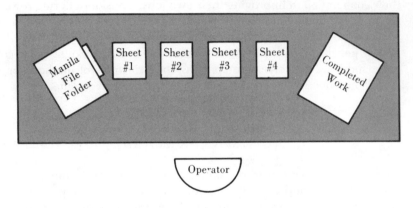

Nancy's Work Table

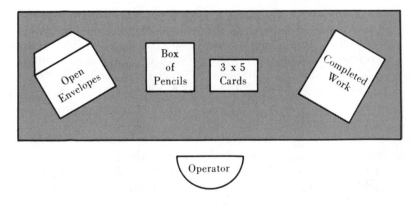

FIGURE 18-9.
Layout of Mary's and Nancy's work places. (From George, *Management In Business*, p. 392.)

Nancy's work, on the other hand, consisted of placing a 3" × 5" card and a pencil in a standard envelope. She was situated at a table as shown in Figure 18-9. In performing her job, Nancy picked up an open envelope with her left hand. Then, holding the envelope in her left hand, she picked up and placed a pencil in the envelope with her right hand. Still holding the envelope in her right hand, she placed a 3" × 5" card in it, transferred the envelope to her right hand, and disposed of it on her right.

The girls had hardly completed 50 units when they saw that it was going to be a long and tiring task.

1. Construct an operations chart of each job.
2. Using the charts and the principles of motion study, devise a better and easier way for Mary and Nancy to do their work.
3. Illustrate your improvements by constructing operations charts of the new methods.

A Case Study
BURLINGTON MACHINE WORKS

The Burlington Machine Works was organized in 1950 to fabricate and manufacture metal parts and subassemblies for other manufacturing concerns. The plant makes a variety of products, but the major portion of its business consists of (1) fabricating a bracket assembly, (2) assembling a small gear train in a housing, and (3) fabricating a control lever for a vending machine. These three items are relatively easy to handle, are about the same size, and are manufactured in approximately the same quantities.

During the manufacturing process, the three items must go through the following departments in the sequence indicated:

Bracket Assembly	*Gear Train*	*Vending Machine Lever*
Storeroom	Storeroom	Storeroom
Machine Shop	Plating Shop	Machine Shop
Assembly Shop	Assembly Shop	Plating Department
Paint Shop	Paint Shop	Inspection Department
Packing & Shipping	Packing & Shipping	Machine Shop
		Assembly Shop
		Inspection Department
		Plating Department
		Paint Shop
		Inspection Department
		Packing & Shipping

The layout of the plant, shown in Figure 18-10, was developed by Mr. Kingsley, the owner, without too much thought or study. With the three items taking up a major percentage of his shop's productive capacity, however, he is very much aware of the extra handling of material caused by poor layout and is trying to rearrange his plant so as to have a minimum movement of items and thus a smooth flow of material.

To accomplish this objective, Mr. Kingsley is willing to swap or move the departments about in any fashion. For example, if it would improve the flow of items through the plant, he would move the assembly department to the area now occupied by the plating shop, or put the paint shop where the machine shop is, etc. However, Mr. Kingsley doesn't want to move the packing and shipping department because he feels that it should remain at the rear of the building where the exit doors and the shipping platform are located.

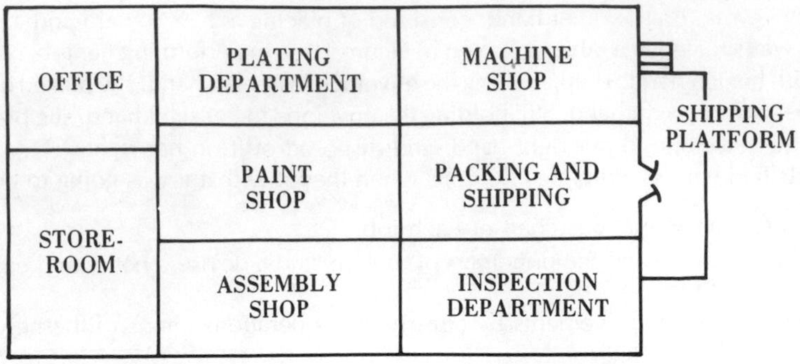

FIGURE 18-10.
Layout of Burlington Machine Works Plant.

1. Considering the three products manufactured, what layout would you recommend for Mr. Kingsley?
2. Construct flow diagrams for each of the items as now manufactured.
3. Construct flow diagrams for each item in your improved layout.
4. Why is your layout superior to Mr. Kingsley's?

19
HOW TO MEASURE WORK

This chapter explains—

- Why you need time standards
- How you can develop time standards
- What to tell your employees about time standards

$\mathbf{H}$ave you ever stopped to think that we buy coffee by the pound, coal by the ton, and gasoline by the gallon—yet when we buy an hour's worth of work from a man we don't know what we are buying? Workers have different capacities, and although they may be making the same amount of money per hour, the amount of work they turn out varies widely. In fact, in some plants it is not unusual for the output of employees doing the same job to vary as much as 100%—that is, the best employee would be producing twice the amount of the poorest employee. The reason for this difference might be that one employee is more skilled than the other, that one employee might be working faster than the other, or that one employee knows and uses a better and shorter way to do the job. To help even out these situations and to instruct your employees as to how they should do a job, you as a supervisor will need to know the best way to do a piece of work and *how long* it should take the average employee to do it. In other words, *you need to know the standard time.*

WHAT IS STANDARD TIME?

allowed time

Standard time is the time that is allowed to do a specified quantity and quality of work. It is the time that is allowed for an average employee, working at average pace, to do a job day after day without ill effects. You might find, for example, that you should allow 1.80 minutes for an employee to buff a part to the required brightness. To buff 100 parts, therefore, you would allow him $100 \times 1.80 = 180$ minutes or three hours.

Standard time includes:

1. How long it should actually take an average employee to do the work if he works at a normal pace.
2. An allowance for work interruptions, fatigue, and personal time.

WHY DO YOU NEED TIME STANDARDS?

Once you know how long it should take an average employee to do a job, then you can figure out how much work an average employee *should* turn out in an hour or a day. Or you can figure out what would constitute a fair day's work.

Other reasons for knowing how long it should take an employee to perform a task are:

1. As a supervisor, you can assign jobs more equally and fairly since you know how much work is involved in them.

2. You can plan and schedule your department's work load better.

3. Your employees can be paid fairly and equitably according to the quality and quantity of work they do.

how much time to allow

4. The costs in your department can be calculated more easily.

5. The relative efficiency of an employee or a group of employees can be easily calculated by comparing how much work they actually completed with how much they should have done. For example, if they should have turned out 100 pieces and only did 80, then their efficiency would be 80% (80 ÷ 100 = 80%). If they turned out 120 pieces, their efficiency would be 120% (120 ÷ 100 = 120%).

WHAT EQUIPMENT IS USED TO DEVELOP A STANDARD TIME?

In many situations, you can time a job by using an ordinary wristwatch with a second hand. At other times, however, you'll need to measure time in shorter intervals than seconds and minutes. For these shorter intervals, a stopwatch is used that measures times in hundredths of a minute.

HOW DO YOU DEVELOP A STANDARD TIME?

First of all, you should *select an operator* who knows how to do the work using the right equipment and method. Select a good, average worker, not a speed demon because most employees think that if you study a fast worker, the time allowed will be less than if you study a normal worker. This is not true. As we will see later in our discussion of performance rating, the end result is the same regardless of the operator chosen. You should not, however, select an unskilled employee, or one who is nervous and prefers that you not watch him work.

Second, *be sure the working conditions are standard*—that the raw materials, tools, layout, lighting, etc., are the same for each employee. It wouldn't be fair to time an operator using machines and raw materials different from those used by the other workers.

Third, *break the job down into steps or elements* of short duration. A step or element has an easily identifiable beginning and ending. For example, the elements in the job of testing a lock in a lock manufacturing plant might be:

steps in developing a standard

1. Get key from box and insert in lock.

2. Turn lock twice to be sure bolt works freely.

3. Remove key from lock and return to box.

These three elements make up one cycle of work.

291

You need to break the job down into elements rather than time the whole job because some elements in a job do not occur during each cycle. For example, an operator might have to make slight changes in the machine every few cycles. If you timed the whole job for several cycles, you would get different times for each cycle, which you could not explain. These differences in times would be caused by the operator's making adjustments in the machine every few cycles. The cycle in which he made the adjustment would be longer than the other cycles. You wouldn't be able to explain these time differences unless you had broken the job down into steps or elements and thus became aware of the adjustment step. Also, you get the best description of the job and how it is performed when you break it down into its basic elements.

Fourth, *record the elements* on a piece of paper in the sequence in which they are performed.

Fifth, *time the work*. Time enough cycles so that you have a good sample of what the operator is doing.

Sixth, *determine the selected time*. The selected time is the time you select from your observations as being representative of each element. You might select the time that appears most frequently, or you could simply average the times to get the selected time. For example, assume that the times for the lock-testing cycle are:

	Time in Minutes					
Element	*Cycle 1*	*Cycle 2*	*Cycle 3*	*Cycle 4*	*Cycle 5*	*Cycle 6*
1. Get key from box and insert in lock	.25	.26	.24	.25	.23	.27
2. Turn lock twice	.50	.50	.48	.52	.51	.49
3. Remove key and return to box	.25	.23	.28	.25	.25	.24

The time appearing most frequently for element # 1 (get key and insert in lock) is .25, which you could use as your selected time for element # 1. Or you could average the times required to perform element # 1. If you average the times required to perform each element and use this average as your selected time per element, you get the following:

1. Get key and insert in lock	.25 minute—selected time for element #1
2. Turn lock twice	.50 minute—selected time for element #2
3. Remove key and return to box	.25 minute—selected time for element #3

Selected time per cycle (all three elements) =   1.00 minute

Seventh, *determine a performance rating.* All operators don't work at the same pace; therefore, it would not be fair for you to set a work standard based on the time required by either a fast or a slow operator to do the job. Some allowance for speed, therefore, should be made in the time you select as being representative. If the operator you timed worked faster than the average employee, you would need to add some time to the time you observed in order to get a fair time. If the operator you timed worked slower than an average employee, then you would need to subtract from the time you observed.

Time study men are trained to evaluate an operator's speed and thus rate the operator's performance. With this training as a background, a time study man watches an employee work and rates or compares the operator's speed or pace with his concept of a normal pace. If he determines that the operator is working 10% faster than normal, he would rate him at 110%. If he determines that the operator is working 20% slower than normal, he would rate him at 80%. He would rate him at 100% if he determines the operator is working at a normal pace.

Eighth, *apply the performance rating.* Assume you rated the operator in the key-lock example at 120%. The time required by an average employee working at average pace would be the time you selected for the cycle (1.00) multipled by 120% (or 1.20). This would give: 1.00 min. × 1.20 = 1.20 minutes. Since you rated the operator as working 20% faster than normal, the time that an average employee would take to do the job working at normal pace would be 20% longer than the 1.00 minute, or 1.20 minutes. This is called the *normal time.*

Ninth, *add allowances.* To determine a standard time, you need to make some allowances for:

1. Normal work interruption (the boss speaks to you or you drop a part on the floor).
2. Fatigue—as you work longer, you become tired and work slower.
3. Personal needs such as cleaning your glasses, going to the washroom, etc.

In a normal work environment, we commonly find 10 to 15% added for these allowances. If we use 10%, this would be the equivalent of allowing 48 minutes per eight-hour day to cover allowances.

Using our same example, you take the normal time of 1.20 minutes and add 10% of it for allowances. This would give you 1.20 minutes + .10 (1.20 minutes) = 1.32 minutes. This means you would allow an operator 1.32 minutes to test each lock. Or you would expect him to test 45.45 locks per hour (60 minutes ÷ 1.32 minutes = 45.45). Stating it otherwise, the standard time per lock is 1.32 minutes.

Figure 19-1 illustrates a time study of assembling electric coils. Note that under each element are columns headed R and T. The R is the reading

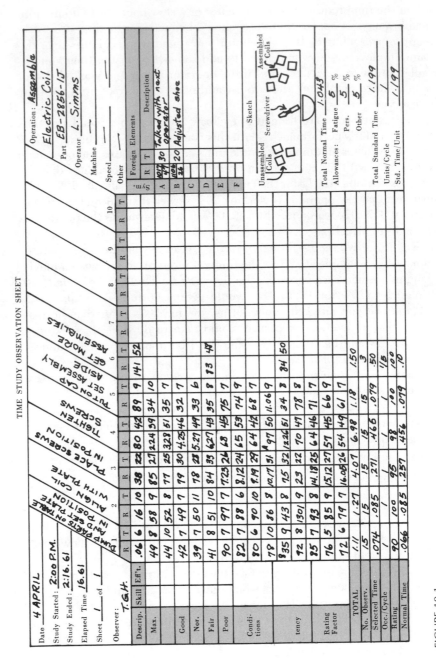

FIGURE 19-1.
Time study of assembling electric coils. (From George, *Management for Business*, p. 441.)

from a watch, and the T is the time it took to do the element. For element 1, the reading was .06, for element 2 it was .16, for element 3 it was .38, and so on. You determine the actual time for each of these elements by getting the differences in these watch readings. Thus for element 2, it took .10 of a minute to perform it (the difference between .06 and .16); for element 3, the actual time is .22 (the difference between .16 and .38), and so on. Note the rating, allowances, and standard time on this study.

HOW IS STANDARD TIME LINKED WITH PIECE RATES?

At this point, you know that the standard time for the lock problem is 1.32 minutes with a standard output per hour of 45.45 locks. You can convert this to wage rates per unit (piece rates) as follows. If the going rate of pay in the community for this type of work is $6.82 per hour, then you would pay an operator at the rate of 15¢ per unit ($6.82 ÷ 45.45 = 15¢). If an employee worked faster than average, he could test more locks per hour, say, 60. This means for one hour of work he would receive $9.00 (60 × 15¢ = $9.00).

DO TIME STUDIES MAKE FOR POOR QUALITY?

The idea behind a time study is to set a pace at which an *average* worker can perform day in and day out with no detriment to his health or well-being. *pay and work* This should not make for a decrease in work quality. However, if one particu- *quality* lar employee has more skill than the average employee, he can produce more and therefore earn more if he is working at piece rates. But the catch is that only production that passes inspection and meets the company's quality standard will count. Thus, if the employee tries to go too fast at a sacrifice in quality, he won't get paid for the extra production. An employee soon learns to pace himself at a level of output that he can sustain and at which he can produce a product of acceptable quality.

DO YOU NEED A TIME STUDY TO GET A STANDARD TIME?

No, you do not need a time study to get a standard time—if standard data are available. If many time studies have been made of highly repetitive work, these time values (standard data) can be used instead of making new time studies. For example, a standard operation in a furniture factory is drilling the same diameter hole in a standard-size board. The only variation in the *standard data* job is the depth of the hole, and over the years data have been recorded in chart form (Figure 19-2) showing the time needed to drill various depths of

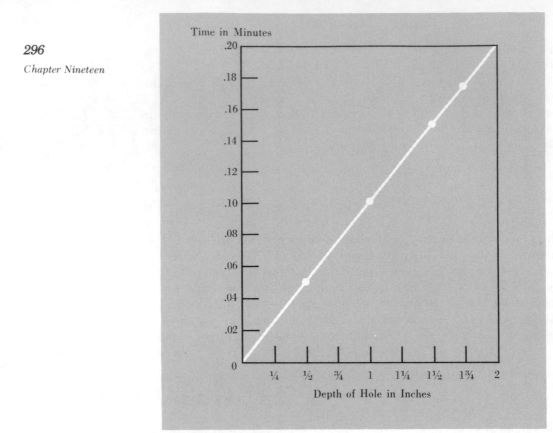

FIGURE 19-2.
Leveled time for drilling ¼″ hole in white pine board.

¼-inch holes in white pine. Thus, to get a standard time for a new job of drilling a ¼-inch hole in a white pine board, all you need to do is look up the time values (derived from time studies over the years) for picking up a board and placing it on the drill press, drilling the hole, and removing the board from the press. This is a quick and reliable way to get a standard, and, inasmuch as the times have been used on hundreds of studies before, they are not apt to be contested by the workers.

WHAT IS A PREDETERMINED TIME STANDARD?

A predetermined time standard is one that you can calculate by analyzing the movements (basic motions) required to do a job and assigning predetermined and fixed time values to these motions. For example, the motions required to pick up a pencil might be as follows: (1) *reach* to the pencil, (2) *grasp* the pencil, and (3) *move* the pencil to the required location. Time values for the *reach, grasp,* and *move* basic motions have been predeter-

Distance in Inches	Reach	Move
5	.01	.02
10	.02	.03
15	.03	.04
20	.04	.05
25	.05	.06
etc.		
	Grasp: .01	

FIGURE 19-3.
Leveled times for "reach," "grasp," and "move."

mined and recorded (see Figure 19-3) and can thus be assigned to these motions. Adding the three time values for each distance specification will give you a *normal time* per distance; that is, no allowances are included. From this normal time, you could calculate a time standard by adding the desired time for allowances.

In addition to setting time standards for jobs currently running in a plant, using predetermined time standards also allows you to calculate the time that will be required to perform a job *in advance* of its actual production. Using blueprints or other information, you can visualize the work that will need to by done, assign predetermined time values to this work, and thus calculate how long it will take to get the job done *in advance* of actually doing it.

Several basic types of predetermined time systems are used in industry: MTM (Methods-Time Measurement), Work Factor, and Basic Motion Time Study—to name a few.

WHAT IS WORK SAMPLING?

Work sampling, or ratio-delay study as it is sometimes called, is another way to measure work. It is a statistical technique you can use to get information about the work performance of an employee or a machine. For example, *statistical technique* suppose you want to know how much time an employee spends oiling his machine. To get this information, you visit the machine at random intervals throughout the day for several days or weeks and record whether or not the operator is oiling his machine. Suppose that in 1,000 random observations you found him oiling his machine 150 times. This means that the operator spends 15% of his time oiling his machine. You could make the same sort of study on any other part of a job, but for accuracy, the observations must be random, and the number must be large enough to insure accuracy.

Suppose, for example, that a certain machine needs an adjustment at *irregular* intervals. It would be quite time-consuming to run a time study over the weeks or months necessary to find out how frequently this occurs. You could, however, make a ratio-delay or work sampling study as follows.

1. Set up a sheet of paper showing that the operator is either adjusting the machine or doing other required work.

2. Visit the machine at random intervals, and tally what the operator is doing. The visit must be random or the procedure won't work. You shouldn't, for example, observe what the operator is doing every hour on the hour because, of course, this is not random. One way to make it random would be to write down the times of the workday in five-minute intervals on individual pieces of paper. Thus, one piece of paper would have 8:00 A.M. on it. Another would have 8:05 A.M., another 8:10 A.M., and so on throughout the workday. Put all these pieces of paper in a hat, mix them up, and draw out, say twenty-five pieces. You would observe the operator at the times shown on these twenty-five pieces of paper.

3. Make a large number of visits to insure accuracy. Your study after two months might show:

Element	Number of Times Operator Was Performing This Element When Observed	Percent of Total
Adjusting machine	769	3
Doing other work	24,861	97
Total	25,630	100

This would indicate that your employee was spending 3% of his time adjusting his machine; therefore, this amount of time should be added to the other time allowances to establish a standard time.

WHAT DO UNIONS THINK OF TIME STUDIES?

The stopwatch used to be a cause for war between unions and management. Today, however, the attitude has changed from hostility to acceptance. The reason? Union officials and their members have a better understanding of what time studies are, how they are made, and how they can be fairly used. In many plants, the unions even make their own time studies when grievances arise over a standard. Recognizing that they can protect their members from improper use of time studies, many unions today are more open-minded about the fairness, value, and reliability of time study procedures. Thus, although they aren't advocating them outright, neither are they actively fighting time study procedures.

WHAT ARE LOOSE STANDARDS? FAIR STANDARDS? TIGHT STANDARDS?

A loose standard allows an *average* employee, working at about normal pace, to easily produce many more units per hour than the standard calls for.

A fair standard allows the *best* workers to produce about 20 to 25% more than the standard calls for. If an *average* worker can also produce 20 to 25% more, then it is no longer a fair standard—it is a loose standard.

A tight standard is just the opposite: an average employee working at normal pace can't meet the production requirements, and even the best employees can't exceed it by more than, say, 5 to 10%.

ARE LOOSE STANDARDS A RESULT OF POOR TIME STUDIES?

Loose standards can be a result of poor time studies but probably aren't. In all reality, they probably developed gradually over time as the result of creeping changes. For example, suppose that in an original time study, a particular tool was used. Some employee finds that by changing the tool slightly, he can produce a unit in less time. Not a significant decrease in time *evolved over time* but about 1 or 2%. Then later, the specification for the raw material is changed, which also makes it quicker to make a part. It doesn't decrease the time much—about 2%. By themselves, these changes don't amount to much, but when they creep into the picture over time, they can be significant, changing the time standard by as much as 15 to 20%. This would make it a loose standard—easier to achieve.

The reverse could also be true—creeping changes could cause a tight standard. Employees, however, are more apt to complain about tight standards than loose ones. As a result, tight standards are more quickly corrected.

As a supervisor, you should be ever alert to any changes that would affect a time standard. You are obligated to your employees to protect them from tight standards that will cause a decrease in their pay. Likewise, you owe it to your employer to make sure the standards are fair and will not cause an increase in cost.

WHAT DO YOU DO WHEN AN EMPLOYEE SAYS A STANDARD IS WRONG?

Most standards are put into effect for a trial period, say, 30 days. During this period, either the employee or management can suggest changes to make the standard a better one. If both sides agree that it is OK, then it goes into effect and cannot be changed unless there is a change in methods, tools, materials, or conditions of work.

When an employee complains that a standard is not right, listen to his complaint. He may have a legitimate beef. Also, be sure he is following the prescribed method. If he isn't, this may be his problem. If he is and still has problems, call the time study man to reexamine the study.

SHOULD YOU EXPLAIN TIME STUDIES TO EMPLOYEES?

By all means explain time studies to your employees because these studies affect their jobs and their pay. Time studies are not secretive or underhanded, but failure to explain them will make the employees think they are. If your employees come to know the time study man and understand time study procedures, they will have more confidence in the fairness of the *explain* procedure. Knowing that you are not trying to hide something will build *fully* their confidence in you and will minimize gripes and complaints.

When you explain time study procedures, don't try to give your employees a "snow job." This will make them even more suspicious. Instead, use one of the jobs in your department and show precisely, step by step, how the study was made and how the time standard was set. Don't dodge issues

"By all means, explain time studies to your employees because these studies affect their jobs and their pay. Time studies are not secretive or underhanded, but failure to explain them will make employees think they are."

RALPH, I THINK WE'RE IN TROUBLE...

like rating. Show how it is done, and explain that this keeps from setting a standard that is too high and not fair to the employee—or too low and not fair to the company. Be sure to explain how additional time is allowed for fatigue, personal needs, etc., to make the standard a just one.

If you have done a good job in explaining time study to your employees, they should be impressed with the fact that you want them to get everything that is coming to them, that you are looking out for them as well as for the company, and that neither one will be sacrificed for the other.

A Case Study
LUCAMA PACKERS

One of the operations in the pickle plant of Lucama Packers consisted of packing small, party-type pickles in a glass jar by hand. The pickles had to be uniformly placed around the side of the jar to make an attractive appearance and to add sales appeal.

Until three years ago, the employees performing the work had been paid by the hour. Although most other jobs in the pickle plant were on an incentive basis, management felt that this job could not be placed on incentive because of the varying number of pickles per jar caused by the variation in shape and size of cucumbers. However, with the new sorting and grading operation recently installed, the pickles were much more uniform in size, and management believed that the job could be placed on incentive pay. Accordingly, one of the company's older and more experienced time study men observed the operation and came back with the data shown below.

In addition to these times the time study man indicated that the operator's performance should be rated at 120% and that an allowance of 5% should be made for personal time, as well as 5% for fatigue.

1. Using these data, determine a time standard for packing a jar of pickles.
2. What would be the standard output of jars per hour?

Element	Time in Minutes Per Cycle										Occurrences Per Cycle
1. Pick up 2 jars and place on fixture	.08	.07	.08	.08	.06	.07	.08	.10	.09	.08	1
2. Pick up 3 pickles from conveyor and pack parallel in jars	.12	.14	.12	.14	.14	.14	.13	.13	.12	.14	*
3. Place jars aside on rack	.08	.06	.07	.08	.06	.08	.08	.07	.08	.06	1

*The number of pickles per jar varied from 19 to 23.

A Case Study
BLACKWELL CLEANING

In 1976, Bob Johnson doubled the capacity of his cleaning plant and purchased all new equipment. New equipment meant that his employees would have to learn new techniques, new routines, and new work methods. With these changes, Bob decided that this would also be a good time to install some type of wage incentive plan. Therefore, after this new equipment had been in operation for about a week, Bob announced to his employees that he was going to give them a chance to get extra pay for extra work—that beginning the next week their pay would depend on the amount of work they produced.

The spotters (those who check the clothes and clean spots), the wet cleaners, and the dry cleaners worked as a team in Bob's plant; therefore he installed a group incentive plan for these employees. Theirs was the basic job of cleaning the clothes. The pressers and the ironers, however, were independent workers and were placed on individual piece rates with a guaranteed base equal to 75% of their old hourly rate. The markers and sorters were on the same type of individual incentive system, i.e., piecework with a guaranteed base.

Bob used previous production records to establish his standards, and inasmuch as the equipment was newer and easier to operate, he raised the standards and used the adjusted figures as production quotas. The employees seemed eager to earn more money and worked hard the first week. In fact, the total work produced increased; however, when the paychecks were handed out, there was considerable grumbling. Although none of the employees complained directly to Bob, remarks similar to the following could be heard: "I work twice as hard and get $1.50 more." "My bonus was only $3.25—but I don't know how he figured it." "I pressed more suits than she did—but she made more money!"

Output for the second week dropped slightly, and by the end of the first month, production had dropped below the old levels of output despite new equipment and an incentive system.

In an effort to make the system work, Bob decreased everyone's production quota by 10%. The decrease, however, had little effect on output the first week following its incorporation. According to Bob, the net effect at this point of his new equipment and the wage incentive system was to increase the cost of processing a garment—rather than decrease it as he had planned. By the end of the first month following the 10% decrease in standards, however, the workers seemed to have settled down and output was back at its old level. Three weeks later the number of garments cleaned and pressed exceeded the old average by 22%, and the employees seemed happy with their increased pay and the new system.

The delivery drivers and the girls who waited on the cash and carry customers began receiving complaints, at this point, about clothes not being clean, two creases instead of one, soiled spots on dresses, and the like. If allowed to continue, this could have had a drastic effect on his business. Recognizing this, Bob stated that his first objective was to clean and press clothes properly. Therefore, he called his employees together, told them of the customer complaints, and asked for suggestions. All of his workers indicated that the quality of their work had not decreased and could not understand the reasons for the complaints. None of them made any suggestions as to how the condition could be corrected.

Bob disliked the idea of discarding his incentive system but was undecided as to what action he should take.

1. What do you think was wrong with Bob's installation?
2. What do you think is causing the poor quality of work?
3. What would you recommend that Bob do now? Why?

20
HOW TO SELECT A PAY PLAN

This chapter explains—

- The basis for paying your employees
- The most frequently used wage payment plans
- What makes for a successful wage plan installation

Good wage payment plans that are well administered have a healthy effect on employees—the employees are happier in their work, morale is higher, productive output is up, and quality is better. What the employee earns is one of the most important factors affecting the relations between labor and management. In fact, more open strife and grievances are generated over pay than over any other single factor. For these reasons, it is important to management to find a wage plan that is mutually agreeable and easy to understand and administer.

Most companies are interested in paying fair and just wages to all employees. If wages are too high, the company will suffer by increased costs and loss of sales. If wages are too low, they will produce a negative effect on the employee's attitude and output. An employee's pay establishes his standard of living, it provides him with the necessities and luxuries of life, and it affects his home and home life as does no other single contribution by management. Considering all this, there's no wonder that pay is such an important factor between labor and management.

To help you find the right pay level and thereby determine a fair wage, a technique known as *job evaluation* is used by many companies.

WHAT IS JOB EVALUATION?

Job evaluation is a systematic way of determining the relative worth of each job in a company. A window washer and a cashier are both important to the firm, but how would you compare their jobs for pay purposes? This is what job evaluation does. It establishes the *relative worth* of each job but not the

"Good wage payment plans that are well-administered make employees happier, make morale higher, and make them more productive."

wages that go with the job. It sets up a hierarchy in a company from the lowest to the highest ranking job. Employees are not only interested in what they get, but also in what the next fellow gets. So when jobs are fairly rated on their hierarchy and employees are paid accordingly, management usually has fewer gripes about pay.

DO YOU NEED JOB DESCRIPTIONS AND SPECIFICATIONS?

Yes. Before any job can be evaluated, you'll need to know what the duties of the job are. A job description gives you this information. From the job description, you can prepare an individual job specification. This job specification shows the abilities and qualities an employee would need to perform the job covered by the job description. Before you use any job specification for evaluation purposes, however, it would be a good idea to review both the description and the specification to be sure they are up-to-date and contain the correct information. Also be sure that both union and management agree on their contents.

HOW DO YOU EVALUATE JOBS?

You can use several systems to evaluate jobs. The *ranking* method is the easiest to understand, the least costly, and the simplest. Using job specifications, you simply rank the jobs from the lowest to the highest. In a super-   *systems used* market, for example, the lowest job might be the sweeper or the stock clerk, and the highest would be the store manager. You can easily use the ranking system of job evaluation in small organizations, but when you have a large number of employees, it is difficult to get agreement on the ranking order. Some other system, therefore, must be used.

A second system, which is really a refinement of the ranking system, is known as *job classification*. Using this technique, several grades or classifications of jobs are determined for the company, and then all the various jobs in the company are fitted into these grades. For example, in a machine shop you would have three classifications of work: Class 210 would include the top jobs where skills like tool and die work are required; Class 205 would include jobs requiring skills to run lathe and milling machines; and Class 200 would include all other less skilled jobs like drill press operators, punch-press operators, and the like. In similar manner, classes are set up for all types of jobs in the company. You have classes for maintenance work, clerical work, and so on. The system is simple and is used successfully in many government jobs.

The system that over 75% of the companies making job evaluations use, however, is the *point rating* system. Under the point system, jobs are broken down into common factors such as skill, effort, education, and so on. Next, each factor is assigned a range of numerical values. For example, education may have a range of 100 to 300, whereas working conditions may have a range of 5 to 20. Finally, point values are assigned to each factor in a job. Thus, for the job of stock clerk, education may be assigned 100 points and working conditions 8 points. In a similar manner, you would assign points to skill, effort, and the other factors of the job. For the store manager, education might be assigned 280 points, and working conditions 5 points; and so on, according to what you thought each factor was worth. Adding up the points assigned to each factor in a job gives you the point rating for that job. One job might have a total number of 670 points; another, 920 points; another 785 points; and so on. The job with the most points would be the highest ranking, the next highest number of points would be second, and so on down. In this way, the relative worth of each job has been set.

WHEN DOES PAY ENTER THE PICTURE?

pricing the job

When you've ranked and established the relative worth of all jobs using a system of job evaluation such as the point system, you next have to price the job. Before you attempt to set the wage for a particular job, however, you first need to look at various factors existing in the community that have a bearing on wages, namely:[1]

1. Union wage scales.
2. Prevailing wage rates in each occupation in the community.
3. A comparison of the experience, education, skill, and the like required for the company's jobs with other jobs in the community.
4. The general living standards represented by each job classification.
5. Legal requirements and existing wage laws.
6. Estimated supply and demand of labor.
7. Cost of living indexes.
8. General level of labor productivity.
9. Anticipated profits.

Considering all of these factors, you have to set wages for the key jobs in the company—jobs that everyone understands and jobs that can be compared with similar jobs in other companies. A clerk typist, a key-punch operator, and a computer program specialist are examples of key jobs. Once

---

[1]The following list is from Claude S. George, Jr., *Management for Business and Industry* (Englewood Cliffs, N.J.: Prentice-Hall, Inc., 1970), p. 467. Reprinted by permission of Prentice-Hall, Inc.

you price these key jobs, then other similar jobs can be priced by the number of points and point spread from the key job.

WHAT ARE THE LEGAL PAY REQUIREMENTS

Every supervisor should be aware of two laws about legal pay requirements: The Wage and Hour Law of 1938 (Fair Labor Standards Act) and the Walsh-Healey Act (Public Contracts Act).

The Fair Labor Standards Act regulates methods of payment, hours of work, and minimum wages for firms engaged in interstate commerce. It requires a 50% increase in pay for every hour over 40 worked in a week. As amended in 1966, the Act set the minimum wage at $1.60 per hour effective February 1, 1968. It also restricted the employment of children between sixteen and eighteen years of age from working on hazardous jobs. In 1974, Congress raised the federal minimum wage for most workers to $2.10, with an increase to $2.30 effective January 1, 1976.

federal minimum

In November 1977 the President signed into law a bill boosting the federal minimum wage rates to the following levels:

Minimum Wage	Effective Date
$2.65	January 1, 1978
2.90	January 1, 1979
3.10	January 1, 1980
3.35	January 1, 1981

The Fair Labor Standards Act applies to all wage-roll and clerical employees but exempts most professional employees and employees who do original and creative work in recognized fields of artistic endeavor. Also exempt are employees who earn a minimum of $115 per week, exercise discretion and judgment, and spend less than 20% of their time on routine tasks. If an employee earns $150 or more per week, there are even fewer restrictions on what he can do and still be exempt from the overtime provisions. Salespersons working in retail trade must have salaries between $95 and $125 to be exempt from overtime provisions.

The Walsh-Healey Act applies to employees working for companies that are directly or indirectly engaged in federal contracts in excess of $10,000. Under its provisions, time and one-half must be paid for all hours worked over eight in a day (instead of 40 per week as in the Fair Labor Standards Act), and the minimum wage is established in accordance with the going rate in the community (rather than a specified minimum as in the Fair Labor Standards Act). The Act also forbids hiring boys under sixteen and girls under eighteen years of age.

Once you decide how much you should pay for getting a job done, you next have to decide what system of wage payment you will use.

WHAT IS THE MOST FREQUENTLY USED WAGE PAYMENT SYSTEM?

One of management's toughest and most critical jobs in deciding how to pay employees is what type of wage plan to use. The choice of the plan not only affects company earnings and profits but also affects employee satisfaction, turnover, morale, etc. Despite its critical role, however, a lot of managers seem to fall into a system of wage payment without really thinking about it.

Regardless of the type of system management selects, an employee has to be paid either on the basis of the *time* he works for you or on the basis of the *amount he produces* for you. Time is commonly used but has the disadvantage that no significant recognition can be given for differences in output since all like employees doing the same work are usually paid the same rate *time as a basis* per hour. Also, using time as a basis for pay, management doesn't know in advance what the cost per unit will be to make a product. For these reasons, a lot of companies like to use productivity as a basis for wages.

A lot of unions, however, are against incentive pay systems and have caused management to back off from using them. In addition, some poor incentive installations have given incentive systems a black eye. Despite these troubles, however, incentives are relatively popular with both labor and management, with about 30 to 45% of all employees covered by incentive pay.

WHAT ARE THE EFFECTS OF AN INCENTIVE PAY SYSTEM?

A good incentive pay plan will benefit labor and management in the following ways:[2]

For management

impact of
incentive system

1. Unit cost is usually less under incentive wage plans.
2. Individual differences in employee output can be recognized and rewarded.
3. Unit cost can be established with fair certainty.
4. Morale is often better under a well-administered plan where an employee can see the relationship between his work and his pay.

[2]Ibid., pp. 477–78. Adapted with permission.

5. Costs can be estimated with greater accuracy.

6. Less supervision in terms of output is required.

7. Improved cost control leads to more consistent, more uniform, and less variable production costs.

8. Improved utilization of facilities results.

For labor

1. An opportunity to earn money in proportion to individual effort is available.

2. The opportunity is present for recognition of individual performance.

3. The opportunity is present for labor to partially control their standards of living by their own efforts.

ARE THERE DIFFERENT INCENTIVE PAY PLANS?

There are dozens of different incentive pay plans. And every day brings a new twist to some basic concept. The fundamental plans, however, around which most companies develop their own particular incentive plans, are as follows:

1. Straight piecework.

2. Straight piecework with a guaranteed base.

3. The Halsey 50–50 plan.

4. The 100% bonus plan.

WHAT IS THE STRAIGHT PIECEWORK PLAN?

The straight piecework plan simply pays the employee so much money for each unit produced. If he doesn't produce anything, he doesn't get paid. The unit price is calculated by dividing the standard hourly output, as determined by study, into the "price" assigned the job. Thus, if the standard is 25 units per hour and the job is priced at $4.00 per hour, then the piece rate for the job is 16¢ per unit. If an employee produced 20 units per hour, his pay for an eight-hour day would be $25.60, calculated by multiplying the total output for the day (8 hr × 20 units per hr = 160 units per day) by the rate per piece (16¢). If he produced 30 units per hour, his daily wage would be $38.40.

pay for each unit

This plan is simple and easy to understand, and it provides a constant labor cost per unit. The big drawback is that workers are not guaranteed any minimum earnings regardless of output. Also, every time that wages are changed, new piece rates have to be calculated for every job.

IS THERE A PLAN WITH A GUARANTEED BASE?

Yes. One of the most commonly used plans is the straight piece rate, with a guaranteed base. It is the same as the straight piecework plan except that an hourly base rate equal to the going rate for the job is guaranteed.

Using the illustration above, an employee would be guaranteed $4.00 an hour regardless of how little he produced. Thus, if he produced 20 units per hour, his pay for an eight-hour day would be $32.00. If he produced 30 units per hour, his pay would be $38.40 for an eight-hour day (16¢ × 30 × 8).

WHAT IS THE HALSEY 50–50 PLAN?

This was one of the first incentive plans that deviated from some form of straight piecework. The Halsey plan guaranteed the employee a certain base rate plus a percentage of the time he saved on the job. Standards of output for this plan usually came from previous production records rather than from time studies. The bonus for the time saved was split between the employee and management in some proportion varying from one-third to one-half, with a 50–50 split being most common.

guaranteed base plus a percentage of savings   Using a 50% division in savings, an employee's wages under this plan would be equal to the hourly rate for the hours worked plus one-half of the time saved multiplied by the hourly rate. This can be expressed as a formula by letting:

$$W = \text{wages}$$
$$H = \text{hourly rate}$$
$$S = \text{standard time}$$
$$A = \text{actual time}$$

By using these symbols, the formula for the Halsey Plan with the savings split 50–50 would be:

$$W = HA + \frac{(S - A)H}{2}$$

Using our same illustration, if the employee produced 20 units per hour for eight hours, his pay for the day would be $32.00. If, however, he produced 30 units per hour, he would be producing five extra units per hour. Therefore, at the end of eight hours, he would have produced 240 units of output (30 × 8 = 240), or in terms of standard hours, 9.6 standard hours (240 ÷ 25 = 9.6). His pay, therefore, would be:

$$W = (4.00 \times 8) + \frac{(9.6 - 8)\$4.00}{2}$$
$$W = \$32 + \frac{\$6.40}{2}$$
$$W = \$35.20$$

Thus an increase of 20% in output enabled the employee to receive a 10% bonus because the bonus was split 50–50.

Using previous output as a standard is not acceptable today because it penalizes past good workers and rewards past poor workers. Past good employees would have produced well and could not exceed their past production very much; therefore, they could not earn a very large bonus. On the other hand, a poor worker who produced only a nominal amount in the past could exceed his standard easily since it is based on his past output, and he could, therefore, earn a large bonus.

Although it is relatively easy to understand, workers don't like the plan because they don't understand why they should split their bonus with management.

WHAT INCENTIVE PLAN IS MOST COMMONLY USED?

The 100% bonus plan, also known as the *hour-for-hour plan,* is the most commonly used plan. It is identical to straight piecework with a guaranteed base except that allowances are made in terms of time for each unit of output instead of in terms of money.

Using our same illustration of 25 units per hour as standard and a base rate of $4.00 per hour, an employee would be allowed 2.4 minutes per unit of output (60 minutes ÷ 25 = 2.4 minutes) instead of a piece rate of 16¢ per unit. Thus, if he produced 20 units per hour, his daily wage would be $32.00 since he would receive the guaranteed base of $4.00 per hour, but he would not receive a bonus because he did not exceed the standard of 25 units per hour.

allowances in time

If his rate of output had been 30 units per hour, he would have received an allowance of 2.4 minutes per unit for the 240 units he produced during the day. He would have earned, therefore, 576 minutes of pay (240 units × 2.4 minutes allowed per unit = 576 minutes) or 9.6 hours. This, multiplied by $4.00 per hour, equals $38.40, his rate of pay for the day.

This plan is simple and easy to understand and has the added feature that piece rates do not have to be refigured every time the wage rate changes. It is the most universally suitable incentive plan that uses carefully set standards based on an accurate system of time studies. Wages can be easily calculated by the employee regardless of what his hourly rate is. And, finally, management likes the plan because efficiency can be figured for individual employees, groups, departments, or the whole plant using the formula.

$$\text{Efficiency} = \frac{\text{Standard hours earned}}{\text{Actual hours worked}}$$

Using this formula, you could calculate employee efficiency, for example, using the figures above. Thus, for 30 units per hour for a day, an employee's efficiency would be:

$$E = \frac{\text{Standard hours earned}}{\text{Actual hours worked}}$$

$$E = \frac{9.6}{8}$$

$$E = 1.20 \text{ or } 120\%$$

WHAT ARE THE REQUIREMENTS FOR A SUCCESSFUL INCENTIVE PAY PLAN?

Obviously, the requirements for a successful incentive pay plan must suit both labor and management. If they suit both, you've gone a long way in making the plan successful. In addition, you should be sure to follow these points in undertaking any incentive pay installation:[3]

1. Explain the plan to everyone before you install it. If you talk out problems before you install it, employees will better understand and accept the plan.

2. Be sure the earnings are in direct proportion to output above the standard. Employees don't like to share their earnings. Instead, they like plans where they get the full benefit of their extra effort.

agreement between management and labor

3. Be sure it is simple and easily understood—so simple that the employee can easily calculate his wages. Lack of understanding plants seeds of doubt. If employees don't understand the plan, they won't trust it.

4. Reward extra effort by extra pay in the next pay envelope. Most people don't like to get their extra pay next month for work done today.

5. The differential in pay between guaranteed and incentive rates should be large enough to make extra effort worthwhile—usually about 25%.

6. Be sure the plan has a guaranteed base.

7. Never change a work standard unless an error was made in calculations or changes have been made in work methods or conditions of work. It is grossly unfair and unjust to change a standard simply because someone thinks the employee is earning too much.

8. Be sure the standard has been fairly and accurately set. Use only recognized procedures and then only those agreed upon by your employees.

9. Always maintain standard working conditions. Without standard conditions, employees cannot be expected to achieve or surpass the output standard.

10. Always make prompt and fair adjustments in pay for employees who do not meet the standard for reasons beyond their control.

11. Insist on production being up to the designated quality. Employees should not be paid for poor quality.

[3]Ibid., pp. 486–87. Adapted with permission.

12. Once the standard has been achieved, unit costs should be constant.

13. If an employee is not meeting or exceeding the standard, check immediately to see why. If improper training or a change in working conditions is responsible, it should be corrected. Every employee should be able to earn a bonus if he tries.

14. Once installed, keep the incentive plan rigidly maintained. Be sure that conditions of work, materials, and methods remain standard; or if changes have to be made in any one of these, be sure they are reflected in the time standard. Any system of incentive pay that is worth installing is worth keeping up to date.

15. Be sure all employees understand what you expect from them and what they can expect from you. A changing and weak policy toward incentive problems can easily destroy your employees' confidence. In case of doubt, rule in favor of the employee.

DO UNIONS APPROVE OF INCENTIVE SYSTEMS?

Labor is keenly interested in any plan affecting the wages of its members. Some unions, like the miners, textile workers, clothing workers, cigar makers, shoe makers, iron and steel workers, potters, and flint glass workers either prefer incentive pay systems or accept them willingly. Of course, some unions vigorously oppose incentive pay for their members. Much of labor's opposition, however, can be blamed on the malpractices of unscrupulous management in the application of incentive systems. During recent years there are signs that these unions are not as opposed to incentives as they were previously. This has been brought about mainly by better personnel policies, better labor relations, better worker education, and more enlightened management practices.

In fact, when morale is high and when trust and good relations exist between labor and management, almost any wage incentive system can be made to work. Millions of workers are moderately satisfied with their wage incentive plans, and many more employees accept them as a result of their positive experiences.

WHAT IS MANAGEMENT'S POSITION?

Labor's attitude toward an incentive system should be the deciding factor for management on whether or not to install an incentive wage plan. If labor favors it, if the work can be adapted to incentive pay, and if the characteristics of the industry are such as to make incentives feasible, then management can move in that direction. Without all of these "go" signals, management should stay clear.

Incentives don't make the work of supervisors easier. To the contrary, more supervision and better management are required under incentive plans. Incentive pay plans need more in the way of good organization, more careful planning and control of production, better and closer supervision, and more attention to maintaining standard working conditions. Not only should management acknowledge and assume these responsibilities at the outset, it should also recognize the added obligation to its employees to maintain and continue the plan as agreed upon.

consult with labor then decide

Finally, management's position should be the acceptance of the responsibility of generating and warranting its employees' cooperation, faith, and confidence. In the final round, employees have the power to make a plan succeed or fail. With understanding and faith, a plan will work. But without mutual trust and confidence even the best plan will be ineffective. Winning and meriting its employees' trust has to be recognized by management as a cornerstone for successful incentives. Finally, management must recognize that incentive systems demand more of management than other pay plans, and management's position must be one of recognizing and accepting these responsibilities.

A Case Study
THE ROUGEMENT CASE *(B)*

The Rougement Company owned and operated eighteen textile plants employing a total of 5,400 employees. Many of these plants engaged in the same types of textile operations, such as spinning, throwing, dyeing, weaving, etc.

The Rougement Company was founded in 1938 and got its real start during World War II. During and immediately after the war, the management, in an effort to round out and complement its activities, acquired a series of small mills scattered over a radius of 300 miles from the home office. In acquiring these plants, the Rougement Company maintained, insofar as possible, the same local administrative and operative officials, the same policies, and the same labor, and in every way attempted to make the local unit autonomous. Each plant was considered as a profit center, and each plant manager operated his plant in the way that he thought best for sound business operations and maximum profits. This practice was apparently successful, and the company continued to grow.

Sixteen months ago, however, a textile union began a campaign to organize the company's eighteen plants. The union has not, to date, been successful in its mission. Many of the employees expressed the feeling that they would wait and see what management planned for them under the new ownership of the Rougement Company before they definitely decided on union representation. Even though the union organizers have not succeeded in their drive, they have planted some seeds of doubt and distrust in the employees' minds. For example, they have demonstrated to the employees that no consistent wage scale has been adhered to by the company. The union showed that employees performing the same work but in different plants received wage differentials as great as 26% in some situations. Even within some plants, it was pointed out that no systematic attempt had been made by the company to establish fair and just relative wages. In one plant, for example, the union representatives pointed out that the plant janitor was making 3¢ per hour more than employees who were doffing (doffing is a job requiring manual dexterity in removing and placing bobbins on textile machines).

Many of these wage ills, of course, were acquired with the various plants. And some of them were brought about because the several plants were brought together under one common owner. How the company acquired the troubles, however, was of no interest to the union. But what the company did about them was vital to organized labor. Labor's emphasis had been on adequate and just wages.

The management of the Rougement Company preferred that the workers not be organized but was taking no active part in a campaign to influence employees and thus prevent the union from getting established. The company felt that many of the so-called wage inequities could be justified and explained, although they would be difficult for the employees to understand. Whatever its course of action, the management recognized that it had to answer the union's charge—as well as indicate what it was going to do to correct the situation.

1. What has the Rougement Company done wrong?
2. If you were called in to advise the company, what steps would you suggest to correct the problems?

A Case Study
MOUNT VERNON WASHING MACHINE COMPANY

The Mount Vernon Washing Machine Company was one of the oldest and largest manufacturers of home-type washing machines. About 60% of the parts used in the washers were fabricated by the company, and the remaining 40% were purchased from outside suppliers.

Inspection procedures for the items made by the company were routine. Various combinations of floor inspection, first piece inspection, process inspection, and key point inspection were used to inspect material as it proceeded through the various manufacturing processes. Inspection of items purchased from the outside varied. Some of them were inspected by Mt. Vernon's inspectors at the plants where they were manufactured; others were inspected in Mt. Vernon's plant in their incoming inspection department. Various inspection procedures were employed here. For example, many of the parts were small and because of their critical nature, 100% inspection was not uncommon. Other items, such as electrical switches, were inspected on a sampling basis.

Recently, Mr. Morven, the manager of the inspection department, had received several complaints from the shop about how long it took material to get inspected. In addition, top management for the past seven months had pointed out that his inspection costs were higher than those in any of the other plants owned by the company. In an effort to reduce costs, Mr. Morven established some new inspection procedures that helped streamline the movement of materials. He also procured some newer and faster measuring devices to speed up the flow of materials through his department.

In an attempt to control his labor better, Mr. Morven also planned to install an incentive system of wage payment. His plan was deceptively simple. Inasmuch as he had inspection records for the past fourteen years showing the average output for inspectors on different types of work, he reasoned that these could be used to establish work standards. Using these standards, he planned to pay his inspectors on a 100% bonus plan.

When he talked over his plans for an incentive pay system with his four supervisors, Mr. Morven met with divided reaction. One was enthusiastic about the proposal and indicated that he believed it would be a real stimulus for the workers to inspect a larger number of pieces per day. One of his older supervisors said that he did not believe it would work because inspectors were temperamental—they were artists—and that artists could not be placed on incentive pay. A third supervisor said that in his opinion it would be a lot of trouble to administer and that considering the extra costs of administration, he did not believe that inspection costs would be reduced. The fourth supervisor indicated that he felt an incentive system such as the 100% bonus plan should never be applied to inspection because it would be asking for a speedup that would probably result in improper and poor inspection and thereby higher costs. He did state, however, that he believed a measured day work plan could be worked out that would be satisfactory.

1. What do you think of Mr. Morven's proposal?
2. What are your reactions to the comments of his four supervisors?
3. What do you recommend? Why?

21
WHAT TO DO ABOUT PREVENTING ACCIDENTS

This chapter explains—

- Why you need to stress accident prevention
- What you can do to reduce the number of accidents
- How safety can be measured

Any lost-time accident is a waste of human values, to say nothing of the suffering and expense involved. And when you add together all the accidents that occur each year, it represents a tremendous loss of manpower and skills.

Despite compensation and company aid, a lost-time accident frequently means a serious financial loss to your employee and his family. It could be a loss of wages during his time out of work. It might mean a reduction in his pay when he gets back on the payroll because of his physical inability to perform his old job. It might even mean total disability and loss of his job, not to mention the high costs of medical care.

Companies also incur losses from accidents in such forms as decreased production, damage to machinery, spoiled or poor quality products, excessive waste, and idle time. These costs, however, are usually hidden in some overall cost of manufacture, but they can be determined. One cost we do know, however, and that is that the industry in the United States pays about $3.5 billion dollars annually to employees for job-related injuries and illnesses.

Preventing accidents is one of your important jobs as a supervisor. You must devote a considerable portion of your time to fostering effective safety practices among your employees. If you don't, safety will be regarded by them as being secondary or even unimportant.

WHAT ARE THE REASONS FOR STRESSING ACCIDENT PREVENTION?

The major reason you as a supervisor should be interested in your employees' safety is to *prevent personal injury and death*. Whenever one of your employees is injured in your department, you may well be responsible for it if an investigation shows that the accident could have been prevented. A severe accident is uncalled for, and no supervisor wants to feel a part of such an occurrence.

A second reason for you to stress accident prevention is to *reduce operating and production costs*, thus putting your department in a favorable profit position in the company. Not only do you save obvious costs, but *loss, injury, and* indirect costs (like insurance rates) are lower if your department has a good *costs* safety record. Along this line, another cost that might not be so obvious would be the cost that results after a member of a work team is injured. His replacement is frequently not as familiar with the job, thus causing a disruption in work harmony among the other employees and a resulting decrease in output.

The relationship between sound safety practices and productive efficiency is, of course, well recognized. Our mass production techniques in large plants depend on the careful planning and control of every operation in the manufacturing process, and accidents that cause interruptions in the manufacturing process mean costly delays in operation.

Safety is also important to small firms because an injured worker is a nonproductive worker—or at best a less productive employee. And in small firms, an employee is typically more important to the productive process than in large firms. Also, when an employee returns to his job after an accident, it is not unusual for the quality as well as the quantity of his work to drop as a result of his accident.

In addition to these obvious reasons for practicing safety, you should stress safety to your employees because of its *effect on employee relations, community relations, and employee morale.* Although you cannot measure these factors in dollars and cents, your common sense points out how safety can help all three. The reputation that a company develops in a community as being a good, poor, or dangerous place to work has a decided effect on the quality and quantity of employees who apply for work. In like manner, it has a decided effect on the morale of those already employed. Workers lose their confidence and trust in supervisors who do not stress accident prevention. They see a manager who doesn't stress safety as being one who is more concerned with output than with providing a safe place for his employees to perform their jobs.

ARE EMPLOYEES ACCIDENT-PRONE?

Some employees seem to be accident-prone; however, all individuals don't appear to be equally susceptible to accidents. Some seem to have a greater chance of accidents than others. Those who have more than their share are known as *accident-prone* employees. Some people "explain" this by saying bad luck comes in "threes"—when you have one accident, you'll have two more. A more logical explanation is that because of their physical or mental makeup, some workers are more apt to have accidents.

Accidents by such employees are caused by factors like:

1. Poor sight, poor hearing, or lack of stamina.
2. Distaste for the job, dislike for the supervisor, or similar faults.
3. Low level of intelligence.
4. Not enough manual skill to perform the job the way it should be done.
5. Poor usage of plant and equipment.
6. Existence of hazards.
7. Carelessness.
8. Poor training in safety practices.

*cause of employee
accidents*

A correctable defect, like poor vision, doesn't make an employee accident-prone if the defect is corrected. But those employees who do not respond to training and correction are the ones who are more liable to injury than the average worker. You should place these employees in jobs where their efforts can be effectively and safely used, or you should discharge them. Working them under hazardous conditions is a menace to other employees as well as to themselves.

Accidents can and do happen anywhere. However, as a supervisor you should be aware that some spots are more dangerous than others and that employees who are poor accident risks should not be placed in or near these locations.

Where are these danger spots? First, wherever materials are handled—particularly heavy materials. In fact, improperly handling materials is one of the prime causes of back and foot injuries. You should, therefore, be sure that your employees in these areas are adequately trained in lifting, moving, and handling the materials. In addition, you should make sure that the proper types of materials-handling equipment—such as hand-trucks, cranes, hoists, and forklift trucks—are available and that your employees know how to use them.

danger spots A second hazard spot in most companies is wherever you find moving parts, conveyors, machines, gears, and the like. Great strides, of course, have been made in designing machines that operate more safely as well as in adding safety features to old machines. Many people, in fact, think of such things as guards around machines when they hear about industrial safety. Despite this, machines are still far from being safe. In fact, machine injuries exceed all others in both number and severity. Thus, whenever your employees work around moving hazards, you should take extra precaution to

"Don't be too confident. Accidents can happen anywhere, anytime."

insure that they are well trained in operating the machine. In addition, you should be sure that you have taken all possible precautions to isolate or minimize the hazard.

Finally, employees hurt themselves by tripping and falling over objects, slipping on floors, and falling down or up stairs. Adequate precautions, therefore, should be taken to call attention to hazards such as stairs, rough or slippery floors, unusual objects, and so on.

WHO IS RESPONSIBLE FOR SAFETY?

Although top management can't personally assume the role of safety director, it can make crystal clear to all employees that top management is strongly behind a concerted effort to reduce accidents and to make the plant a safer place for employees to earn their livings.

However, the person who actually stresses safety is you—the supervisor. You are the one who must enforce safety procedures, and you will have to answer for poor safety practices in your area. To help promote safety, your company should make available to you and to your employees safely operating tools and equipment, and it should install safety guards on machines where feasible. You, in turn, should be ever alert to discovering and correcting unsafe practices. In addition, you should try to plan production operations with safety as a central theme. Finally, as a supervisor you should try to develop an atmosphere in your department that is conducive to general employee health and safety. Safety is not something that you can *supervisor's role* "turn on" once a month. You should, instead, organize safety in your department on a continuing basis and make sure that every employee through proper training and supervision has a desire to work safely.

DOES THE INDIVIDUAL EMPLOYEE HAVE ANY RESPONSIBILITY FOR SAFETY?

In the final analysis, the individual employee is the one responsible for an accident. Your job, therefore, is to make your employees think and practice safety and make this so much a part of them that practicing safety becomes second nature for them. Do this through demonstrations, lectures, informal talks—any way you can get the information across to them. You've got to educate and train employees as to what is or is not a safe practice. You've got to tell them how they should or should not lift an object. In other words, you've got to give them the benefit of your knowledge and experience in safety practices. Explain to them their possible loss in pay, the suffering they might incur, and the possibility of losing their capacity to make a living. In other words, instill in them the desire to want to practice "safety first."

WHO IS RESPONSIBLE FOR SAFETY IN LARGE COMPANIES?

safety director

As stated previously, safety is the responsibility of individual supervisors. Although they are closest to the job and should want to promote safety practices, it often happens that their primary concern is to meet a production schedule. This concern with output along with dozens of other matters that press the supervisor often pushes safety to a secondary position. Because of this, large companies frequently place responsibility for safety planning under an individual whose only job is that of safety director.

The safety director usually reports to some top management individual who can exert considerable influence in the company to make accident-free work a reality. The responsibility of the safety director is only to *plan* for safety. Putting it into effect is still your job as a supervisor.

How large does a company have to be to have a safety director? This varies with the company and its activities. One rule of thumb is that you should have a safety specialist for each 2,000 employees. However, in plants where conditions are hazardous, a safety man for every 1,000 or 1,200 employees may be normal.

WHAT DOES A SAFETY DIRECTOR DO?

The safety director works closely with individual supervisors to design safety programs and to see that certain safety practices are implemented. He inspects all operations in the plant to detect safety hazards. He analyzes jobs for safety content. He is responsible for employee training and education in safety principles and practices. He has to keep up with the latest improvements in safety products that are available for employee protection, and communicates all of this to the supervisors concerned.

He investigates accidents to determine their cause and takes the necessary steps to prevent their recurrence. Finally, he is the one who is responsible for seeing that the company complies with all local, state, and federal regulations governing safety.

HOW CAN YOU PREVENT ACCIDENTS?

training for safety

Accidents don't happen by themselves. They are caused by people. Likewise, accident prevention doesn't occur by itself. It has to be promoted by both management and labor if it is to have any success.

A well-organized and well-operated safety program can have a dramatic effect on the overall safety record of your employees. The type of program you install can be varied to suit individual company needs, but you should keep several factors in mind. You've got to have complete support and cooperation from the top man in the company to the bottom of the organization, thus making it easy to report unsafe practices. You've got to teach your employees to think and practice safety. Do this through informal meetings, talks, lectures by authorities, and movies. After every accident, hold a meeting to analyze what happened, what caused the accident, what safety practices were violated, and how the accident could have been prevented. Make your safety program contemporary, inventive, interesting. You can use contests, posters, safety rallies, and slogans to convince employees that for their own good, they should look for and discover unsafe working conditions and practices. Safety equipment such as hats, shoes, glasses, and gloves should be generously provided the employees, and they should be required to use them. Put safety equipment on machines. Be sure you have enough light. Use color and lights to call attention to safety hazards.

Finally, help prevent accidents by detecting and eliminating "psychological booby traps"—points of strain and stress in the flow of work, where employee tension and strain might make for carelessness and thus promote accidents. Make your working conditions involving heat, light, ventilation, humidity, and so on, the best attainable.

DOES DEPARTMENTAL INSPECTION HELP?

Absolutely. A safety inspection of a department or a plant is the oldest and most obvious device used to promote safety. Safety inspections turn up hazards such as slippery floors, uneven surfaces, poor lighting, unguarded machines, poor housekeeping, unguarded elevator shafts, irregular steps, inadequate exit facilities, and inadequate washrooms. Once detected, these hazards should not be left to the busy employee or supervisor to correct. These individuals are frequently so concerned with other problems that safety slips their minds. Instead, safety hazards should be reported to the appropriate manager for immediate correction.

WHAT IS JOB SAFETY ANALYSIS?

Job safety analysis consists of going over every aspect of a job to see if any possible hazards exist. Doing this frequently brings out points previously overlooked. For example, you might discover that a fixture is sharp and could cut an employee's hands. Or you may find that a particular reach over a machine could easily result in loss of balance and injury. Or you might note that the job calls for lifting an object in an awkward position—one that is apt to cause back strain. *aids to accident prevention*

In addition, job safety analysis should point out any special qualifications needed by an individual to perform the job. You might, for example, find that to perform a particular job safely, the employee needs certain motor skills, or special muscular coordination, or special visual or hearing ability. These requirements should be incorporated in the job specification that you set up.

WHY IS PROPER PLACEMENT IMPORTANT?

Be sure to match the employee's mental and physical qualifications with those demanded by the job. A poorly placed employee is more apt to incur injury than one whose capacities match the job requirements. If your company doesn't provide tests and other placement aids to match employees and jobs, then you should carefully supervise the new employee. Watch for any demonstrated inability or any unsafe practice so that it can be corrected—or so that the employee can be moved to another job.

WHAT ABOUT PERSONAL PROTECTIVE EQUIPMENT?

More research has gone into developing personal safety equipment and more companies use it as a means of accident prevention than any single item other than plant inspection. An almost endless number of safety items are available. A few of them are:[1]

1. Protection for the head
   a. Hard hats
   b. Hair protection
   c. Ear protectors
2. Protection for the face and eyes
   a. Hoods
   b. Goggles and glasses
   c. Face shields
   d. Welding helmets
3. Protection for breathing
   a. Oxygen or air-breathing apparatus
   b. Supplied air respirators
   c. Canister and cartridge respirators
   d. Filter respirators

[1]Adapted from Claude S. George, Jr., *Management for Business and Industry* (Englewood Cliffs, N.J.: Prentice-Hall, Inc., 1970), p. 375. Reprinted by permission of Prentice-Hall, Inc.

4. Protection for hands, feet, and legs
   a. Gloves
   b. Safety shoes
   c. Foot guards
5. Protection for the body by using protective clothing

The only trouble with personal safety devices is that the hazard is not eliminated. The safety equipment is only a thin line of defense between your employee and the unsafe condition. As the responsible supervisor, you should make every effort to eliminate or at least minimize the hazard calling for the equipment. Then see what you can do to encourage employees to use the equipment provided. Familiarity with the job sometimes makes employees careless with the use of safety equipment, and all it takes to lose an eye is failure to wear safety glasses just once.

To keep employees from forgetting safety equipment, let them in on plans for minimizing a hazard. Let them make suggestions about what should be done, what equipment would be appropriate, and what they would like to have available. If they propose and approve a piece of equipment, they will be more apt to use it. If you have a union, get the steward, or if not, pick one or two "informal leaders" and solicit their help in getting your employees to respect and wear protective equipment. Remember to set a proper example for your employees by wearing the equipment that the job calls for. If employees shouldn't go in a special area without a hard hat, be sure you don't wander in without yours.

DO YOU WATCH HOW EMPLOYEES HANDLE MATERIALS?

Although often ignored, the careless handling of materials is responsible for over 80% of the injuries in some plants. Correction is simple. For light materials, instruct your employees in the fundamentals of how to handle the materials, how to use their legs instead of their backs. For heavy items, study the materials' handling requirements, and purchase equipment capable of efficiently and safely handling the materials.

HOW DOES GOOD HOUSEKEEPING HELP?

Good housekeeping is one of the most important factors in preventing injury and accidents in your department. Littered aisles, stairs, and work areas invite industrial accidents—in addition to being fire hazards. A major portion of all industrial fires start in rubbish, litter, or oily clothing and rags. Good housekeeping includes not only floors and machines but also windows, dusty lights, and dirty reflectors, which reduce light.

WHAT MEASURES CAN YOU TAKE TO MINIMIZE ACCIDENTS?

You can do a lot of things ahead of time that could reduce your accident rate by as much as 30 or 40%. One obvious thing you can do, for example, is make sure that first-aid supplies are available and that emergency telephone numbers are known and are easily available. These numbers would include the company physician and the local police and fire department. You should also be sure that your employees know what to do in emergency situations. In case of fire, they should know what to do and where to go. In case of accidents, they should know what to do and whom to call. And it is up to you to make sure that they are aware of these things by holding fire drills, mock *supervisory* emergency drills, accident drills, etc.

responsibilities

Your employees should also be given written instructions about what they should do in emergency situations. Tell them orally, hold drills, and give them printed instructions. Don't take chances on poor communications. "You never told me what to do" is a poor epitaph to a well-meant communication.

Finally, to get the fullest cooperation in observing safety procedures, give your employees a voice in making the rules. Let them help decide what the best practices should be, how drills should be conducted, what sort of aid an injured person should receive, and how safety rules can best be implemented. Remember that whenever your employees participate in making a rule, they tend to follow it more closely.

WHAT SHOULD YOU DO FOR AN INJURED EMPLOYEE?

What you should do for an injured employee depends on the facilities your company has and what its practices are. If you are well qualified to give first aid and your company supports this, you should do so immediately. If you are not qualified, then you should see that the employee is given first aid quickly by someone who *is* qualified, such as a company nurse, doctor, or safety man. Let only trained people help the employee. Know who these trained people are and where they work so that they can be quickly called for help. Don't move an employee who appears to have any bone or back injury. Call a doctor who knows how to move the injured employee and what can safely be done to make him more comfortable until the ambulance arrives.

HOW CAN YOU MEASURE SAFETY?

You can measure safety by using various ratios and trends to show changes in the status of safety in your department. One simple measure is the quarterly accident rate for your department. You can compare each period with prior

326

ones to see improvements. Departmental figures showing *frequency* as well as *severity* are important to you because they tend to pinpoint trouble spots. *Frequency* shows how often accidents occur. *Severity* tells for how long a time the injured person was out of work.

To develop a figure to measure the *frequency rate* for your department, use as a base a disabling injury—one that makes the employee unable to work one or more days following the accident. This is expressed as a ratio of the number of man-hours worked, with the rate expressed as the number of disabling injuries per million man-hours worked. The formula is:

$$\text{Frequency rate} = \frac{\text{Number of disabling injuries} \times 1,000,000}{\text{Number of man-hours worked}}$$

For example, if you employ 100 people in your department and report 8 disabling injuries in a year, your departmental frequency rate would be: *frequency vs. severity*

$$FR = \frac{8 \times 1,000,000}{100 \text{ men} \times 2000 \text{ hr worked each year}}$$
$$FR = \frac{8,000,000}{200,000}$$
$$FR = 40$$

This says you have 40 disabling injuries for every million man-hours worked.

The *severity rate* for your department shows the number of productive days lost due to injuries per million man-hours worked. This formula is:

$$\text{Severity rate} = \frac{\text{Days lost} \times 1,000,000}{\text{Number of man-hours worked}}$$

To determine the number of days lost, the American National Standards Institute has developed time charges for different types of accidents. For example, a total disability accident charges you with 6,000 days lost. If an employee loses a toe, you are charged 35 days plus the actual time he is out.

To illustrate how you figure your severity rate, suppose you had an employee who lost a toe and suppose your department experienced a total of 20 days lost time during the year. The number of days actually lost would be 20, but you would add 35 days to this because one of your employees lost a toe. Thus, your days lost would be 55, and your severity rate would be:

$$SR = \frac{55 \times 1,000,000}{100 \text{ men} \times 2000 \text{ hr worked per year}}$$
$$SR = \frac{55,000,000}{200,000}$$
$$SR = 275$$

This means you department had 275 productive days lost for every million man-hours worked. This measure shows how severe your accidents were.

By themselves, these rates don't mean much. But when you compare them with similar ratios from other companies in your industry, you can see where you stand. Many of these industry norms can be secured from the National Safety Council in Chicago. They show, for example, that the *average frequency rate* for all industry is 6.54 per million man-hours work, and the *average severity rate* for all industry is 695 per million man-hours worked.

HOW DOES THE OSHA PROMOTE SAFETY?

The Occupational Safety and Health Act of 1970 (OSHA) is an act that makes work places safer for employees. As a result of the act, companies involved in interstate commerce are required to:

1. Provide a work place free of recognized hazards.
2. Comply with health standards set forth by the Secretary of Labor.
3. Keep records of all employee injuries and deaths.
4. Provide physical examinations and check-ups for employees exposed to certain harmful substances.
5. Open their plants for inspections.
6. Post in a prominent place copies of any violations.

Employees who report complaints to the Secretary of Labor are specifically protected by the Act from discharge or any other punitive action by an employer.

The safety standards that companies are required to abide by are those created and administered by the Secretary of Labor. When the Secretary receives a complaint from an employee or his union, the Secretary investigates the situation. If he finds the company guilty of safety and health violations, the Secretary may issue a citation specifying the violations and what the remedies should be. The company can disagree with the citation and appeal to the Occupational Safety and Health Review Commission for relief. If the Commission finds the company guilty, it has the power to assess penalties up to $10,000 for violation of a standard, administer penalties of $1,000 per day for continued violations, and assess a company $20,000 for willful violations resulting in the death of an employee. The Commission can also levy a fine of $1,000 to persons giving advance notice of inspections, as well as fine individuals up to $10,000 for providing false information.

A Case Study
BEAMON PLATING COMPANY

The Beamon Plating Company specialized in cleaning and plating all types of small metal objects. Its service was good, its prices were reasonable, and its work was guaranteed. As a result, it enjoyed a healthy business—mostly from industrial concerns located within a 500-mile radius. Some of its work, however, consisted of silver-plating and gold-plating objects of art as well as silver services and the like.

Several hazards exist in any plating shop, and due precautions must be taken. Fumes from the plating tanks, for example, are very dangerous and can cause sickness, and even death, from prolonged exposure. To preclude such a mishap, the management of Beamon Plating installed one of the most efficient air exhaust systems obtainable. In fact, air purity tests showed that the air in the plating room contained less toxic gases than air elsewhere in the plant. In addition, three emergency showerheads were installed beside the plating tanks. In case an employee spilled acid on himself, he quickly stepped under the closet shower and pulled a chain. This automatically opened a valve sending a full-force shower over him, thus dissipating the effects of the acid. The company also furnished all its plating room employees with special uniforms, rubber boots, rubber aprons, and rubber gloves. These protected the employees from the plating fluids and acids.

Chemicals used in the plating tanks were purchased in 50-gallon drums, and acids came in large glass containers called *carboys.* Both the acids and the chemicals in drums were stored under a shed, which was 150 feet from the main building. Other less bulky items such as cadmium balls, soda ash, etc., were stored in a small storeroom in the plant. When material from either of these storerooms was needed, any one of the employees who wasn't busy at the time was sent to get the material. If it was not too heavy, the employee usually carried it by hand. If it was heavy or bulky, the employee could choose one of the several handtrucks that were always available. Occasionally, the material fell off and spilled on the floor. In several instances, an employee dropped material on his feet, causing a lost-time accident. Some of the workers complained of straining their backs from lifting, but this could not be positively linked to lifting the material for the plating shop.

Despite all the precautions and the provision of protective equipment, the company had some trouble in the plating room. Several of the employees almost refused to wear the rubber boots and aprons provided by the company. In fact, they removed them quite frequently, claiming they were bulky, hot, and uncomfortable. Management realized that this was a dangerous practice, but if the employees would not wear the safety equipment, management admitted it did not know what to do about the situation.

Several accidents of a minor nature occurred recently. For example, one of the girls who wired parts to racks so they could be individually plated stuck one of the sharp parts in her finger. This would not have happened if she had been wearing the gloves furnished by the company.

Although this may be looked upon as a minor item, the Beamon Plating Company does not want its employees to forget that serious injuries can occur. It also wants them to realize that the company is trying to provide maximum protection for its workers during their workday.

1. What do you think of the safety program of the Beamon Plating Company?
2. What changes, if any, would you recommend? Explain why.

A Case Study
HILL CREST SCHOOL

On a surprise visit by the town Safety Officer, the Hill Crest School received a substandard report. Specifically, the officer cited violations resulting in the following:

1. Three or more accidents involving the same students on the playground.
2. Several serious eye injuries during basketball practice.
3. Falls on the school steps.
4. Two broken ribs and one dislocated shoulder at football practice.
5. Multiple cases of burns and cuts.
6. One crushed finger.
7. One slight concussion.
8. Two cases of back strain and/or injury.
9. Two sprains caused from slipping.
10. One broken arm.

1. What things could have caused these injuries?
2. Where and under what conditions do you think the injuries occurred?
3. What would you recommend to minimize or prevent similar accidents from occurring in the future?

22
HOW TO CONVINCE MANAGEMENT TO BUY NEW EQUIPMENT

This chapter explains—

- Why you should consider replacing equipment
- How you assemble the cost figures you will need
- How you can prove to management that new equipment will pay for itself

$\mathbf{H}$enry Ford once said if you need a new machine and don't buy it, you pay for it without getting it. In other words, if you don't buy a new machine, the high costs of operating an old machine will pay for the new machine, and you will not be getting the benefits of the new machine.

Knowing *when* to replace a machine, however, is a difficult problem. A lot of people think a piece of equipment should not be replaced until it is worn out. However, just because a piece of equipment has not *physically collapsed and fallen apart* is no reason not to replace it if it has been superseded by newer machines that can do the job more effectively, in less time, and at a lower cost.

A lot of supervisors find themselves in this spot today. They are operating old machines that are expensive to run when they could be operating new machines at a lower cost. The problem they face is how to convince top management that a new machine should be purchased. This is not an easy job but one that you can handle with a little study.

The first step, of course, is to single out a process or operation for study. It could be studying whether or not to switch work from a hand-operated job to a machine or studying whether to move from an old machine to a newer model. You might, for example, have a hand-cranked spirit duplicator and are considering the wisdom of buying a new power-operated duplicator. Or you may be concerned with whether or not a new model delivery truck would be cheaper to operate than the old jalopy you are using.

Whatever you choose to study, you face the problem of proving to management that the proposed process or machine is economically justifiable, that it will save money and be cheaper to run. In most instances, the proof rests on determining whether or not total operating costs can be lowered enough to make the new machine a wise purchase.

WHY REPLACE MACHINES?

We need new equipment for one of four reasons:

1. *Deterioration.* When a machine wears out, it needs replacing. A 1927 typewriter may still be working, but in all probability it is so worn that you are losing money on labor costs, decreased production, poor quality of product, and increased maintenance. Your question is not *whether* to buy a new typewriter, but *which one to buy.*

   no longer useful

2. *Obsolescence.* A new piece of equipment may be available on the market that is more efficient than the machine you currently use. However, your present machine may be functioning well mechanically, and the need to buy a new one may be hard to prove. For example, a

This chapter is adapted with permission from Claude S. George Jr., *Management for Business and Industry,* Englewood Cliffs, N.J.: Prentice-Hall, Inc., 1970), pp. 288–97. Reprinted by permission of Prentice-Hall, Inc.

"A lot of supervisors are running old machines that are expensive to run when they could be operating new machines at a lower cost."

manual typewriter that is only two years old might be obsolete because it cannot do the job as effectively and quickly as a new electric typewriter.

3. *Inadequacy.* New products may make old machines inadequate. Thus, a new form that is 14 inches wide that must be typed would make a typewriter with a standard carriage inadequate.

4. *Working conditions and morale.* Employee dissatisfaction, lack of safety, and low morale resulting from the unpleasantness or hazardous nature of a process might be reasons to consider new equipment.

HOW DO YOU DEFINE THE PROBLEM?

If deciding when to replace a piece of equipment were as simple as deciding when to replace a ball point pen, you would not have any problem. You'd get a new one when the old one gave out. Unfortunately, this is not the case. Most pieces of equipment, like automobiles, require a series of maintenance expenditures, which often increase as the equipment ages. With age, most equipment deteriorates and, in addition, is subject to obsolescence as newer, better machinery is produced to perform the same job more effectively. In fact, today most supervisors find that their equipment is more often superseded technologically rather than worn out by deterioration. The problem that you as a supervisor will face, then, is one of equipment *dis-*

*displacement vs.
replacement*

placement rather than *re*placement because improvements tend to *displace* a piece of equipment long before it is worn out. Few of us, for example, wear out a car. Instead, we *replace* it with an improved model.

The problem in business is to determine *when* you should purchase a new piece of equipment and *how* you can convince management that you are right. You can do this by following a systematic and logical approach to solving the problem.

WHAT TYPES OF COSTS ARE INVOLVED?

The costs involved in buying a new piece of equipment are of two types:

1. *Recurring costs* are those that continue year after year as the equipment is used and include such items as direct labor, material, taxes, insurance, and power. Although these costs may vary slightly from year to year, they are usually a relatively constant amount.
2. *Nonrecurring costs* are those that are incurred only once in the life of the equipment and include such items as the purchase price of the new machine, transportation costs involved in getting the new equipment to the plant, and the installation charges.

When a company decides to buy a new piece of equipment, it usually does so only after the best estimates indicate that the money invested in the new equipment will be recovered, and a reasonable return will be forthcoming. This return is figured on the difference between the recurring operating costs for both the present and the proposed equipment and is known as the *cost saving*.

HOW DO YOU COMPUTE COST SAVINGS?

You compute cost savings by listing the operating costs of the old equipment and the estimated operating costs of the proposed machine. In listing these operating costs, you consider only those costs that will be *different* from one machine to the other. For example, if a proposed machine will take less labor to run than the old machine, then this type of cost should be listed because the amount varies for the two machines. However, if a cost, such as heating, will stay the same whether or not you replace an old machine, then this cost should not be considered.

steps in cost
computation

After you have listed the operating costs of the old and the proposed machines, you then compare the totals of each to determine whether or not the proposed equipment would be cheaper to own and operate. For example, assume that you are considering the purchase of a new machine at an

costs of the old and proposed machines are:

	Old Machine	Proposed Machine
Direct labor	$3,000	$2,000
Indirect labor	1,500	1,000
Maintenance	800	200
Power	200	800
Taxes and insurance	100	600
Total out-of-pocket expenses	$5,600	$4,600

In addition to these costs, you should also include such costs as fringe benefits, floor space, tools, set-up time, materials, and materials handling, if they apply.

As you can see, you would save $1,000 per year if the proposed machine is purchased. However, these figures represent only the *out-of-pocket* costs with no allowance made for interest and depreciation. Both interest and depreciation are expenses and should be considered.

WHY INCLUDE INTEREST CHARGES?

The new equipment mentioned in our illustration above will cost $5,000. If this amount is borrowed, the costs involved in this transaction, such as interest, must be paid. If, instead of borrowing, the company has the funds necessary to purchase the equipment, you would still have an interest charge. This is reasoned as follows. If the $5,000 available for purchase of the equipment were *not* used to buy the machine, it could be invested elsewhere, and a return could be realized on the money. It could, for example, be placed in a bank and earn interest at the rate of, say, 5% per year—a return of $250 per year. However, if the company uses the $5,000 to purchase the new equipment, this interest return of $250 would not be received and should therefore be considered as a cost for the new equipment.

In all probability, the interest rate of 5% used above is not a good figure. Instead of placing money in a bank, many firms invest it in their own or other companies with greater risks but yielding a higher rate of return than that normally paid by a bank. You should, therefore, determine what rate of return you could get from an investment of a similar risk; then use this rate of return to figure the interest charges, which you would add to the annual operating costs. For example, assume that you find that from an investment of comparable risk, you can get an interest return of 10%. This figure of 10%, then, would be used and would add an annual interest charge of $500 (10% of $5,000) to the total out-of-pocket expenses of $4,600. Al-

an
operating
expense

though next year's interest charges on the new equipment would be $500, the interest for each succeeding year would, of course, be less as the amount of money you have tied up in the machine decreases by depreciation. For the purposes of replacement, however, this annual decrease in interest charges is not usually considered significant.

Next, you must determine what interest charge, if any, should be applied to the old equipment. The same reasoning as that used for the proposed equipment is applied to the old equipment. For example, if you can determine that the company is giving up a possible interest return on the money invested in the old equipment, then this loss in interest should also be charged as an annual operating cost against the old equipment. Determining how much money or capital the company has invested in the old equipment is simply a matter of determining the current market price of the old equipment. For example, assume that the old piece of machinery could be sold for $1,500. If it is sold, the $1,500 could be invested at 10%, and a return of $150 per year would be realized. This $150, therefore, constitutes a charge because it is something the company gives up or "pays" when it keeps the old machine. If the old machine had no market value, then you would have no interest charges.

By listing the interest charge of $150 for the old machine and $500 for the proposed machine, you can now compare the two machines as follows:

	Old	Proposed
Total out-of-pocket expenses	$5,600	$4,600
Interest expense @ 10%	150	500
Total	$5,750	$5,100

The proposed equipment still shows a net annual savings of $650.

DO YOU NEED DEPRECIATION COSTS?

Yes. Depreciation is a decline in asset value. It is an accounting concept that is used to allocate the charges for a piece of equipment in some equitable fashion over the operating life of the equipment. In one sense, depreciation can be thought of as the "rent" paid for use of the equipment during a period of time.

There are many ways in which depreciation can be figured, but for simplicity, use the straight-line method. You can figure it as follows. You know the proposed equipment will cost $5,000. Assume it will have an operating life of four years, after which it can be sold for $1,000. Subtracting the $1,000 salvage value of the machine from its original cost leaves $4,000 that must be charged as depreciation over the four-year life of the equipment. This $4,000 divided by four years yields an annual depreciation charge of $1,000. Thus, the equipment, like a resource, is being used up at the rate of $1,000 per year. An annual charge of $1,000, therefore, should be made in your analysis against the proposed machine in addition to those charges already listed.

The depreciation charge for the old equipment, however, is nothing but its loss in value from *this time on.* This loss-in-value figure has no connection with the depreciation estimates that were made by the accountants when the equipment was originally purchased.

To illustrate depreciation charges on the old equipment, assume that the old machine will last two additional years and at the end of that time will have a salvage value of $500. You have already determined the current market value of the old equipment to be $1,500. At the end of two years, therefore, it will be worth only $500, declining $1,000 in market value during these two years. This $1,000 decline in market value over a two-year period represents the depreciation on the old machine and is an annual equivalent of $500 ($1,000 divided by two years). This $500 figure, then, is the annual amount you should charge off as depreciation against the old equipment. Obviously, if the old machine did not decline in value over this two-year period or if it had no current market value, then no annual depreciation charges would be made against it.

*decline in asset
value*

Your annual cost figures now read:

	Old	Proposed
Direct labor	$3,000	$2,000
Indirect labor	1,500	1,000
Maintenance	800	200
Power	200	800
Taxes and insurance	100	600
Interest expense @ 10%	150	500
Depreciation	500	1,000
Total	$6,250	$6,100

This leaves you an annual *cost saving* of $150 if the new machine is purchased. Is this sufficient to warrant investing $5,000? Other factors are often considered before this final decision is reached. For example, the proposed equipment may increase the capacity of the plant in line with a sales forecast, or it may be more flexible equipment and make for ease in product variation. Both of these factors would also favor the replacement, not to mention the $150 annual cost saving. In addition to these factors, however, management is interested in how long it will take to get its investment back.

WHAT IS THE CAPITAL RECOVERY PERIOD?

Many companies establish a standard pay-off period during which time any investment in new equipment must "pay for itself." For example, one large meat packer will not invest in any tool that will not pay for itself in one year or any piece of major equipment that will not pay for itself in five or fewer years. This capital recovery period is sometimes expressed as a *rate of return on investment*. Actually, both concepts are identical. If your company has a pay-off period of two years, then the rate of return is 50%. A one-year recovery period would obviously be a 100% return, whereas a five-year recovery period would be the same as a 20% rate of return on investment.

rate of return   You can figure how quickly a proposed machine will pay for itself by dividing the annual saving plus depreciation on the new equipment into the investment necessary to realize the saving. For example, in our problem, the new machine costs $5,000, but we could realize $1,500 by selling the old machine. The net investment, therefore, would be $3,500. To determine the recovery period, this $3,500 is divided by the sum of the annual cost saving ($150) and the depreciation on the proposed machine ($1,000), yielding a recovery period of 3.04 years ($3,500 ÷ $1,150 = 3.04 years). The $1,000 depreciation charge is added to the annual saving of $150 because in addition to the $150 saving realizable each year, $1,000 will be set aside as a depreciation allowance that is also applied to recovering the $3,500 net investment. Or you can look at it another way. If the total annual operating costs for the old and proposed equipment were the same, then the proposed equipment could still be "paid for" through the depreciation charge set up for the proposed machine. Thus, $1,000 as a depreciation charge is available annually to help pay for the new machine, and, *in addition,* a total net saving of $150 is also available. Therefore, to figure the recovery period, $3,500 is divided by $1,150, yielding 3.04 years. This means that in approximately 3.04 years, the net investment of $3,500 in the new machine will have been recovered, and after that time, the $1,150 return will be "pure profit."

Deciding whether the pay-off period will be two, four, or eight years is mostly a matter of "business judgment," or "sound business reasoning." In general, however, management seems to feel freer to invest money that will be recovered in two to five years rather than longer periods of, say, ten or twenty years. They indicate that beyond the relatively short range of two to five years, their estimate of future economic conditions is much more uncertain; therefore, they are hesitant to commit large sums of money for longer periods, sums that might involve a loss.

CAN DEPRECIATION BE OMITTED FOR THE PROPOSED MACHINE?

Although the previous discussion of depreciation indicated that it would be included as a cost factor for the *proposed* piece of equipment, this is not actually necessary. Depreciation can be entirely omitted on the *proposed* machine with no difference in the final answer. This is true because the depreciation charges included in the operating costs were "taken out" and added to the annual savings, with the net effect that no numerical difference occurred in the final figure.

added to annual savings

To illustrate this fact, consider the depreciation charges for the proposed equipment in the problem previously discussed. By adding the $1,000 depreciation charge to the annual saving of $150, you determined that the total amount that would be available to help pay for the new equipment would be $1,150. Look at what this figure would have been if you had not included depreciation. With the $1,000 depreciation figure omitted from the proposed equipment, your total operating costs would have been $5,100. Your annual saving would have been the difference between this figure and $6,250, or $1,150—the same as that calculated previously. Therefore, because depreciation on the new equipment has no net effect on the final figure, it is often omitted from replacement calculations.

HOW DO YOU TREAT THE UNDEPRECIATED BOOK VALUE OF THE OLD MACHINE?

The book value of a machine is the amount the accountants show on the company books as the undepreciated value of the machine. Some people feel that depreciation for the *old equipment* should be figured on the basis of this book value and not market value. They say, for example, that if a stamping machine that is expected to last ten years is purchased for $10,000, then annual depreciation would be $1,000 if the machine is expected to have no scrap value. At the end of eight years, the book value of the machine would be $2,000. Assume, however, that at the end of eight years the stamping machine has a market value of $1,000 and is expected to have a scrap value of $200 at the end of ten years. This means that the machine will lose $800 in market value during the ninth and tenth years, or depreciate at the rate of $400 per year. Which depreciation figure should be used for equipment replacement problems? The $1,000 depreciation based on the book value as estimated by the accountants, or the $400 figure based on actual market value.

forget the book value

Because accountants most frequently use the $1,000 figure in their various statements and because the government accepts that figure for the purpose of income tax statements, some managers see no reason why they should not use the same figure in computations arising from equipment replacement analysis.

Replacement problems and accounting problems, however, are not the same. The accounting figure of $1,000 was the best estimate of the stamping machine's decline in value *at the time the machine was bought.* This figure is the result of actions taken in the past. Actually, it has no relevance to equipment replacement problems because no current decision can alter the figure. The current market value of the stamping machine is relevant, however, because the machine may be sold and the money applied toward the purchase of a new machine. Therefore, depreciation for the old stamping machine should consist of the annual decrease in market value that the business would actually experience if the old equipment were retained.

use current market value

Looking at it another way, you could say that if the $1,000 depreciation figure is used, you would actually be overcharging the old equipment's operating costs and thus tend to make the proposed machine more attractive. Conceivably, this could lead you to replace the machine prematurely. For example, if operating costs for the old stamping machine, including the $1,000 book depreciation charge, totaled $5,000, and if operating costs for the new machine were $4,400, then you would probably say that you should buy the new machine because of the annual "saving" of $600. If, however, you use the true depreciation figure of $400, then total operating costs for the old stamping machine would be $4,400, or equal to those of the proposed equipment. With other things equal, replacement of the old machine obviously would not be made.

IS THE BOOK VALUE OF THE OLD MACHINE A COST OF THE NEW MACHINE?

When a new machine is purchased, some people feel that the undepreciated book value of the old machine should be a part of the total cost of the new machine. This is incorrect. The book value of the old machine is a sunk cost. Nothing can be done about it. Regardless of whether or not you buy the new machine, the sunk cost of the old machine will be written off by your accountants.

sunk cost

To illustrate this fact, assume that you have a machine with an annual depreciation of $1,000, an undepreciated book value of $5,000, and no scrap value. Also, assume that a proposed new machine will cost you $10,000. If you buy the new machine, do you need to recover $15,000 in order to cover the $10,000 cost of the new machine plus the $5,000 book value of the old? Of course not!

Regardless of whether or not you buy the new machine, the undepreciated balance of $5,000 for the old machine will be written off. Thus, if you keep the old machine, the $5,000 balance will be written off in five years at the annual rate of $1,000 per year. If you buy the new machine and discard the old, then this undepreciated book value will be written off as a loss. In either event—whether you buy the new or keep the old—you write off the undepreciated balance of the old machine with the same ultimate effect on company profit. The undepreciated book value of the old machine, therefore, can be ignored and not treated as capital to be recovered through cost savings resulting from the purchase of a new machine. To do otherwise would place an undue burden on the proposed piece of equipment.

You can. It is possible that the proposed replacement would enhance profits and that annual federal taxes would be higher as a result. In fact, it is possible that because of the tax structure, a proposed investment in new equipment though providing an "annual operating cost saving" could cost more to own and operate because of the increase in resulting taxes. Or it may be that from a tax standpoint, purchasing the new machine could save money.

easier to omit

Many companies, however, omit the question of income taxes from replacement decisions because they feel that the situation that offers the greatest saving (or profit increase) before taxes will usually offer the greatest saving (or profit increase) after taxes. For this reason, forget about the effect of taxes when you figure replacement problems.

WHAT IS THE TOTAL-LIFE AVERAGE METHOD?

The total-life average method is another approach to justify buying a new machine. Some companies figure replacement analysis by lumping *all* costs involved in owning and operating a machine into one total figure and dividing this total by the estimated life of the machine, thus giving them the average annual cost. It works as follows:

average cost per year

Old Machine		Proposed Machine
Given: $1,000 market value		$10,000 installed cost
no scrap value		$ 1,000 scrap value
2 years of life		9 years of life
$4,600 annual operating costs		$ 3,700 annual operating costs
excluding depreciation		excluding depreciation
10% interest		10% interest
Costs: $ 1,000	Depreciation	$ 9,000
9,200 (2 yr)	Operating costs	33,300 (9 yr)
150	Interest @ 10%	5,400
$10,350	Total life cost	$47,700
$ 5,175	Average cost per year	$ 5,300

Interest is figured each year on the value of the equipment. For example, the old machine is worth $1,000 today and will have no scrap value in two years. Therefore, it depreciates at the rate of $500 per year. Thus, interest for the first year would be $100 on the full $1,000. For the second year, however, interest would be computed on only $500, the value of the machine at that time, and would be $50. The interest for the two years, therefore, would be $150. In like manner, interest for the new machine for the first year would be computed on $10,000, for the second year on $9,000, and so on.

On the basis of this analysis using the total-life average method and considering no other factors, the old machine would be cheaper to own and operate. The new machine, therefore, should not be purchased at this time.

HOW CAN YOU CONVINCE MANAGEMENT TO BUY?

Most of the time, if you can show through cold, hard facts that the purchase of a new piece of equipment will save money and pay for itself—then top management will go along with you. One of the best ways to demonstrate this is through a cost analysis of the old and the proposed equipment using the procedures covered here. It might look like hard work and a lot of figuring, but when the smooth operation of your department depends on it, the end result is well worth the time and effort you put into it.

A Case Study
TRAMWAY POWDER COMPANY

In 1968, the Tramway Powder Company installed a new packing machine to package poultry disinfectant; this machine replaced an old machine designed and built by the owner. The new machine installed, cost $4,800 and produced 800 units per eight-hour day. It averaged running 2,000 hours per year and consumed three kilowatts of electricity for each hour it ran. At the time of the installation, the estimated life of the machine was ten years.

In 1974, a salesman called on Mr. Tramway and tried to interest him in buying a new multiple unit machine for $9,000 installed. He indicated, however, that he could not allow the company a trade-in allowance on the old machine because it had no market value. The salesman claimed that the new machine would produce the same number of units per hour as the old machine—but at a lower cost. For one thing, he showed that labor on the new machine would not have to be specialized, thus reducing hourly labor costs from $4.25 to $2.60. In addition, he pointed out that his machine consumed only two kilowatts of electricity per hour at the current rate of 6¢ per kilowatt-hour.

One of his strong points was that his new machine would not have to be set up each time the package size was changed, as was necessary on the machine the company then owned. In fact, he showed that the company averaged changing the setup for its machine every 25,000 units at a cost of $100 per setup. These savings, coupled with an estimated life of fifteen years (no scrap value), would enable the machine to pay for itself in two years, he claimed.

The company averaged 250 working days per year.

1. Using an interest rate of 10%, was the salesman correct?
2. If Tramway's policy was to buy only if a new machine would pay for itself in three years, should he buy?
3. Do you think the three-year policy is a good one? Why?

Marcie McCain desperately wanted to get new electric typewriters for her typing pool employees. The manual ones currently used by all twenty employees had been requisitioned by the previous supervisor, Gloria Brown, who was firmly convinced that manual typewriters were superior to and more efficient than electric typewriters. As a consequence, Gloria had persuaded management two years ago to purchase the latest and best manual typewriters with an expected useful life of at least eight years.

Marcie, however, felt that the manual machines were inferior, were slower, cost more to own and operate, and had a definite impact on the overall morale of the department. Her problem was to convince her bosses that the new machines were desirable, were needed, would cost less to keep, and would be the most efficient in the long run.

1. If you were called in to give Marcie help, what would you suggest that she do?
2. List the things that Marcie should consider in preparing a report showing the need for new typewriters.
3. How can you justify discarding typewriters that are in excellent operating condition?

GLOSSARY

Agenda. A memorandum or list of things to be done or discussed.

Authority. The right to command. The power you have over others.

Brainstorming. The development of ideas without evaluating them. Innovative thinking without regard to feasibility of ideas.

Capital Recovery Period. The time period during which investment in new equipment must pay for itself.

Checkoff. The collection of union dues by the employer who then turns them over to the union.

Classroom Training. Training that takes place in a classroom rather than at the work place.

Closed Shop. One where an applicant has to join the union before he will be hired. (Now outlawed.)

Collective Bargaining. The activity involved when management and the union get together to bargain over and agree upon wages, hours of work, and working conditions.

Communication. The transfer of information and understanding from one person to another.

Communication Feedback. An indication of understanding (or lack of understanding) of a face-to-face communication, usually taking the form of a nod, puzzled expression, smile, or some other indication of understanding or not understanding the message.

Controlling. Checking or regulating activities so that activities or events will conform to plans.

Counseling.   Helping an employee get over a problem by listening, understanding, and giving helpful advice.

Craft Union.   One that accepts members only from a single trade or occupation, such as a carpenters union or a machinists union.

Depreciation.   The loss or decline in the value of an asset.

Directing.   Guiding, influencing, or telling another person what to do.

Discipline.   Any action undertaken to get a person to comply with rules and regulations.

Empathy.   Looking at a problem from the other fellow's point of view.

Esteem Needs.   The need for recognition, status, achievement, or sense of accomplishment. Self respect.

Exception Principle.   Checking only those items that fall outside of predetermined limits.

Fair Standard.   One that allows the best workers to produce about 20 to 25 percent more than the standard.

Feedback.   An indication of understanding (or lack of understanding) of face-to-face communications, usually taking the form of a nod, smile, puzzled expression, or some other indication of understanding or not understanding the message.

Flow Diagram.   A map of the movement or flow of a product or a person through a work process.

Forelady.   A female foreman or supervisor who directs the efforts of others.

Foreman.   A male supervisor who directs the efforts of others.

Formal Organization.   The recognized and formalized lines of communication, authority, and control.

Grievance.   A complaint that has been formally registered with an employee's supervisor or some other management official in accordance with the recognized grievance procedure.

Halsey 50–50 Plan.   An incentive pay plan designed by F. A. Halsey in which the employee received a guaranteed base pay plus a percentage of the time the employee saved on the job, usually 50 percent.

Human Relations.   A mode of management that is concerned with getting employees to work together harmoniously, productively, and cooperatively to achieve economic as well as social goals.

Industrial Union.   One that represents all workers in a particular company or industry regardless of what job the worker performs.

Informal Organization.   A hierarchy or organization set up by the employees, not agreed to or recognized by management.

Job Description.   A statement giving the duties and responsibilities of a job.

Job Evaluation.   A systematic way of determining the relative worth of each job in a company, but not the wages that will be paid for doing the job.

Job Safety Analysis.   Going over every aspect of a job or task to see if any possible hazard exists that can be eliminated.

Job Specification.   A written record of the qualities and capacities that an individual would need to fill a particular job. Sometimes called a man specification.

Leader.   An individual who knows where he is going and can persuade others to join him.

Leader, Authoritarian.   One who exercises strong control over his employees.

Leader, Democratic.   One who solicits aid and advice from his employees, thus getting them involved in the solution to work problems.

Leader, Dictatorial.   One who holds the threat of punishment or discharge over his employees to get them to do his will.

Leader, *Laissez-faire*.   One who holds virtually no power over his employees. A leader in name only.

Line Organization.   One that has the power to act or to command.

Line and Staff Organization.   A line organization to which staff assistants have been added.

Loose Standard.   One which allows an average employee working at normal pace to easily produce more units per hour than the standard calls for.

Management.   The formally designated supervisors or bosses in a company.

Manager.   One who supervises and gets work done through the efforts of others.

Methods Improvement.   The process involved in trying to improve the way a job is performed.

Morale.   A person's state of mind—how he feels about things.

Morale Survey.   An opinion poll or attitude survey that tries to measure or find out how employees feel about their jobs, their supervisors, the company, and so on.

Motion Analysis.   The study of the body motions employed by an individual to perform a job.

Motivate.   To make others want to perform an assigned task. To make an employee want to do his work.

Need Hierarchy.   The rank assigned by psychologists to the five basic human needs.

Nonrecurring Costs.   Those costs that are incurred only once in the life of a piece of equipment.

Obsolescence.   The condition of a piece of equipment that functions well mechanically, but has been superseded by a newer, more efficient machine.

On-the-job Training.   Training that is carried on at the employee's work place.

100 Percent Bonus Plan.   A piecework plan in which allowances are made in terms of time for each unit of output instead of money.

Operations Chart.   A "picture" of the simultaneous work that the right and left hands are doing. Sometimes called a left-hand right-hand chart.

Organic functions.   The three basic functions (finance, production, distribution) necessary for any firm to "live" or exist.

Organizing.   The process of coordinating the efforts of employees so that objectives can be achieved in the most efficient manner.

Pay-back Period.   The time required for a piece of equipment to pay for itself.

Performance Evaluation.   A formalized, systematic appraisal of an employee's performance and his potential for development and training.

Physical Needs.   The basic necessities of life such as food, shelter, clothing, etc.

Piecework Plan.   A system of pay in which the employee receives a stipulated amount for each unit of product produced.

Planning. The process involved in deciding what you will need to do to accomplish your objective.

Predetermined Time Standard. One which you can calculate by analyzing the movements required to do a job and then assigning predetermined time values to these motions.

Process Chart. A piece of paper on which you have recorded the steps in a process.

Professional Worker. One with particular educational skills or training such as a nurse or engineer.

Rating Scale Method of Performance Evaluation. A system of rating an employee's abilities by placing a check on a scale that best describes the employee's quality of work, quantity, job knowledge, dependability, cooperativeness, and other factors.

Ratio-delay Study. A statistical technique used to get information about the work performance of an employee or machine.

Recurring Costs. Those that continue year after year as a piece of equipment is used, as opposed to one-time or nonrecurring costs.

Responsibility. The obligation that an employee has to his boss to do a job that has been assigned to him.

Safety Need. The desire or need to protect yourself from danger, to be secure.

Self-realization Need. The need to feel that you have accomplished things to the best of your abilities and potentialities. The need to realize what you are capable of becoming.

Social Needs. The need to belong, to be a part of a group, to be accepted and respected by members of the group.

Span of Management (or Control). The number of people an individual can effectively supervise.

Staff Organization. One that is advisory in nature, helping other people know what should be done and how to do it.

Staffing. All the activities involved in recruiting, hiring, and retaining employees on the job.

Standard Time (Time Standard). The time allowed to do a specified quantity and quality of work.

Straight Piecework. A pay plan in which the employee gets paid only for each acceptable unit of output. If he doesn't produce, he doesn't get paid.

Straight Piecework with a Guaranteed Base. The same as the straight piecework plan, except that an hourly base rate equal to the going rate for the job is guaranteed.

Supervisor. One who gets things accomplished through the efforts of others. An overseer. A boss.

Theory X. A system of supervision in which the supervisor appeals to his employees through their lower-level needs.

Theory Y. A system of supervision in which the supervisor appeals to his employees through their higher-level needs.

Tight Standard. One which an average employee working at normal pace cannot meet. Even the best employees cannot exceed a tight standard by more than 5 or 10%.

Time-Analysis Chart.   An accurate account of what you do throughout a day showing when you did something and how long it took. Usually made by listing vertically on a sheet of paper the hours of the day in fifteen-minute intervals.

Union.   An organization of employees that seeks to improve its members' economic, social, and political interests through the process of collective bargaining.

Union Shop.   An agreement whereby an employee must join the union within a given period of time after being hired, or lose his job.

Unity of Command.   The authority relationship that exists where an employee in an organization has only one boss—where only one person gives orders to an employee.

Vestibule Training.   Training that takes place in a classroom (vestibule) where an attempt is made to duplicate working conditions, with machines and other equipment set up.

Work Sampling.   A statistical technique used to get information about the work performance of an employee or a machine. Ratio-delay study.

Work Simplification.   The process involved in trying to improve the way a job is performed.

INDEX